TAROT FOR SCEPTICS

TAROT FOR SCEPTICS
The Practical Usage of Divination for Psychic Results

Ari Freeman

AEON

First published in 2025 by
Aeon Books

Copyright © 2025 by Ari Freeman

The right of Ari Freeman to be identified as the author of this work has been asserted in accordance with §§ 77 and 78 of the Copyright Design and Patents Act 1988.

All rights reserved. No part of this publication may be reproduced, stored in a retrieval system, or transmitted, in any form or by any means, electronic, mechanical, photocopying, recording, or otherwise, without the prior written permission of the publisher.

British Library Cataloguing in Publication Data

A C.I.P. for this book is available from the British Library

ISBN-13: 978-1-80152-167-3

Typeset by Medlar Publishing Solutions Pvt Ltd, India

www.aeonbooks.co.uk

TABLE OF CONTENTS

ACKNOWLEDGEMENTS	vii
INTRODUCTION	ix
Questions and answers	x
Possible models for how Tarot works	xx
LEVEL 1	
Tarot reading	1
Reversals	2
Card relationships	3
The four suits	4
Quick explanations for the Rider Waite Smith and Marseilles Decks	12
Understanding Tarot numerology	16
The journey from one to ten through the suits	22
The Court Cards	29
The Major Arcana	33
Example readings	36

LEVEL 2
Advanced Tarot reading — 67
   A deeper dive into the cards — 67
   The Major Arcana in depth — 71
   The Minor Arcana in depth — 145
   The Court Cards in depth — 217
   Reversals revisited — 263
   Example spreads (advanced interpretation) — 266
   The history of Tarot — 286
   The evolution of Tarot decks, and Tarot Reading — 296
   Oracle cards — 315

LEVEL 3
Understanding Tarot — 319
   Congratulations, you are psychic! — 319
   Finally understanding what is going on with Tarot — 328
   You might not actually be psychic — 332
   Dealing with problematic querents — 341
   Outro: Bullshit that works — 345

BIBLIOGRAPHY — 347

INDEX — 349

ACKNOWLEDGEMENTS

This book is for Ciaran MacConneach, who introduced me to Tarot reading, asked me to write this book about Tarot and was my consultant and collaborator. Many of his ideas have found their way into this book and many of my ideas were discussed with him. He also provided me access to many of the papers and books I asked for, and some of his own suggestion. Thanks Ciaran, your friendship is one of a kind and continues to inspire me.

I would also like to thank: John David Ebert, for his astrology readings and philosophy. Lionel Snell (Ramsey Dukes) for his experience and magical theory. And those sceptics and curious people who participated in my Tarot experiments.

INTRODUCTION

This book can be used as a gradated course that will take the reader from an absolute beginner to a professional-level expert, with a focus on giving readings that work. Results of the course depend on the reader practising as they go.

This book is for everybody, including the hard-nosed sceptic who has decided to give divination a go out of curiosity. I am not going to ask you to adopt a particular belief system or assume one before we start. If Tarot works, it ought to work whether you or the person you are reading for believes in it or not, right?

To my knowledge, no other book provides both an accessible and respectful guide to the traditional occult methods of Tarot, while also answering sceptical questions to their logical endpoint.

It has been said that great art changes the way you see the world. Magic has often been referred to as 'the Art', and Tarot, as a form of magic which is an interaction between visual art and fortune-telling, is an incredible way to hack your 'reality tunnel'.

While this book has been designed to be readable in the order it is written, it is also understood that like any textbook, you may want to first skip to the sections that most interest you, or read it in a different order. This is especially the case if you have already started using Tarot before reading this book, or if you plan on using it as an aid to teaching others. If, however, you haven't done a Tarot reading before, there is no better place to start than the beginning.

Questions and answers

What is a 'querent'?

A querent is the traditional name for the person for whom a Tarot reading is being done. Most of this book is about readings done with two people, one Tarot reader and one querent. It is also possible to do Tarot readings for yourself, in which case you will be both the querent and the reader.

What is Tarot reading?

Tarot reading can be used in many ways. Some of the uses which we will explore in this book are:

- A narrative card game for one or two people.
- A story construction set.
- A type of counselling.
- A method for predicting the future.
- A way for you to talk to the 'back of your head'.
- A system of symbols that help reframe your experience of the world.
- A technique to distract your rational mind in order to engage your intuition.
- A framework and interface for understanding conscious states and transcendent experiences.

What are the core parts of a Tarot reading?

- The Tarot deck and the Tarot method.
- The Tarot reader.
- The querent, for whom the reading is being done.
- The interpretation of the events and the situation.
- A prediction is made and/or advice is given to the querent.

For this book, I have experimented with all five components in order to discern how these parameters interact.

Are Tarot readers psychic?

This is a big question that we will explore throughout this book. In summary:

- I have had great readings from sceptics who claim not to believe in psychic phenomena.
- I have had bad readings from people who self-identify as psychic.
- While I don't identify as psychic, I have had the type of experiences that people who do claim to be psychic report as 'hits' or take as evidence for their psychic ability. I also believe that you, or anyone who practices will be able to tap into these experiences. The difference between my approach and that of 'true believers' is that I don't require you to believe, I only ask you to try it yourself. Then you can make up your own mind as to whether this is a 'trick', a deception, or evidence of psychic phenomena. Even if you decide it is a trick, I hope to show you that it is a useful trick which is fascinating in its implications.

If you are reading and you get an inkling, a voice in your head, an image or a flash of experience from the querent's point of view rather than your own, the 'rules' of the Tarot game (and of magic in general) are that you should factor that in for the duration of the experiment.

A good approach to Tarot is to treat it as a performance. You have done a good reading if the querent agrees that you have done a good reading. If they don't think you have done a good reading, then you need more practice or knowledge. In this sense it is similar to any other performance, be it theatrical, musical, comedic or otherwise.

In my experiences performing and teaching Tarot reading, no belief in the supernatural is necessary in order for it to work. Some strong beliefs in magic or spirituality may actually get in the way of becoming a better Tarot reader, which is why I frame it here first as a performance. Likewise, a certain suspension of disbelief is necessary for the duration of the game. My favourite Tarot readings have been from people who are open-minded sceptics, who aren't afraid to try magic and who are open to discussing what is going on.

When one plays the board game *Monopoly*, one plays as if one is a capitalist. Likewise when one 'plays' divination, then one ought to play 'as if' one is a psychic. In neither case, however, is it required that you carry these beliefs outside of the game.

Magic, including divination by cards, for our purposes is inherently about the manipulation and creation of personal and shared experiences. If magical results were objectively measurable, then they wouldn't be 'magical' but rather part of science. If one is worried about the ethics of making predictions for a querent, then it is wise to offer a disclaimer beforehand. Tarot is, however, among other things, a game of predictions, and avoiding making predictions, in my opinion, diminishes the game.

Okay, but do you REALLY believe in psychics?

Okay, yes … But only when I feel like it. The rest of the time I am super-rational. More rational than Richard Dawkins and James Randi! You've never met anyone as sceptical as me! Honestly though, the point is you should try it for yourself. I suggest you stop worrying about what other people claim they believe. My core belief is that beliefs ought to be experimented with if they are to be understood.

Can Tarot results be explained by cold reading?

Cold reading is simply the factoring in of clues given by the subject from how they look, how they talk, their body language, their age and other observable details. Cold reading is bound to be a part of what Tarot reading is. The results of good Tarot readings, however, are almost always far too specific to be explainable by cold reading alone. The same goes for 'rainbow statements', the 'Forer effect' and all the other sceptical theories that I have come across. I will address all of these near the end of the book. If you find yourself stuck at this hurdle, you may want to read the Level 3 section of the book after this introduction. In any case, I urge you not to make up your mind before getting some readings under your belt.

In my experiments reading and teaching Tarot, it is very clear to me that those who study the tradition get better results than those who try and get by with cold reading and the Forer effect alone. The system works.

It is usually a fool's errand to try and alter a game before one has learnt how to play it (I know this from personal experience). On the other hand, as I frame Tarot as a performance, I don't see anything wrong with using some cold reading as part of divination. In fact, in face-to-face readings it's probably not possible to exclude cold reading, as Tarot is a game of grasping at clues.

Another reason is that the symbols of the cards have purposefully been refined over hundreds of years. No matter how smart one is, it's simply too hard to compete with that many competent Tarot readers and deck designers.

If you want a quick start, don't be afraid to look up the meaning of the cards as you go. I have witnessed and orchestrated great readings by readers who know nothing about the Tarot, with the help of a print-out of the meanings of the cards. It is not required that you memorise the cards straight away. You have this book, feel free to refer to it during your reading.

What is a 'good' reading?

For our purposes, at least to begin with, a good reading is a reading that 'wows' the querent. If you focus on this initially, then you'll be honing your abilities in the right way. For some of you, a good reading might be one which gets the querent out of a problem, or which offers a prediction which comes true. These are higher aspirations. I recommend you start playfully at first. You don't have to begin by being a fully fledged prophet, it's perfectly fine to start with a parlour trick and then work your way up.

What is a 'bad' reading?

A bad reading is either one where the reader projects their own psychology or prejudices onto the querent, rather than giving them a story they can personally connect to, or it is a reading with a high number of 'misses'. Don't be afraid of one or two misses during a reading, you are learning. However, if you don't get anything right, or barely so, then it's time to change your methods.

Should I avoid making predictions?

Certainly not. Predictions are part of the tradition and part of the fun. Some readers avoid making predictions because they don't want to be proved wrong. I feel this is a shame. Without making predictions, there is very little, or no falsifiability[1] to a Tarot reading. For some people,

---

[1] Falsifiability is a principal of the scientific method. If there is no way for something to be proved wrong through testing, then there is also no way to prove it correct. A scientific theory is established when it survives all attempts to disprove it. This term was coined by Sir Karl Popper (1902–1994 CE), one of the most famous philosophers of science.

aversion to the idea of 'fate' can get in the way of wanting to make predictions. I personally believe in free will. A prediction is not a certain future. There is always a way to act to prevent an event from happening. While playing the game of Tarot, I prefer to frame predictions as things that the querent is being 'drawn towards'.

In the ancient Chinese philosophy of Taoism, there is a metaphor in which fate is described like the current of a river. One can swim against the current for a short distance, but eventually one will run out of energy, at which point the river will carry one where it wants. If, however, one swims with the river, one still has the choice to swim left or right, manoeuvring around any obstacles that come. In this direction, one swims with the power of the river, which is much less tiring. This is a less fatalistic and more pragmatic way to consider future predictions.

Some cultures other than my own[2] have no problem with fatalism and predictions and expect them. I advise that you tailor your readings to the needs of your querent.

Knowing something about the future doesn't affect your free will. Instead, it gives you power over being swayed by chance. In a sense it actually allows you to exercise your free will.

This is somewhat related to spiritual ideas like the Dao or Karma. Lack of knowledge about what will come may mean that you are at the mercy of forces that you can't see coming. Having a forecast, like a weather report, gives you more opportunity to avoid pitfalls and to grasp opportunities. One use of Tarot can be to provide a kind of 'emotional forecast'.

For those of you who dislike the idea that Tarot can predict the future, I urge you to test it. The results are probably, at first, going to be more subtle than you expect, and yet if you follow my instructions I expect that you will have 'hits'.

Are Tarot predictions a self-fulfilling prophecy?

If you treat them as such, then yes. However, one could just as easily try and rebel against what the cards suggest for us. Either way, the reading has exerted its effect. Call me a contrarian, but I think the more interesting question is: 'Can self-fulfilling prophecies be used for beneficial effect'. In my experience, a good self-fulfilling prophecy can be a tool in the magician's arsenal.

---

[2] I am a New Zealander of Anglo-Saxon, Scottish and Jewish descent.

Trickery is part of all magic. The thing is that the more one studies which parts are the trick and which parts are a legitimate bending of reality, the more one discovers that even every day ordinary human perception is full of tricks. As the best scientists will admit, the choice is never between a trick and perfect objectivity. The choice is between more tricks and fewer tricks, better tricks and worse tricks. True objectivity is a goal that one orientates oneself towards, rather than being something that one ever truly achieves. For this reason, it is better to go into Tarot with this expectation. Furthermore, all magic including Tarot reading is in large part a manipulation of one's subjectivity. Objectivity is rarely the goal.

During readings, most querents will open up and tell you about their lives as the cards are turned over and explained. However, I always offer the querent an option of withholding all information in order that they may test what I can find out about them.

If the exercise were one of cold reading alone then one would expect divination to work better when the querent offers comments, than when they stay silent and poker-faced. I have not at all found this to be the case. Instead, I find both seem to work equally well. This weird result is part of what has kept me fascinated by Tarot.

What does Tarot do for us?

At any given moment, many ideas are influencing you. Divination, such as Tarot, presents a realignment of your attention so that you can build a connected narrative out of what otherwise might have been disconnected thoughts, observations, feelings, intuitions and concepts.

By shaping a selection of these ideas into a narrative, one makes a manageable understanding out of information that could have otherwise been nonsensical. Therefore divination gives us an ability to understand and act where one would have not been able to otherwise.

In this sense, divination, and especially Tarot, has a similar use to narrative therapy used by counsellors. Before modern institutionalised counselling, fortune-tellers and seers offered a similar service for their community, albeit in a much less regulated fashion.

The truth revealed by divination is, in this way, not so much in the cards (or other symbol sets) themselves, but in the way they can shed light on real things that are happening to you. The divination acts as a way to change your focus, and this changes your opportunities to act in the world. As I discussed in depth in my first book *Pragmatic Magical Thinking*, what you pay attention to changes what you can do.

Humans require focus in order to act. Nothing freezes up a person more than giving them too many options. In this way it's not always so important which selection is the 'right way', but rather that one way, which gets the job done, is chosen out of an overwhelming many.

Is Tarot originally a card game?

Yes. Tarot evolved from the union of a set of playing cards which Tarot readers refer to as the 'Minor Arcana', and a set of what were originally educational cards, the 'Trumps' or 'Major Arcana'.

I will explain this in detail in the history of Tarot section in Level 2. My first goal with this book is to get you doing Tarot readings quickly. If, however, you wish to learn the history before beginning, then feel free to go to that section first.

The English-speaking world received Tarot cards in the late nineteenth century mostly from the influence of Éliphas Lévi, a famous French occult writer. As such, for the English-speaking world Tarot, has almost always been associated with the occult and divination rather than the playing of card games.

In continental Europe, early decks such as Tarot de Marseilles are clearly intended primarily as playing cards, with divination being, in a sense, one of the 'games' that they are used for. In the Italian-, Spanish-, Portuguese- and French-speaking world, a variety of Tarot card games are still played today.

Do I have to learn the meanings of the cards or can I just read 'intuitively'?

If you want to read 'intuitively', that is, without first learning the traditional meanings of the cards, feel free. You probably don't need my help to do that.

In my experience, however, readings given by people who ignore the traditional meanings of the cards have never been good. I think the main reason for this is that the card meanings, which are complex and interesting, reduce the likelihood that the reader will project their own prejudices or other elements of their personality onto the querent. By learning an external system of meaning, you are forced to think outside of your regular habits. Readers who give their own meanings to the cards tend to fall into this trap.

Why not use a prediction as a way to motivate yourself or the querent?

I have found that the idea of self-fulfilling prophecies is not enough to explain the efficacy of Tarot predictions. If you are concerned about this, then you should test it; for instance, get a friend to do a reading for your future in secret and only have them reveal the reading after the fact. Did the reading still come true without the querent being able to act upon it knowingly? Enough of these tests ought to give you an answer.

What about self-confirming biases?

Part of what makes Tarot work in the first place is the ability to tell a story with any cards in any order. In this sense, the creativity required to create the narrative is where most of the magic happens. So again, the assumption should not be that the discoveries of biases in a Tarot reading would negate its effectiveness. Instead the utilisation of biases, especially where one uses them as tools to break out of ways in which one is 'stuck', might be the very factor that makes Tarot useful.

We are always being affected by our biases. The choice is generally not available to us to live without biases. So instead one has the choice only of better and worse biases. For more on this read the section at the end of the book entitled: 'Bullshit that works'.

Should I remove negative cards to prevent negative results?

You can do anything you like. In my experience, the message will find a way to get through regardless. The more overtly the querent is trying to suppress or steer the reading away from something they find uncomfortable, in my experience the more directly the reader will be presented with that very thing. So the removal of negative cards will not necessarily remove the likelihood of bad news any more than telling an inventive child that she mustn't use curse words will prevent her from coming up with ways to insult a rival.

What if my Tarot reading doesn't work?

Tarot is a creative exercise. Like any complex game, it takes practise. There is always a way to make any reading work if one has the creativity and problem-solving ability to build a story from the cards. If your Tarot reading doesn't work, that's okay. It's a skill that comes with practise. Tweak it and try again. All magicians fail. Great magicians are those who also succeed.

How does Tarot work?

One thing that's important to understand when relating to magic, is that the models for how things 'work' are primarily just means to get results. Magical models often don't reconcile well with other models of reality, or even with magical models from other traditions. This can be frustrating to people who know a little science (though skilled theoretical scientists tend to relate), who come from a dogmatic religious tradition, or simply those amongst us who are a bit more 'black and white' than average.

Artists, musicians and writers tend to understand straight away. The rules produce the results. Outside of striving for those results, entirely different rules may apply.

Tarot is one of these magical practices that according to our standard scientific cosmology 'shouldn't' work, but appears to anyway. As such, it is hard to pin down precisely what it is that is working, and any explanation for how it works will tend to be incomplete. For those of you who have read my first book, *Pragmatic Magical Thinking*, you will already be ready for this. For some of you, my approach in this book might be a little hard to pin down at first. So here's my approach in summary:

- Beliefs are tools. It's normal and okay to experiment with beliefs. Different beliefs allow different things to get done.[3]
- Ordinary people believe different things at different times, and as long as they can compartmentalise these beliefs, they will remain perfectly sane. For instance, when we watch a Superman movie, we allow that Superman can fly in the film. We don't get upset that

---

[3] This is an approach I have inherited from chaos magic, which is a movement which began in the UK in the 1970s. The founding text of which is *Liber Null & Psychonaut: An Introduction to Chaos Magic* by Peter J. Carroll. (Carroll 1987). I also highly recommend the writings of Ramsey Dukes (Lionel Snell) especially *SSOTBME (Sex Secrets of the Black Magicians Exposed)* (Dukes 1978), and *Blast Your Way to Megabucks with My Secret Sex-Power Formula* (Dukes 2003).

nobody in our everyday 'real' life can fly like Superman and walk out shouting 'this is all bullshit!' Likewise, we hold different values in different roles in our life. A security guard can also be a loving father. He isn't going to break up a fight between his two young kids in the same way that he might break up a fight between two drunks at a bar (even though the kids may well behave like drunks and the drunks may behave like kids). There are different values and beliefs in each role.

- While playing the game of Tarot divination, or any fortune-telling, 'spooky results' are part of what is allowed and expected in the game. Outside of the game, you can go back to your disbelief in spookiness. What happens in-game doesn't have to affect what happens out of the game.
- Cognitive dissonance is not so much the holding of conflicting beliefs, as an inability to compartmentalise them. We all have conflicting beliefs that we use for different things. It's part of the human condition. I propose that the ability to compartmentalise conflicting beliefs, so that they don't interfere with your mental health should be called 'cognitive harmony'. Sane people have this cognitive harmony. It is not the case that sane people believe the same thing all the time. Nobody does. Trying to rid yourself entirely of contradictory beliefs will not result in you being less insane. Rather you will start to go insane from the impossible task. This is the usual true cause of cognitive dissonance, that is, trying to be right all the time. It is a state that fundamentalists and mind-control cults exploit in their followers.

I try not to attribute truth claims to stories formed from incomplete data. Regardless I will outline here a few possible models for how Tarot might work. I use all of these at different times, depending on what I am trying to get done and I am more interested in the results than whether the models are true *all* the time. This approach to truth is called 'Pragmatism', and its most important proponent was the American philosopher William James (1842–1910 CE). In a nutshell, Pragmatism holds to be true those things that produce real results. If a phenomenon can be repeated, then something about it must be true. This is the philosophy that underlines the scientific method, and it applies just as well to magic and fortune-telling.

Possible models for how Tarot works

- **The conscious universe model.** The universe is inherently symbolic, meaningful and in some sense conscious. The things that happen to us, including things conventionally considered to be beyond our control, are, in part, determined by our thoughts and our will and intent. What we wish for, or expect, has some effect on how the universe appears to us. We don't always get what we want because there are many willpowers at play all the time.

    Symbol sets such as Tarot can somehow tap into the symbolic structure of the universe that precedes matter and action. Everything that happens, that could have happened a different way, is preceded by a 'decision' that the universe, (or an entity in it) makes. Magic is the ability to interfere with these decision points and persuade the universe or entity to go one way rather than the other. Divination is the scanning of these decision points. This model or something like it is used by many adherents of New Thought and New Age. It is also part of the magical theory behind chaos magic.
- **The synchronicity model.** Though they have no direct causal relationship, our lives are full of meaningful coincidences that reflect our psychology. These were termed 'synchronicities' by the famous psychologist Carl Jung (1875–1961 CE) who was vying for a compromise between scientific thinking and spiritual thinking. Tarot can become 'synchronistic', showing us things about ourselves and each other that we have trouble accessing otherwise. It works for us by conveying an inherent meaning which is part of the background of the universe. Because the universe is structured by meaning, meaningful coincidences will occur in union with a Tarot reading. Carl Jung remained vague about the exact mechanics of this. It was enough for him to notice synchronicities and to negotiate a meaningful structure for his patients that allowed them more agency in their lives.[4]
- **The deterministic model (fate).** Our future is partly or wholly written. Linear time is an illusion. In truth, all things happen all at once. Because, in some sense, everything has already happened, predicting

---

[4] For more on this look into 'neutral monism', the idea that neither the physical world nor the mental world is fundamental, but rather that both are outcomes of an inaccessible meta-reality. For this reason the mental realm and the physical are intertwined, yet their precise interaction remains irreconcilable. This can be used as a partial explanation for all sorts of things from quantum physics to psi phenomena, psychics and magic.

the future is not impossible, and with practise humans are able to do it through Tarot and other means.

Even though determinism is even used in physics by some theorists, I generally don't like it as it robs us of free will and reduces us to automatons. In the West, free will is a necessary part of our ideas about ethics, religion, the soul and our pursuit of happiness. For this reason, most of us will reject determinism. It does however have its proponents and I have mentioned it here regardless.

- **The psychic model.** The mind and all it can contain exists separately from the brain. A certain part of our minds exists in a shared space, and sometimes we can receive thoughts from another person in this space where two or more minds overlap. Despite this, we never have full access to someone else's mind-space. Tarot somehow 'taps us in', most likely through shared attention to this shared mind-space, and allows a certain amount of 'mind reading'. As fruity as this may sound, there is over a century of real scientific study on psychic phenomena. The most well-known modern scientists proposing and testing this theory are Rupert Sheldrake and Dean Radin. Their results are statistically valid and scientifically sound … However the findings are not dramatic enough to build a new model of reality inclusive of psychic phenomena, so we are for now in a kind of stalemate. Despite this, the model works well enough to become a good Tarot reader.
- **The psychic energy model.** People give off 'vibrations' or 'auras' or some other 'energy' signature. Certain people, psychics, can sense or see these signatures and interpret them with some level of accuracy. Tarot reading somehow focuses on the ability to sense these 'energies'. This model is common amongst New Age practitioners, spiritualists, and some occultists, and it has precursors in Chinese medicine as 'chi', 'prana' in Hinduism and Buddhism and 'virya' in Buddhism and some forms of yoga. Most cultures have an equivalent or similar concept of spiritual energy. While it is actually a very old concept, it has been rightly or wrongly dismissed by sceptics for so long that many won't give it the time of day. Because of this, I try to come up with other ways of explaining magical phenomena. The psychic energy model is easy to grasp, however, so many people like it.
- **The spirit model.** The universe is made of information, an idea which is more or less confirmed by modern quantum physics. Given that matter is, in a sense, condensed information, that your body is made of matter, and that you are conscious, the question

is this: Can information become sentient without first becoming matter? If the answer is yes, then the spirit world can be said to exist.

Though we in the West are educated to be sceptical of this idea, if you talk to many people you will find that most people actually do believe in spirits, at least some of the time. Likewise, spirit experiences, real or trickery, are commonplace. Most people just don't like to openly talk about them. Because of this, people don't know what to do with these beliefs or experiences and they are never fully incorporated into our model of the universe.

Belief in, and interaction with spirits is in truth, a near human universal worldwide and it has been as far as we can tell, since prehistory. For this reason, spirits are not so easily explained away as disbelieving sceptics would hope. To do so is to suggest that all of our ancestors and most human cultures have been deceiving themselves for all this time. I'm not keen on this idea. I think it's clear that spirit experiences in a general sense are real, even if spirits themselves are in some way illusory. On the other hand, the existence of any particular spirit is not easily proven, and there seem to be great limitations on the ways spirits can be communicated with, and the types of information they can impart. So we appear to be stuck. In the future, I am planning an entire book that will try and get to the bottom of this, but for now it is enough to address the problem and move on.

The logical endpoint to a belief in the spirit world, and one that is in line with Plato's theory of forms; one of the core philosophies on which the history of Western occult thinking depends, is that all information is capable of being sentient. This means that the spirit world is not only inhabited by ghosts, gods, angels, demons, jinn, fairies, elementals etc. But also by 'living' numbers, words, symbols, songs, poems, etc. The spirit world can be engaged with, at least in a limited sense by attributing personhood to a concept and asking what it is trying to get done. What does the number two want? What is the rain trying to do? How does a tree talk? This is a very useful story-telling game, a great way to brainstorm, and good practice for the type of thinking that allows us to become good Tarot readers.

- **The confirmation bias model.** Tarot reading is a trick. We deceive the querent (and ourselves) into believing the story. Explanation done, everyone can go home now.

    No wait, even this self-deception can be pragmatically useful. Given what we understand scientifically about the nature of human perception, the choice is not between believing in reality or believing in a trick. No matter where we look it's tricks all the way down. We simply do not have perfect access to reality and our perception of the world is always full of tricks. The only choice then, is which trick we believe in. This is as true outside of Tarot reading as it is within the confines of the game. Tarot can help us find a 'better' trick. A trick that helps you achieve what you want or need.

- **The psychological model.** We get so stuck in our psychological thought habits and the stories that we tell ourselves, that we become blind to alternative ways to see the world. Tarot, by its random sorting of cards, acts as a lever and gets us into alternative narratives. These are useful precisely because they break our habits and allow us new ways to see situations, and therefore new ways to act. In this model, precisely which story you tell is not particularly important. Most important is that you are able to break out of a story in which you have been stuck, and which has not been serving you, and into a new one. Many forms of counselling work the same way.
- **The self-fulfilling prophecy model.** Human beings are highly suggestible. So suggestible that telling them a story about what is going to happen might subconsciously set them on that path. This is 'enough' to explain why Tarot readings often become true.

  This is the perfect model if you want to blame your Tarot reader for anything that goes wrong. It's the worst model to choose, however, if you want to feel self-empowered, and can be easily dismissed by all the times that you were sceptical of a story that was told to you. Despite this, the self-fulfilling prophecy may sometimes play a part, and Tarot readers need to be aware of it.

* * *

So which model is the right one? I will let you be the judge. I recommend that you try at least a few of these out and that you draw conclusions from the results you get.

The mind-opening game of 'what if', and 'as if' as a precursor to scepticism

The term 'sceptic' comes from the ancient Greek word for 'inquiry' (σκέψις, *skepsis*). The original intent of the term is the withholding of judgement until the evidence is clear, and implicit in this is that true sceptics try things out before claiming to understand them. This is the attitude that underpins the scientific method, and it is also the best approach for a magician or Tarot reader, especially if your goal is to become the best magician or Tarot reader that you can be.

Though some use the term, 'sceptic' to mean 'naysayer' this is not the use of the term that I am interested in with this book.

Attributed to Aristotle is the adage: 'It is the mark of an educated mind to be able to entertain a thought without accepting it'. This is the philosophical game I am using. It is enough to ask, 'What if Tarot can tell the future?' and then test it. It is enough to try a reading 'as if' Tarot is capable of magically retrieving information from the mind or situation of the querent. It is not required that you hold these ideas to be true outside of the game, any more than playing *Dungeons & Dragons* requires that you behave as a 'level three half-elf wizard outside of the confines of the game'. With that said, I will continue henceforth by accepting Tarot on its own terms. In the final part of the book I will revisit these sceptical questions after having thoroughly explored the game of cards, and as always I will let you make up your own mind.

LEVEL 1

Tarot reading

> As poetry is the most beautiful expression of the things that are of all most beautiful, so is symbolism the most Catholic expression in concealment of things that are most profound in the Sanctuary and that have not been declared outside it with the same fulness by means of the spoken word.[5]
>
> —A.E. Waite

> The true Tarot is symbolism; it speaks no other language and offers no other signs. Given the inward meaning of its emblems, they do become a kind of alphabet which is capable of indefinite combinations and makes true sense in all.[6]
>
> —A.E. Waite

The aim of this section of the book is to get you reading the Tarot cards effectively with minimum effort so you can start practising. Later, in Level 2, we will take a much more in-depth look at the cards in order to allow for more detailed readings.

---

[5] Page 1 of the Preface (Waite 1910).
[6] Page 7 (Waite 1910).

The two best decks to start with are either the Rider Waite Smith Deck, which has a symbolic scene pictured on every card, or the Marseilles deck which has 'pip' cards for the minor arcana, these are similar to regular numbered playing cards rather than full images. Most people nowadays start with the Rider Waite Smith, and there are the most resources for learning how to read with this deck.

However, the Marseilles Tarot is the version from which almost all other divination decks have been derived, including the Rider Waite Smith, and starting with this deck is not only a little more straightforward but also makes the learner aware of the numerological structure, via the pip cards, which underpin all other divinatory Tarot decks. The Rider Waite Smith Deck, however, with its attractive Art Nouveau imagery, is a little easier for visual thinkers and being a 'higher information' deck, it leads one's story-telling down a more specific narrative.

The Marseilles deck has less information, and the minor cards must be deciphered using numerology. This is a good place to start for those who are natural storytellers, or those to whom ideas come easily, as it offers more room for interpretation. Most other Tarot decks are derivatives of these two. Crowley's 'Thoth' deck, for instance, is a little closer to the Marseilles Deck but has a common ancestor with the Rider Waite Smith, in the Golden Dawn Tarot Deck and could be considered a third style of deck. As Crowley's deck is more esoteric I don't recommend starting with it though I will also include it in this book from level two onwards.

I also don't recommend starting with one of the many thousands of novelty decks based on pop-culture references: Themed decks involving, cats, witches or characters from movies or books, or decks that are largely art pieces. These are sometimes quite unbalanced in the way they tell stories, though they can be fun for experiments later on.

Once you are proficient in the tradition of Tarot, it can be fun to try out different decks, and you may well choose a non-traditional deck as your primary one. Personally, before reading I often prefer to show querents a few different decks, including the aforementioned ones, and let them choose the one they want me to read with.

Reversals

When reading with reversals, the orientation of the cards matters, and the cards are shuffled accordingly. When a card is upside down, it is usually read as being 'blocked', or negatively aspected (or positively aspected if it was already a negative card).

Whether or not to read with reversals is one of the most hotly argued aspects of Tarot reading. Though in Level 2 we will explore reversals thoroughly I will not be teaching them to start with, as they can be overwhelming for the beginner. There are already 78 cards to learn and reversals potentially double that amount of information. For now, all you need to know is that many professional-level readers read without reversals, so their inclusion is entirely optional. I usually ask my querent whether or not they want me to read with reversals before starting a reading.

Card relationships

The logic of Tarot, and of magic in general, is one of associative thinking. This is to say, that pulling a story from the cards requires a mode of thinking similar to how one might use words to write a poem or musical notes to write music. Each card can be used to say many things and the story becomes more precise as more cards are turned over.

In music, a single note could have a potential relationship with any note not yet played, and to fully define a key requires seven notes. From the first note in a song, the listener's relationship to the music is cemented by the arrival of more notes, be they parts of the bass line, the melody or the chords. Leaving notes out creates ambiguity, and the inclusion of more than seven notes, or of notes outside of the parent scale creates a modulation, also known as a 'key change'. The listener's understanding of the music becomes simpler when they can understand the key.

I read the cards similarly. Their meanings are not precisely fixed, but instead they change their context in relation to other cards, and also with their position in a spread. Despite their face meanings, or their tendencies, there are ways for all the cards to be positive and all the cards to be negative. Similarly in music, minor chords, which are in isolation, gloomy, can be made to sound cheerful given the right context in relation to major chords, and major chords which are in isolation, contented, can be made to sound 'brooding' or 'dark' when in a dissonant relationship with preceding chords. Because of this, learning Tarot can, at first, seem airy-fairy or even arbitrary. However, things will become clearer and more precise as one gets used to doing readings.

Tarot reading, like composing or improvising music, is highly personal. It is an interaction between a reader, their cards and the querent. Just like performance art, one has done a good reading, if the querent is moved by the reading. One has done a bad reading if the querent doesn't relate at all to the story.

Sometimes a querent will come back a week later and explain that a reading they thought was bogus, is in retrospect, profound. Similarly, not all readings are going to make the querent happy. Sometimes a little tension is what a querent needs. Without tension, we are loathe to get moving.

While there is no objective 'black or white' way to decide whether a reading is good or bad, there are most definitely bad readings and good readings, just as there is good and bad music and art. Having said that, a heavy metal gig is not going to easily move a bluegrass audience, and a skilful performer is one who knows how to tailor the performance to be well received.

The four suits

Everyone will be familiar with the four suits of playing cards. These have a common root with the four suits of Tarot. For divination, the four suits act as groups of categories and concepts. These concepts are largely drawn from European and Islamic alchemy and the four classical elements: Fire, Water, Air and Earth, which were first clearly defined as a symbolic system by Empedocles (approximately 494–434 BCE). The history of this will be explained in a later part of this book.

In Tarot, the four suits are Wands, Cups, Swords and Pentacles. These suits are actually older than the four used in normal French-style playing cards. Wands were originally called Batons, or clubs, Swords were sometimes called Pikes, and Pentacles were originally called Coins and sometimes Discs. One will still find these variances and more amongst different Tarot and playing card decks.

The attributions for each of the suits are as follows:

Wands (Batons)

Element: △ Fire.
Qualities: Hot and dry.
Gender: Active or 'masculine'.
Traditional social class: Peasantry, agriculture, artists.
Sense: Sight.

Meanings: Creativity and will, personal ambition, personal goals, inspiration, animus in women.[7] Connected to the Kings amongst the court cards.

Humour: Choleric temperament: Dominating, assertive, fiery, striving, competitive, defiant, controlling, leading, intuitive.

Roles: Artists, musicians, inventors, solo sports, magicians.

Cups

Element: ▽ Water.
Qualities: Cold and wet.
Gender: Receptive or 'feminine'.
Traditional social class: Clergy.
Sense: Taste.

Meanings: Emotions and love, personal relationships, the ability to receive, Anima in men.[8] Connected to the Queens amongst the court cards.

Humour: Phlegmatic temperament: Curious, experiencing, accommodating, reacting, supportive.

Roles: Singers, poets, nurses, parents, counsellors, healers, childcare.

Swords

Element: ☐ Air.
Qualities: Hot and wet.
Gender: Active or 'masculine'.
Traditional social class: Nobility, lawyers and judges, academics and military.
Sense: Smell.

Meanings: Ideas, the world of concepts, maths, design, reason, problem-solving, maintenance, ambitions of status. Connected to the Knights amongst the court cards.

---

[7] In Jungian psychology the 'Animus' is the hidden male aspect of the psyche in females.
[8] In Jungian psychology the 'Anima' is the hidden female aspect of the psyche in males.

Humour: Sanguine temperament: Joyful, talkative, impressionable, expressive, social, extroverted.

Roles: Inventors, designers, engineers, mathematicians, scientists, teachers (especially tertiary), comedians, marketers and advertisers.

Pentacles (Coins/Discs)

Element: ☐ Earth.
Qualities: Cold and dry.
Gender: Receptive or feminine.
Traditional social class: Merchants, makers, craftspeople.
Sense: Touch.

Meanings: Body and possessions, time, work prospects, commerce, economics, craftspeople, workers, connected to the Pages amongst the court cards. Melancholic temperament: Gentle, irritable, relating, critical, soulful, feeling, sensual, sensitive.

Careers: Tradespeople, factory workers, builders, manufacturers, salespeople, retailers, models, fashion industry.

The four sensible qualities

In Western and Islamic alchemy, all substances were attributed to four qualities: Heat, cold, wetness and dryness. These were used to explain the relationships and behaviours of chemicals and states of matter. Alchemy was not pure chemistry, however, and the same concepts were used for psychological types, roles and behaviours of human beings and for aspects of nature.

Though alchemy has been largely superseded and split up into chemistry, psychology, magic and other fields of study, there are still many cultural remnants of alchemical theories and esoteric Tarot reading is among these.

The Qualities and their directions

- Heat goes up.
- Cold goes down.
- Wetness is horizontal.
- Dryness has no directionality, it is fixed.

Fire was considered the lightest substance which wants only to go up. It is hot and dry. Air is heavier so it moves both upwards and horizontally. It is hot and wet. Moisture is heavier but still fluid. So it moves downwards and horizontally. It is cold and wet.

Earth goes only down. It is cold and dry. It is the only classical element which is solid rather than being fluid. If you apply fire to boil water, the cold changes to hot and becomes steam, which is considered in alchemy, a type of 'air'. If you remove the heat from fire, it becomes cold and dry, earth, which is ash.

I will not go into much more detail, but you can now get a feeling of how alchemists understood the world. Everything was thought to be filled with these four fundamental qualities which determined the behaviour of all substances and beings.

Likewise in Tarot, the four elements Fire, Water, Air and Earth are used to understand every card, and via the cards all situations relationships, and personalities.

The four elements

- Fire represents the first drive to action, inspiration and the energy to change one thing into another. Fire acts and imposes itself on its environment, actively changing it. In human beings, it is the willpower, artistry and craftsmanship. In our modern era, Fire also incorporates electricity. In physics, Fire would be the phase of plasma, and energy. In human behaviour, Fire is assertiveness, aggression, passion and anger.
- Water responds to its environment and allows its form to be changed to conform to its surroundings. It represents the emotions (tears), which are our reactions. It also represents emotional relationships. It is aesthetics in the arts. It is the 'feeling' stage of getting something done. In physics, Water would be the phase of liquid and fields such as gravitation and electromagnetism. In human behaviour, Water corresponds to love, relationships, joy and sadness.
- Air is the least tangible of all the elements. It represents the mind, ideas, teaching, language and the realm of pure concept. It is the planning stage of getting something done. In the modern era, Air also incorporates flows of information such as the internet. In physics, Air would be the phase of gas and information.

- Earth is the most tangible of the elements. Earth can be cut or divided into separate objects that stay separate. It is the practical doing stage of getting something done. It is the manifestation of will. In Kabbalah Earth is described as the combination of the other three elements. In readings, Earth is our resources, time, money and energy to get things done. Traditionally Earth is associated with shields, protection and also stone. In physics, Earth would be the solid phase, and all matter.

Active and passive

These are often also referred to as 'masculine' and 'feminine'. However, it is important to understand that these concepts do not, in readings, generally refer to our bodies. In Western magic, alchemy and the Tarot everyone is understood to embody some combination of masculine and feminine qualities, regardless of their primary gender.

In nature, a flower would be feminine and the bee masculine. The bee is the active force, and the flower attracts the bee. Both parties get something out of their interaction. That bees are biologically assigned 'female' by modern science is not relevant to the mode of thinking we use for Tarot.

In a musical performance, the musician is masculine/active, and the audience is feminine/passive.

In romance, the partner who woos is masculine/active and the partner who attracts is feminine/passive. For this reason, despite tradition, many men do well in courting, by playing a 'feminine' role, and many women do well by actively wooing a man. An example would be a beautiful male actor, such as James Dean, that women like to look at pictures of, or a rockstar, such as Elvis, who is pursued by female 'groupies'. To fully realise all you are capable of it is worthwhile to learn both active/masculine and passive/feminine roles. I find that this understanding comes up in nearly every Tarot reading and is perhaps one of its best lessons.

Do not think of the active as being more powerful than the passive. One is not more powerful than the other, and they are complementary. An active power needs a goal to pursue and a goal needs an active power to carry it out.

The Temperaments

Preceding modern psychology, the humours represented an early idea of how the body affects the personality. The Temperaments derive from 'Humourism', the idea that the balance of four categories of fluids in the body were central to a variety of health and psychological traits and diagnoses. The Temperaments were a foundational part of medicine and early psychology from the classical era until the beginning of the scientific age, with ongoing influences felt today.

As far as we know, the Greek physician Hippocrates (460–370 BCE) created the theory of humours, and it was later expanded by Galen (129–c. 200 CE), a Greek-Roman, who was influential to medical literature for centuries, and who applied humourism to his medical practice.

These Temperaments can be used by Tarot readers in order to apply personality traits to the four suits. They especially affect the meanings of the court cards, which stand for people (or roles people play) in a Tarot reading. The Temperaments can be thought of as a precursor to modern personality tests such as the Myers–Briggs Type Indicator test, and the Big Five personality test.

The word 'temperament' comes from the Latin temperare, 'to mix', and a balance of humours was considered necessary for good bodily and emotional health.

Blood was believed to consist of proportional amounts of the other three humours, just as the element Earth is often described as being a condensation and mix of Fire, Water and Air.

Somewhat confusingly for the modern reader, the meanings of the four fluids have changed somewhat in comparison with modern biology.

When blood was drawn and settled in a test tube, it was found to split into three sections. Black bile was the collection of dark red blood cells at the bottom of the vessel, phlegm was a layer of white blood cells and yellow bile was the clear serum at the top. The fluid phlegm was also used as a general term for colourless secretions such as pus, mucus, saliva, sweat, or semen. It did not relate to solely to mucus as is the case today.

Temperament	Tarot Suit	Humour	Planet	Element	Qualities	Organ	Season	Personality	Star Signs
Choleric	Wands	Yellow Bile	Mars, Sun	Fire	Warm and dry Combustible	Gallbladder	Summer	Dominating, direct, ruling. Extroverted.	Aries, Leo, Sagittarius
Phlegmatic	Cups	Phlegm	Moon & Venus	Water	Cold and moist	Brain & Lungs	Winter	Agreeable, peace-seeking, empathetic. Introverted.	Cancer, Scorpio, Pisces
Sanguine	Swords	Blood	Jupiter	Air	Warm and moist	Liver	Spring	Sociable, impressionable, cheerful. Extroverted.	Gemini, Libra, Aquarius
Melancholic	Pentacles	Black Bile	Saturn, Mercury	Earth	Cold and dry	Spleen	Autumn	Depressive, cautious, conscientious. Introverted.	Taurus, Virgo, Capricorn

The four personality types followed the sensible qualities described in alchemy.

- The choleric personality is like Fire, hot and dry. Like combustible material, they 'ignite' (become passionate or angry) quickly yet take a long time to be put out. They are energetic and quick-acting. They are quick to develop emotion but slow to lose it.
- The phlegmatic personality is like Water, cold and moist. They take a long time to 'boil' but quickly condensate in comparison to other types. Slow to act, but amenable. They become emotional slowly but lose it quickly.
- The sanguine personality is like Air. They heat up quickly and cool off quickly. They are the most impressionable type, quickly taking on the properties of those around them. They are 'flighty', quick to develop emotion and quick to lose it.
- The melancholic personality is like Earth. They take a long time to heat up and a long time to cool down. They are the most stubborn of the personal types, and the most steadfast. They are slow to develop emotion and slow to lose it.

Wait is this pseudo-science?

It would be if we were trying to use it instead of modern science. However, in this case, these are story-telling elements. Consider the game *Dungeons & Dragons*. The four suits are like different classes.

In this way in *Dungeons & Dragons*:

- Wands would be magic-users.
- Cups would be bards, clerics and other healers.
- Swords would be fighters.
- Pentacles would be druids, monks (because they fight with their bodies), and defensive 'tank' characters.

The four Temperaments are like alignments:

- Choleric is Chaotic.
- Phlegmatic is Good.
- Sanguine is Lawful.
- Melancholic is Neutral.

These types of thought experiments are useful when learning Tarot.

Quick explanations for the Rider Waite Smith and Marseilles Decks

Here are some 'low definition' descriptions to get you started. These will also function as a list of memory prompts later on when you have learnt about the cards but have not yet memorised them.

The Minor Arcana

Aces: Beginnings, something new.
Twos: Crossroads. A Choice.
Threes: Advancement. Creativity. Growth. Looking at options.
Fours: Stability. Routine. Dependability, Predictability.
Fives: Unpredictability, Change. Rearrangement.
Sixes: Overcoming obstacles. Perseverance.
Sevens: Confidence in experience.
Eights: Advancement. Freeing yourself up.
Nines: Curveball or Attainment. Coming to terms with something.
Tens: Completion.

Pages: Newbies/Trainees/Apprentices/Students. Those younger than you. A new role. Being led by others.
Knights: Journeymen. People of action. People your own age. Those who take initiative and do a job directly.
Queens: Feminine authorities. Mothers and grandmothers. Patience and understanding (or the absence thereof).
Kings: Masculine authorities. Fathers and grandfathers. Knowledge, wisdom, big decisions information.

The Major Arcana or Trumps

0 The Fool: A noob or beginner.

I The Magician: A master of their craft.

II High Priestess: Artemis. An intuitive feminine talent. Spiritual knowledge, wisdom gained through direct experience.

III Empress: Demeter. Mother Nature, motherhood, pregnancy, agriculture.

IV Emperor: Solomon. A diplomatic ruler. A wise judge. A high authority.

V Hierophant: One who initiates others into an institution, or the institution itself.

VI Lovers: Faith in love. A trusted partnership.

VII Chariot: A skilful and ambitious tactician. Balancing forces to get what you want.

VIII Strength (XI in some decks): Taming a wild force. Overcoming mental adversity.

IX Hermit: A stage one wiseman (on his way towards becoming the magician). Time spent learning alone. Self-discipline.

X Wheel of Fortune: The completion of a cycle. Fate. A gamble.

XI Justice (VIII in some decks): A conflict resolution from outside.

XII Hanged man: A self-Martyr. Choosing to suffer 'on principle', or undertaking a personal ordeal or a rebellion. Play 'the heretic'.

XIII Death: A painful change.

XIV Temperance: Moderation. Healing.

XV Devil: An addiction, or associating oneself with an immoral institution.

XVI Tower: An established power collapses, usually due to corruption. A loss of faith at the societal level. War.

XVII Star: A lofty idealistic goal.

XVIII Moon: Inspiration from shadow. Hidden things come to light. A journey of self-discovery.

XIX Sun: Innocent joy. Everything is what it seems. Or in some contexts, 'rose-coloured spectacles'.

XX Judgement: The uncovering of old crimes. A wide-scale rebalancing of power. Comeuppance.

XXI World: A new wide perspective. Travel.

Wands

Ace of Wands: Inspiration from novelty. A new creative undertaking.
Two of Wands: A new exploration.
Three of Wands: Ambition. Making a decision.
Four of Wands: Early results.
Five of Wands: A struggle for an initiation. Friendly competition.
Six of Wands: A parade under leadership. A group success.
Seven of Wands: 'Kick against the pricks'. Taking on a battle on principle where one is certain to take a loss.
Eight of Wands: A speedy delivery or sudden change.
Nine of Wands: A last stand, usually successful.
Ten of Wands: A burden.

Page of Wands: A young person or beginner seeking validation.
Knight of Wands: A *Prima Donna*, a charmer.
Queen of Wands: A smothering mother. A woman who is an active power.
King of Wands: A cult leader.

Cups

Ace of Cups: A new emotion or potential relationship.
Two of Cups: Mutual benefit. A new relationship.
Three of Cups: An emotional connection with others.
Four of Cups: Dissatisfaction with what one has.
Five of Cups: Crying over spilt milk. A failure to focus on what one has.
Six of Cups: Nostalgia.
Seven of Cups: Debauchery/hedonism. Temptation.
Eight of Cups: Quitting.
Nine of Cups: Hospitality.
Ten of Cups: A family celebration.

Page of Cups: An imaginative child. An emotional youth.
Knight of Cups: A unique escapist talent or a troubled poet.
Queen of Cups: A poetic woman who makes beautiful things from old trauma. A female counsellor.
King of Cups: A loyal defender of others.

Swords

Ace of Swords: A new endeavour. A new debate or a new field of study.
Two of Swords: A rational decision.
Three of Swords: A heartache. Ideas negatively affecting the emotions.
Four of Swords: Time out. A rest for one's mental health.
Five of Swords: Spoils of war. A debate won, sometimes by trickery.
Six of Swords: An old trauma. Taking one's problems with one.
Seven of Swords: The theft of ideas. A sneak.
Eight of Swords: Self-doubt.
Nine of Swords: Anxiety, depression, nightmares.
Ten of Swords: Defeat, despair.

Page of Swords: A noob 'gatekeeper'. An 'edge-lord' a 'know-it-all'.
Knight of Swords: A daredevil. A sophist. A brazen competitor.
Queen of Swords: A successful and ambitious female intellectual or battle leader.
King of Swords: An intellectual judge.

Pentacles

Ace of Pentacles: A career or financial opportunity.
Two of Pentacles: Juggling resources, balancing the books.
Three of Pentacles: An apprenticeship. Showing one's works for the first time.
Four of Pentacles: A miser.
Five of Pentacles: Pride against accepting charity.
Six of Pentacles: Charity to others.
Seven of Pentacles: Impatience.
Eight of Pentacles: Diligence.
Nine of Pentacles: Comfort.
Ten of Pentacles: Affluence.

Page of Pentacles: A hardworking apprentice.
Knight of Pentacles: A responsible conservative.
Queen of Pentacles: A female guardian of an estate.
King of Pentacles: A master craftsman, or keeper of a tradition.

Understanding Tarot numerology

Tarot comes from a time when numbers were not merely logical frames imposed on reality in order that it could be measured. Instead, they were understood as the pre-existing symbolic structures from the 'heavens' (the conceptual and/or spiritual realm) through which the world manifested. This was not a materialist cosmology like that which has dominated the world since the Enlightenment era. Instead, it was an earlier 'informational' model for understanding reality. This was shared in a similar fashion by most, if not all, pre-modern human cultures. Put simply; concept, mind, thought, spirit and consciousness were together considered to be the fundamental aspects of reality, rather than 'emergent' qualities produced by the interactions of matter. Matter was considered to be 'condensed information', rather than information being a property derived from matter.

In chasing the materialist hypothesis, quantum physics has found that the world is not, after all, put together from small bits of matter, like 'Lego blocks'. Instead, zoomed in beyond a certain point, matter ceases to make rational sense and instead of finding truly fundamental particles, we observe 'energy fields', which can just as easily be described as information fields. There is also an amount of randomness to the universe which eludes our abilities to rationalise it.

Information seems to be more fundamental than matter. A universe made out of information fields is remarkably close to the cosmology of the alchemists and almost all ancients before them. The standard model of quantum physics states that every electron in the universe is in communication with every other electron, regardless of the distances separating them. This means that the smallest parts of matter, particles, communicate also at the scale of the of the largest possible 'thing', the cosmos. The smallest, maps onto the largest.

This may be hard to understand, but some theorists describe it as a single universal electromagnetic field in which 'individual' electrons are merely interaction points. Another way to understand it, is that all electrons are indistinguishable from each other and therefore behave in unison despite being different 'points' in space. That is to say that one electron cannot be measured as being truly separate from another.

This is very much in accordance with the alchemical adage 'as above so below' which comes from the Emerald Tablet of Hermes Trismegistus, an Islamic alchemical text from the ninth century that became somewhat of a manifesto for the burgeoning alchemical age.

The only major potential point of difference between the alchemical worldview and that of the standard model of quantum physics is that the alchemists regarded the realm of concepts to be capable of its own agency. That is, the world has a mind and that this 'world mind' overlaps and interacts with human minds.

This may seem to be the realm of 'New Age' claptrap, except that quantum experiments such as the famous 'double-slit experiment' have shown over and over that the universe, in a sense, seems to understand when it is being watched and will change its behaviour accordingly. Make of that what you will.

To the alchemists, the world of concepts, which in their model of reality, precedes materialisation, was considered to be full of entities which could be negotiated with, and therefore the human mind had a part in creating and manipulating the way the universe puts itself together. Likewise, our minds were not considered to be closed off from the 'world mind' and instead, all of our desires, thoughts, ideas and inspirations were caused by interactions with the informational realm, and the entities, be they spirits, angels, concepts or numbers, that inhabited them.

To understand this, consider how an advertisement can create a desire, often subconsciously, in the mind of the potential customer, or how a pop song or jingle can get stuck in someone's head and leap from head to head. These could be considered information constructs that carry a part of the willpower of their creators. To the alchemists, and the ancients before them, something as simple as numbers could carry will and intent. Numbers were, in a sense, 'spirits'.

To begin Tarot reading requires that we entertain the idea that numbers are not only for measuring and counting but also thematic story elements, which harmonise, through tension and release, like music does.

Likewise, because Tarot is a narrative game, numbers in Tarot behave like plot points or even proto-characters, with wants, personalities and even their own morality. So let's put aside the idea that numbers and maths are 'boring' and 'analytical' and instead consider them as elements in our story-game, which can be emotional, symbolic, moving and entertaining.

Duality

In occult symbolism, ideas are not so black and white as in formal logic. Instead, each idea can be understood as a duality that contains within it, its own contradiction.

For example:

Life/death.
Active/passive.
Male/Female.
Good/Evil.
Belief/doubt.

Later I will explain how the positive and negative interpretations of a card can be understood by their position in a spread, their interaction with other cards that have similarities of number, suit or theme, as well as the optional use of reversals, where an upside-down card can constitute a negative expression, or an obstacle to that card coming through.

In this way, all the cards can be negative cards and all the cards can be positive cards. It is to be noted that not all 'positive' expressions of cards are beneficial to the querent, and not all 'negatives' are harmful to the reader. For instance, the Death card might be a close shave that saves the querent, or the 'death' of something which was holding the querent back. It might, also, be an actual funeral.

These dualities of concepts within Tarot, need not be black and white, but rather can be considered as a spectrum. This is expressed and well understood for instance in the Yin–Yang symbol where the white section contains a seed of black and the black section contains a seed of white.

Reading Tarot is more like having a conversation with a set of symbols than it is like learning logic from a set of precepts.

A three-act play

The most useful explanation of numerology in Tarot that I have come across comes from Papus, the pen name of the French esotericist writer Gérard Anaclet Vincent Encausse (1865–1916 CE). Papus described the numbers from one to ten in terms of a three-act play. The following is my own take on his system, modified to be understandable to the modern reader.

* * *

Act One is comprised of the numbers: 1, 2, 3.
Act Two is: 4, 5, 6
Act Three is: 7, 8, 9
10 is the final scene.

- 1, 4 and 7 are the stable beginnings of each act.
- 2, 5 and 8 are the middle situations of tension in each act.
- 3, 6 and 9 are final resolutions of the tension; either a win or a loss, in each act.
- **10 is a transition to a new narrative.**

Act 1: The conceptual realm
1   Stable beginning
2   Tension
3   Resolution
Act 2: The interpersonal realm
4   Stable beginning
5   Tension
6   Resolution
Act 3: The formative realm
7   Stable beginning
8   Tension
9   Resolution
Final scene: Completion
10   Transition to a new story

* * *

Examples of how numerology can be used are the planning a large project such as building a house, maintaining a marriage, running a business, brokering a deal, writing a book, or studying for a degree.

Act one, the conceptual realm

Aces: The first inspiration for a new idea: the creative spark. Papus and other writers influenced by him say that Aces bring more 'power' to cards around them and express this through the element of their suit. This can be understood as 'enthusiasm' for the project from different quarters.

Twos: The first decisions are made, a crossroads is reached, and a first action is employed. A duality is presented by considering what is wanted and what is not wanted. A Polarity of positive/negative.

Threes: Advancement. A commitment is made. The project is conceptualised. A first negotiation is agreed upon. Realisation occurs, which is the offspring of the duality of what is wanted and not wanted. A new concept springs forth from the synthesis of two preceding concepts. A black-and-white viewpoint suddenly becomes grey. To realise a project, compromises must be made. If threes are negatively expressed, then no agreement is reached, or the goal is deemed unrealistic. If positively expressed, then the project moves forward.

Act two, the interpersonal realm

Fours: A stability is found. Plans are drawn up. Stagnation can occur here if the card is negatively expressed. A push is required for further action. Some stress can be felt as what can be imagined is replaced by more realistic expectations.

Fives: Unpredictability. A sudden loss or gain. A small conflict. A 'fifth wheel' upsets the balance. Tensions arise via the entrance of a new character. One's first choice requires compromise or seems 'blocked'. Idealism suffers here and must give way to pragmatism.

Sixes: Elements settle to their practical best. A journey begins towards harmony. A way through is found. If positively expressed, this can be better than the original plan, if negatively expressed it can feel like a compromise which gives up on the most ideal form.

Act three, the formative realm

Sevens: The beginning of the cycle that results in materialisation. This is a vulnerable stage akin to a germinating seed or a newborn infant. There is much hope here but also a risk. This stage is the realisation of a new level of complexity; one that helps to understand a system of individual parts as a whole, for example, the seven notes of the major scale in music, the seven colours of the rainbow, the seven classical planets in astrology, or the 'seven seas', etc.

Eights: Action and change. This can be painful at first even when the outcome is beneficial in the long run. A strong drive to work is needed to finish the project. This is the last chance to abandon the path in this cycle. The phrase 'it always takes longer than you expect' comes in at this point. This is the most productive step as the promise of completion is just around the corner.

Nines: Resolution occurs, whether positive or negative. Either relief is felt that one's idea is now a reality, or a disappointment sets in, that it didn't live up to the idea that one started with. If the latter is the case, then it's important to remember that it is one's expectations that need adjustment rather than trying to adjust the world to fit one's expectations.

Completion

Tens: Finality. A cause for celebration, or feeling fully committed with no way out. This is a full materialisation from earlier concepts. It is a 'payday', whether positive (income) or negative (debt). In its most negative expression, ten is the necessary death that produces new life, or the defeat that forces one to abandon a project and start something new and hopefully better. Tens are hard-earned wisdom.

The journey from one to ten through the suits

Wands: Creativity and willpower

Ace: Inspiration. The first inkling of desire and will that precedes ambition. The desire to create.

Two: An initial awareness of obstacles is reached and the first planning stage of a project is started. Decisions are made as to what a project will and won't entail. High self-belief or doubt will set in, depending on how the cards are placed. Both have their pros and cons. The subject of the reading becomes excited that a project will succeed, and a projection of success in the new domain is imagined. Two of Wands can also be a productive argument or debate, especially one that helps one understand one's own point of view. As I like to put it: 'If you don't argue, how do you know what you think?'

Three: An initial method to plough ahead is realised. One gets a good feeling about getting a new project started. The first pragmatic step is taken. This requires that other projects be put on hold. Every chosen action contains the sacrifice of those other actions which could have been chosen.

Four: A stable foundation is reached or completed. The initial creative needs for the project have already been met. This round of obstacles will be at a higher level of detail and the subject of the reading prepares to push past them. When negatively expressed, the foundation will be insufficient for the magnitude of the project, or further action will be blocked, as fours also denote a 'hump' that requires an effort to get over.

Five: Battling or solving obstacles. Competition with others who have a similar idea. A justification is required to explain why your project is more worthy than others.

Six: Victory or defeat. If it is a group project, and it is successful, then a small celebration is felt with camaraderie.

Seven: The success of the enterprise is forecasted, as most obstacles have now been overcome. However, a big burst of effort is required to secure benefits. Sevens represent the large picture, so a realisation of what the completed project will look like is reached.

Eight: A final round of issues. The project may only be partially successful. 'Pie in the sky' idealism needs to be dropped in favour of pragmatism. A final rush to meet a deadline.

Nine: Compromise or success. A sense of achievement. There is often the feeling of having been through an ordeal, even when the outcome is a success.

Ten: The project takes on a new life. It is required that it be passed over to new hands or else it becomes something new in the hands of the querent. If it is a performance, then it is left to the judgement of the audience, and while it will have a powerful effect, their interpretation may not be exactly what the querent intended, requiring an adjustment of future expectations. An easing of effort to control outcomes is required in order to sustain the project, otherwise a 'burden of success' will be felt.

Cups: Love, relationships and emotion

Ace: A new attraction, romantic, parental or platonic.

Two: The question arises as to whether one's feelings will be reciprocated. Fear of rejection arises on one hand, but also a buzz of possibility on the other. Or, if one is propositioned, one has a choice to reciprocate or not. Alternatively, a loyal attachment is already established and a question about a substantial change in the nature of the relationship is being presented.

Three: Mutual attraction is established or denied.

Four: Obstacles arise from outside the relationship: 'The grass is greener on the other side'.[9] Dissatisfaction or doubt sets in. A first argument or a negotiation of expectations occurs. The relationship is taken for granted and suffers tension as a result. Dissatisfaction may occur, but out of boredom rather than action.

Five: Arguments occur, and a reconsideration of what one wants is required. Emotional recalibration is needed. At this point, some will admit their expectations have changed, while others will blame the other party.

Six: A decision is made to continue or to leave. Either way, emotions have shifted. If one remains in the relationship then one is required to alter one's expectations.

Seven: Success of the relationship is foreseen, as most obstacles have now been overcome. A new layer to the relationship is revealed that was hidden before. A desire arises to explore new things together. You or the partner's shadow nature might appear.[10] This could result in

---

[9] The phrase originates with the Roman poet Ovid (43 BCE–18 CE).
[10] The philosopher Carl Jung (1875–1961 CE) theorised that each of us has a hidden aspect of our personality that we aren't aware of. While not necessarily always negative, this hidden aspect of self contains drives that push us towards behaviours that we and others around us might not understand. These shadow drives often contradict our 'persona' or outward nature. For instance, a beautiful person may fear being seen as ugly deep down, a healthy person may now and then take dangerous risks because of an inner 'death drive', or a person in a stable relationship may fear being abandoned. Jung's therapy involved uncovering these often unpleasant or surprising aspects of our nature and incorporating them so that they may be controlled or even harnessed, rather than being in tension with our conscious self. This process was called 'individuation'.

enrichment or in troubles. 'Spicing up' the relationship could result in later regrets. Keyword: 'Enabler'.

Eight: A final round of issues. The relationship may only be partially successful. A reworking of expectations is needed. One partner may become distant. Positively expressed, acceptance is reached and the querent or partner stops seeking fulfilment from the relationship that is beyond what is on offer. Though the relationship may continue, they will start looking elsewhere for some of the things they want.

Nine: Compromise or success. The establishment of a new home, a pregnancy, or a new phase in the relationship. A heart-to-heart connection is established. A routine is set to meet up with one or a group of friends.

Ten: The relationship takes on a new life. Possible parenthood, moving in together, marriage, etc. The relationship is accepted by the wider family.

Swords: Intellect, debates and competition

Ace: A new battle, a debate, a rivalry, an entrance into academia, a war, a test. Striving for status in a new field.

Two: An obstacle makes one question if one should get involved. A decision arises between two possible modes of conflict. Usually, people will get roped in.

Three: One becomes committed to the battle. Black and white becomes grey. An oath between two parties is broken. In the case of an argument, things become heated to a point where a relationship or friendship reaches a breaking point. In a debate 'things become personal'. In a fight or battle, pretences to 'play fair' are dropped. Keywords: Heartbreak, 'butthurt'.

Four: An initial hit is scored against the rival, the test or the institution. This usually causes resentment in the losing party. If positively expressed, then success comes to those who have swords but keep them sheathed.[11] The conflict has hit a nerve. One party pulls back in order to consider how to respond (or pull out) without losing grace.

Five: Just as the querent feels they might have won the game, the opponent scores against them. A civil debate turns petty. The opponent is underhanded or comes from an unpredictable place. If the querent 'wins' they will soon discover that they have gained nothing. Often one feels stuck between feeling a need to move on but an inertia to keep fighting. This is the type of emotional momentum and escalation that causes arguments in comment sections on the internet.

Six: The enemy is defeated in this round. Intelligence, or cleverness has won the goal.

Alternatively, one party pulls away, but resentments and some lasting damage have been done.

Seven: The querent or subject of the reading suffers a defeat from overconfidence. An artful and unexpected move takes place, which will be

---

[11] Possibly the figurative meaning of 'the meek shall inherit the Earth' Matthew 5:5. The original Greek word is πραεῖς (*praus*), which means roughly 'strength under control' and was used in this meaning for horses that had been tamed. The English word 'meek' which is a synonym for 'gentle' is a poor translation.

considered 'sneaky' by the victim. The enemy gains the upper hand. Alternatively, the querent makes a move that is surprising and is considered underhanded by their opponent. A gap in armour is found, or security is overcome. Keyword: 'Sneaky'.

Eight: A reworking of expectations is needed. The querent undermines the attack but will still suffer a loss. Damage control. One's ambitions have restricted their movements. If one continues a fight at this point, they will score diminishing returns.

Nine: Stalemate. The tension becomes balanced but not released. There is no win for either side while they continue the rivalry. A stability is reached from the threat of mutually assured destruction. Hurt feelings can arise and must be managed. If the aggrieved party can't win from this point on, they will sabotage, so one must give their enemy an exit path or a way to save face. Shock arises at the behaviour of another which ends a relationship. Keywords: Sour grapes.

Ten: The rivalry is abandoned, or is rendered irrelevant by circumstances. A refocus of attention takes place. To continue the rivalry is 'flogging a dead horse'. Despair will arise if one cannot let go of one's attachments.

Pentacles: Time, money, resources, body

Ace: A new inheritance, a raise, or a new job position arises with new benefits.

Two: An initial struggle to understand the terms by which one will receive this benefit takes place.

Three: The benefit arrives, or the job begins.

Four: A partial loss of money or time or energy occurs as one learns to deal with this new responsibility. There is stress from managing a new role.

Five: A rebalancing secures the resource. Sacrifices might need to be made in other areas. There is stress from overthinking.

Six: A realisation is reached as to how this may change one's life. Either a feeling of prestige, or regret arises depending on whether this card is positively or negatively aspected.

Seven: Success is secured. The querent, or subject of the reading, becomes used to the new arrangement.

Eight: Unforeseen costs arise. A new challenge presents itself. Reality hits home about what one has taken on. One goes through a period where they have to work harder or put in more time than they signed up for.

Nine: Overcoming issues. A new stability is found. The work becomes the new 'normal'. One has mastered the role.

Ten: The next readjustment comes into view.

The Court Cards

Pages

Apprentices, debutantes, youth, beginners, people younger than the querent. Or young women.

Page of Wands:
A beginner or one who is seeking prestige and is attention-seeking to those who have more power. For example, first-year art students.

Page of Cups:
A kind, innocent, idealist. A true believer and a romantic. Example: Juliet from Romeo and Juliet.

Page of Swords:
A beginner who feels they are an expert as soon as they have taken a 101 class. An internet troll. A 'gasbag', and sometimes a bully. In a game of manipulation, they can be a 'useful idiot'.[12]

Page of Pentacles:
A hardworking apprentice. Down to earth. Most likely working with their hands.

---

[12] Though erroneously attributed to Vladimir Lenin, the term was nevertheless used during the Cold War to describe those idealists living in democratic countries who bought into communist propaganda, and showed support, or gave money to Soviet Russia despite (supposedly) not understanding the downsides of actually living under a communist regime.

Knights

Journeymen, skilled practitioners, workers, peers, people around the same age as the querent, or young men (for modern readings I tend to interpret knights and pages as both male or female, as gender roles have shifted a lot since the traditional Tarot decks were designed).

Knight of Wands:
A Prima Donna. A singular talent who is difficult and dramatic. They externalise their insecurities.

Knight of Cups:
An escapist, romantic, poet type. Very talented but unstable, prone to addictions. An artist, musician, writer or actor. Very charming to a group of people.

Knight of Swords:
A brash, over-confident daredevil type who often achieves extraordinary things and creates jealousy in their detractors. They are powerful until they face a true master. They are quick to act, and this is often misunderstood as skill.

Knight of Pentacles:
A skilful, hardworking and down-to-earth masculine person who works with their hands. They can be stubborn as well as conscientious. They can be an engineer, electrician, mechanic or farmer type. They value, maintain and protect well-made things.

Queens

Matriarchs, women of prestige, community leaders, and female bosses. (Occasionally males can be 'Queens' and as per the slang use of the term, they will be acting somewhat outside of male norms.)

Queen of Wands:
A feminine artist, actor or musician or an imaginative mother. They can be a control freak, but may also overcome extraordinary odds. They have an otherworldly charm. As Wands are masculine and Queens are feminine, they may 'gender-bend', i.e. a woman with masculine traits or a very feminine man, or they may be a man in a role traditionally ascribed to women. As women, they find active, assertive and ambitious power in an otherwise feminine role.

Queen of Cups:
A mystical woman or feminine person with great intuition. A counsellor to their friends and family. They are caring, but can also be manipulative. They are prone to depression, but also a great help to others. If artistic, then they are emotional in their art.

Queen of Swords:
A feminine scholar, politician, activist, military commander, or public authority. An expert. She has power in her community. She has pain in her past and a wisdom which comes from life experience. She is a powerful and inspiring communicator. She doesn't suffer fools. She is not motherly.

Queen of Pentacles:
A woman of means who is a protector of nice things. Practical and successful in her own right, or a matriarch of a dynasty. She is not artistic. She likes to 'keep face'. She is a conservative in the original sense of the term; dedicated to the preservation of traditions and things.

Kings

Patriarchs, men of prestige, community leaders, male bosses. Kings can be women if they are in a leadership role that has been traditionally done by men, and they fit one of the King cards more readily than one of the Queen cards.

King of Wands:
A cult leader or successful public, or motivational speaker. Full of charm to a group. He can be brutal to those who don't follow him. He has followers rather than friends.

King of Cups:
An emotional man or masculine person who is loyal and protects his family. He acts from his heart rather than rationally. He is emotionally persuasive. He is able to express the feelings of the group. He promotes civility until there is no other option than to become brutal. As Cups are traditionally feminine, there is room to gender-bend here also.

King of Swords:
A judge, impartial and distant. Rational to a fault. A good advisor for difficult decisions. Can seem cold when exercising judgement. They are fair, but not emotional, and will seek to keep the peace.

King of Pentacles:
A guardian, or keeper of a tradition. A master craftsperson or worker in a highly skilled profession. Slow-moving and cautious. They have a very clear idea of what is going on but can be stuck in their point of view.

The Major Arcana

0 Fool:
An oblivious person with no idea what they are doing, yet who sometimes manages to get things done despite themselves. Or a state of inversion, good from evil, evil from good, order from chaos, etc.

I Magician:
A learned, balanced and measured master who appears to always be in conscious control.

II Priestess:
A person who has command of the hidden, the subconscious and the spirit world. Or the attainment of spiritual wisdom from direct experience.

III Empress:
Mother Nature, fertility, food and the sensual world. Also motherhood and pregnancy.

IV Emperor:
Fatherhood. Ordered society, authority, morality, rules and governance. Belonging to a nation.

V Hierophant:
Institutions, initiations, education, religion, dogma and cultural belief systems. Belonging to a culture. Wisdom from being told rather than from direct experience, i.e. the Bible.

VI Lovers:
Romantic partners, romantic friendships, adolescence, sex and the bond of love between two people. Faith in love or in partnership.

VII Chariot:
Taking control of one's world. Adulthood. Ambition. Actively making one's mark on the world.

VIII Strength (XI in some decks):
Taming oneself toward order. Mental health. Patience. Mentally and emotionally overcoming setbacks. The charming of a wild force, for instance, Beauty and the Beast.

IX Hermit:
Committing to a spiritual path outside of one's upbringing. Introspection. Gaining a spiritual teacher or taking responsibility for teaching oneself. A drive toward personal meaning rather than prestige.

X Wheel of Fortune:
A good or bad fortune. Seeing life events as temporary cycles. Big things that happen outside of our control. Surfing the wave of happenstance instead of being towed under.

XI Justice (VIII in some decks):
Judgement from outside. Being tested by society or an institution. Developing morality. A push toward living honestly or having to face the consequences of dishonesty. Alternatively, receiving justice or getting one's comeuppance.

XII Hanged Man:
Rebelling against societal norms for a cause or for personal identity. A self-inflicted burden in the hope of achieving growth.

XIII: Death:
The difficult shedding of that which has served its purpose in order that new things have space to grow. Grief. The necessary cycle of life and death. The need to sacrifice other things in order to get one thing done. Cycling down into depression. This card rarely refers to literal death.

XIV Temperance:
A rebalancing. Taking time to improve one's health and habits. Taking charge of one's emotions. Coming out of a depression.

XV Devil:
Addictions to things that one knows are unhealthy. Associating oneself with people or institutions that one disagrees with morally. Putting off what one needs to get done because it is unpleasant. Giving in to bad habits and sins. Realisations that an institution or authority is corrupt.

XVI Tower:
A collapse of faith, institutions or authority due to corruption. That which follows the behaviour of the Devil card if it is not addressed. Disasters that unveil corruption. This card usually refers to a group experience rather than an individual one.

XVII Star:
Piety. Taking on a higher purpose or aligning oneself with an idealistic goal. The goal will never be completely realised but it will continue to provide meaning and drive for as long as one is aligned to it. True faith.

XVIII Moon:
Normally hidden things become noticeable to those who look. A journey through the liminal space between consciousness and unconscious, or between body and spirit. An engagement with the occult. Gaining an awareness of hidden powers outside of normal consensus reality.

XIX Sun:
An innocent joy. A pleasant 'lightbulb moment' where things become clear and simple. Being in the moment with love energy. Everything is as it seems. If negatively aspected this card can represent 'rose-coloured spectacles'.

XX Judgement:
Old crimes or pain come back to haunt. A new path is discovered by unburying the past. 'Skeletons in the closet' are revealed so that closure can be reached. Acceptance of the past so that one can move on.

XXI The World:
A perspective of the big picture is gained. An acceptance of one's place in the scheme of things. Finally understanding how the parts fit into a big system. An opportunity to make peace with one's mortality.

Example readings

Now that we've got a good basic sense of all of the cards, let's get straight into reading with a Tarot deck. Here are some example readings with both the Marseilles and the Rider Waite Smith Decks. Don't worry if you haven't memorised the cards, it's fine to refer back to their meanings for as long as you need to.

A Quick start with the Marseilles Deck

1. Shuffle the cards.
2. Come up with a question.
3. Draw the cards into one of the spreads following.

Three-card spread

- The left card is the past.
- The middle card is the present.
- The right card is the future.

Question: The querent is in the process of buying a used car and wants to know if it is a good deal and whether she can trust the salesman.

Example:

Left card: Page (Valet) of Coins. A novice in relation to price (coins). The querent feels out of her depth in regards to the value of cars, their quality and how to negotiate a fair price.

Middle card: Judgement. She feels 'tested' by the car company and the salesperson. Because of this, she is hyper-vigilant, trying to guess the salesperson's every move, her stress is reminding her of other times that she felt out of her depth or judged, and this is further feeding her negative emotions. While the feeling is unpleasant, ultimately this will make it hard for the salesperson to over-sell to her.

Right card: Eight of Swords. Eight is a tension point in the 'third act' of a story. Reality hits home about what one has taken on. Because the other two cards suggested to me a difficulty in her buying the car, I think that this card is negatively aspected. Her ambitions have restricted her movements. The querent succeeds in not being ripped off, but fails to buy a car, as she is too nervous about the price and quality.

* * *

Six-card spread

- The top left card is what you think about the past.
- The bottom left card is an underlying reality about the past that you haven't considered.
- The top middle card is what you think about the present.
- The bottom middle card is an underlying reality about the present.
- The top right card is what you think about the future.
- The bottom right card is an underlying reality about the future.

Example:

Question: An actor has an audition for an action movie and he wants to know how to approach it in order to win the part.

The top left card: Three of Cups. Mutual attraction. The production company is aware of the actor's work and the actor is aware of the company's movies.

The bottom left card: The world (*Le Monde*). An acceptance of one's place in the larger scheme of things is required. The movie is a large project inside a larger industry, with a worldwide audience. The actor's best approach in the audition is not to overplay his case. Instead, he should try to come across as someone who will be easy to work with a good work ethic, who is a team player and is able to bring the goods. The production company also offers the opportunity to allow the actor to be 'shown to the world'.

The top middle card: Ace of Coins. A financial beginning. The actor really wants to earn some money, and to get a foot in in the industry. However, as he is not yet a 'name' in the business, he needs to accept an entry-level pay package.

The bottom middle card: Six of Swords. Intelligence, or cleverness has won the goal. The actor needs to come into the audition having studied their lines, practised their part and to have understood the goal of the script.

The top right card: Ten of Wands. The project takes on new life, and is left in the hands of the audience. The querent has accepted that once he is being filmed, he will be in the hands of the director and the film editor. Likewise, how the audience accepts him will be out of his hands.

The bottom right card: Queen of Cups. A female authority. The audition will be successful if the actor plays well for a female audience, which will be judged by a female casting agent. Bringing romantic charm and nuanced emotion to the part will secure the position.

Cross (six cards)

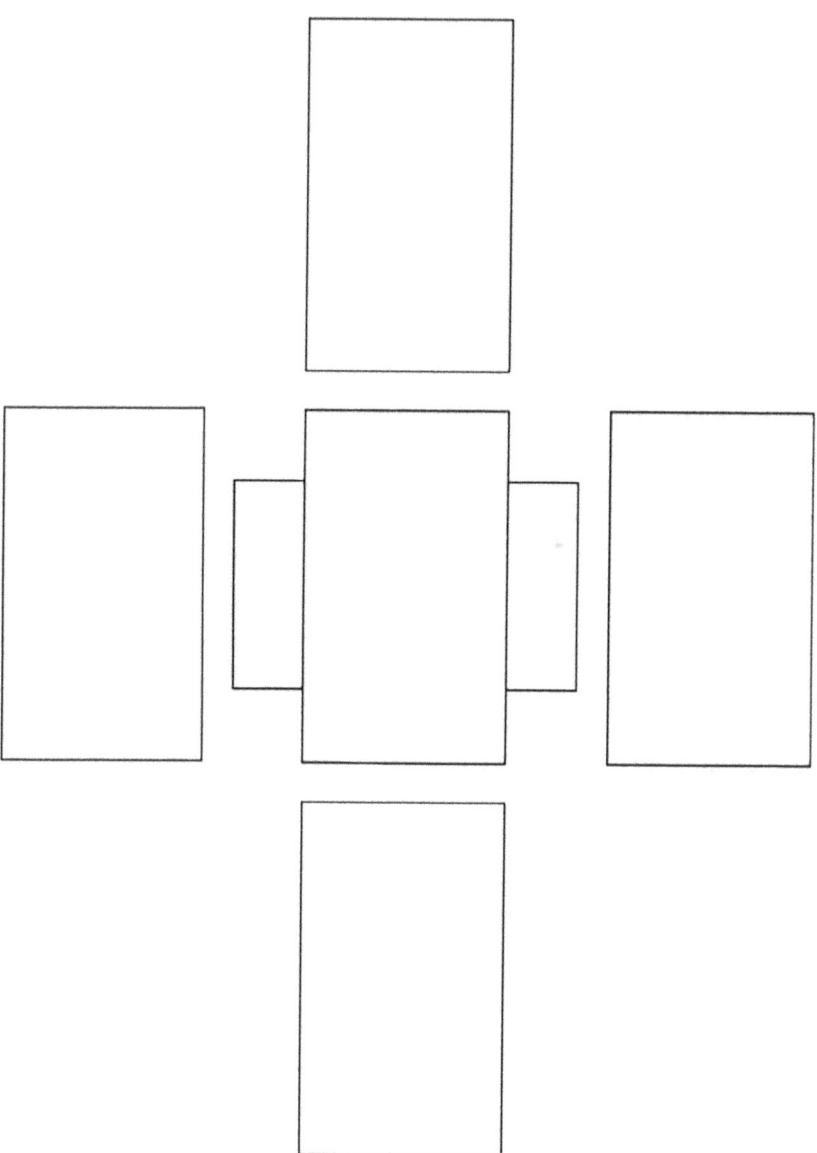

- The middle top card is what you think is going on.
- The middle underneath the card is an underlying reality.
- The left card is the past.
- The top card is what is helping the situation.

TAROT READING 43

- The bottom card is what is not helping the situation.
- The right card is the future.

Example:

  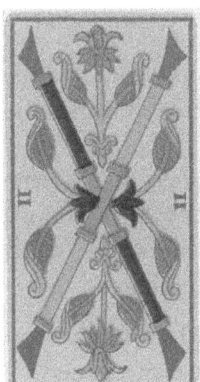

Question: The querent is in her late 20s and is considering going back to university to study psychology.

The middle top card: Two of Swords. If we understand Swords to be ideas, then this fits the question very directly. The querent is weighing up two options. Typical student doubts are relevant. Is the debt incurred from the course and living costs worth the work opportunities at the end? Is she intellectually capable of getting through the coursework? What other opportunities will she potentially miss out on if she takes the course?

A lot of students get interested in psychology because of personal experiences they have had with mental illness, perhaps with themselves or with family. A question arises whether the course will actually help with this, or if it will lead to an unexpected outcome.

The middle underneath card: The Hermit. She needs to know that the course will be personally deeply affecting, causing her to question and change her mind about what it means to be human in a psychological sense. While this can be very enlightening, and life-changing, these questions and the intensity of the workload may cause her to withdraw from those around her.

She may want to be certain that she has a good support network and enough 'time out', as eventually the psychological training may become emotionally heavy. As the Hermit is working towards wisdom through self-sacrifice, the outcome will be rewarding if she can commit to the end.

The left card: Seven of Wands (Batons). In this position, this card shows her preparation. In the journey from one to ten, seven is the beginning of the home stretch. She is more prepared for the course than she may realise. Though it will feel like hard work, a lot of the personal struggles that concern her are actually things she's already been through already and survived. She has a good understanding of the competitive nature of the course and has succeeded in similar situations in the past. Sevens also represent the large picture, so she has a realistic understanding of what the scope of the philosophy course entails.

The top card: Death. Because this is in the position of 'helping' we have to consider the positive nature of the subject of death. She is prepared to deal with the heavy questions of the human psyche, and has a fascination with deep and possibly 'taboo' subjects that other people avoid.

This is necessary as the course will touch on many unpleasant aspects of human behaviour and emotion. In some ways, psychology is to the mind, as being a pathologist (or mortician) is to the human body. One might suggest that criminal psychology or something similar might become an interest of hers. Possibly with a focus on the psychological causes of murder or something similar.

The bottom card: The Lover (*L'Amoureux*). This is in the position of 'not helping' so the hardest part of the course will not be the unpleasantness or pathologies of mental illness or the darker nature of the human psyche, but rather the way that psychology may frame emotions, relationships and love, as something reductive, and perhaps cynical. She must be prepared to manage her faith in love and relationships and not accept too readily that all can be reduced to brain function, hormones, pharmaceutical drugs and other incomplete models of human consciousness. Making time for art, family, music and social interaction is important or she might find the course is a drain on her personal life. This will especially be the case if she dates someone during the course, and even more so if that person is a fellow student. She may be more impressionable than she may realise, and find that she is diagnosing her personal relationships when she ought to just let them live on their own terms.

The right card: Two of Wands. She is ready for the course if she is clear on what she finds important in life, and is ready to debate and defend what is important to her. She may come out of the course with a different viewpoint than her educators and this may lead her into a slightly more unorthodox career within psychology. The life she has led before the course will deeply define her path. I suggest that she does the course, she is more than capable.

Celtic Cross (ten cards)

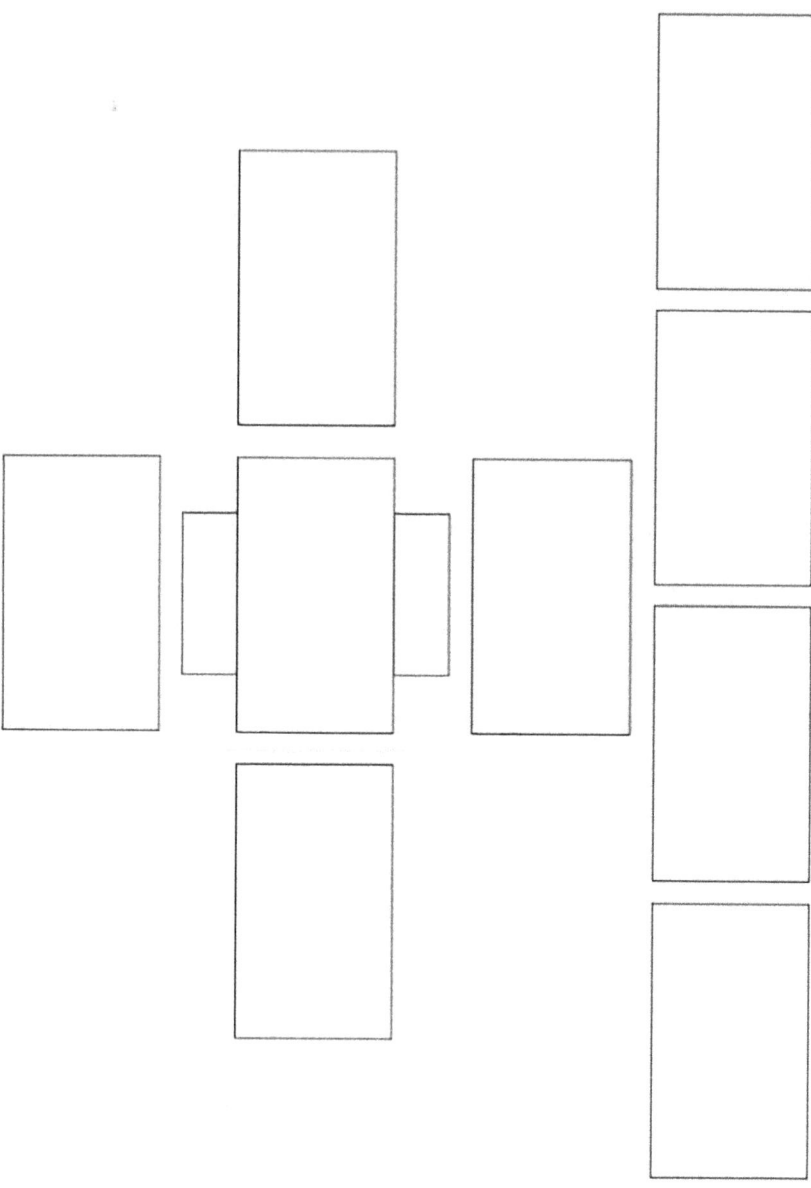

For this spread the first six cards are the same as the cross, except that four additional cards are placed to the right in a column.

- The bottom card of the column on the right is what is motivating the querent.
- The next card up represents the behaviour of people around the querent in regards to the situation.
- The second card from the top represents the hopes and/or fears of the querent.
- The top card in the column is a finality, or conclusion card. What one can reasonably expect to play out unless a large amount of effort is expended to avoid it.

48 TAROT FOR SCEPTICS

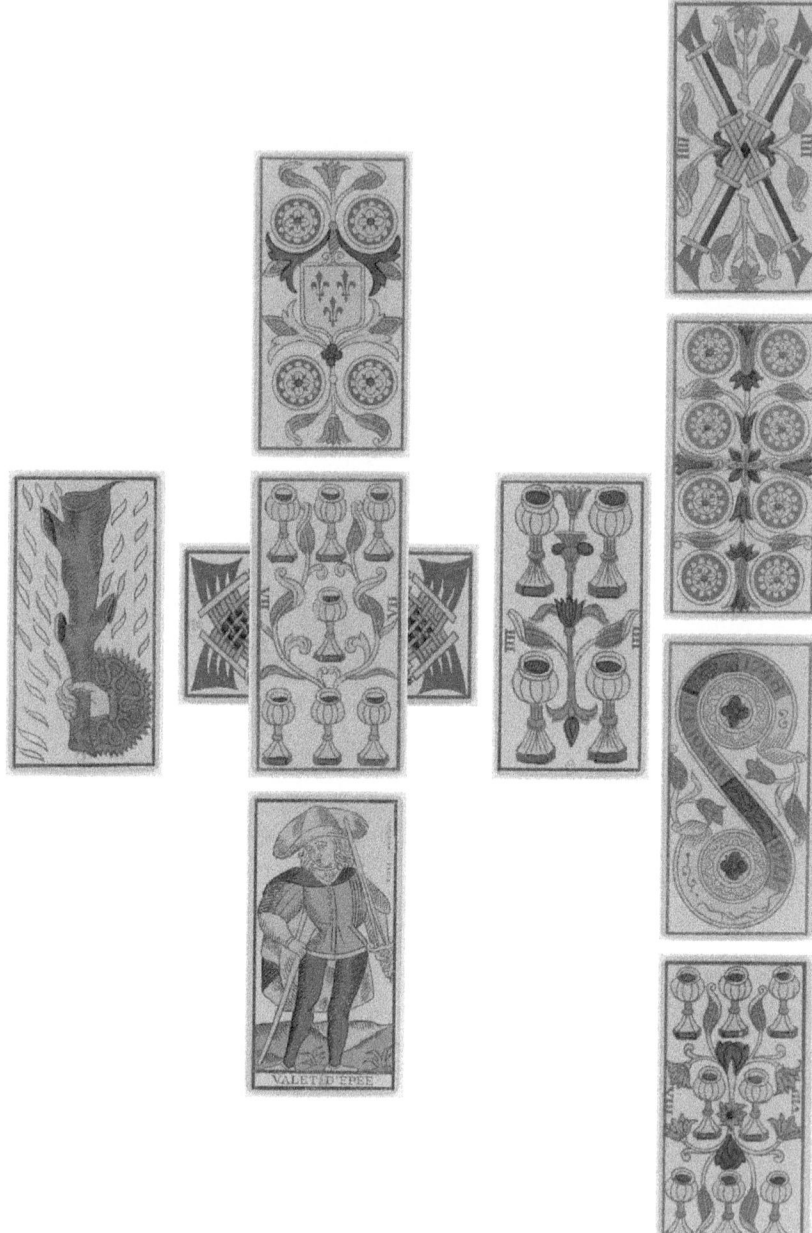

Question: A man around 30 years old has been dating a woman recently, who this week has stopped responding to his texts.

The cross

The middle top card: Seven of Cups. A new layer to the relationship is revealed that was hidden before. The woman is serious about the relationship and is considering taking it further, but she has been withholding some information about herself until she feels certain that she wants to continue. She is making a decision whether to tell him or just to call it off. She is afraid of his response, and also if he is emotionally prepared for the news.

The middle underneath card: Eight of Swords. Damage control. A reworking of expectations is needed. This card suggests that her concerns are valid. When the querent finds out her secret, it will alter his expectations about the relationship. If he is to continue dating her, he will have to reconsider what he expects from her. This suggests that whatever she is facing will diminish the time and emotional energy that she has for the relationship.

The left card: Ace of Wands (Batons). A new inspiration. In the last few weeks, the woman has come to a realisation. It is probable that until now she had been testing the waters. Now that she is considering a more serious relationship with the querent, she is affected by this new decision. It changes the manner in which they will interact.

The top card: Four of Coins. Four is the number of stability. His financial security and career prospects are a plus in her eyes. She could use some material stability in her life.

The bottom card: Page (Valet) of Swords. She has been put off a little by his forthrightness. It has caused her to doubt whether he will be an understanding partner. She is going through something that he is unfamiliar with and she is concerned that he won't understand or be able to see things her way, or worse, that he will behave as if he understands, or knows what he is talking about rather than listening to her side. She doesn't feel he knows what he is talking about sometimes when he is offering his opinion.

The right card: Four of Cups. This suggests that her concerns are founded. He will probably not want to continue the relationship once he finds out her news. The key word for this card is 'dissatisfaction', and the implication is that baggage from outside the relationship, and a feeling that the 'grass is greener' elsewhere will cause him to become dissatisfied as time goes on. Fours often represent hurdles.

The column

The bottom card of the column: Eight of Cups. Emotional baggage. To be motivated to continue the relationship will require an acceptance that what is being offered to him is something quite different from what he expected. It will entail working through an amount of emotional baggage.

The next card up: Two of Coins (pentacles). Interacting with the people around the querent will require a 'juggling' of time and resources. This suggests highly that there is a third person in the relationship vying for her time and attention that the querent was unaware of.

The second card from the top: Eight of Coins. The fear is that the querent will have to work hard to provide for the woman. The reading leans heavily towards the idea that she has one or two dependent children that she hasn't mentioned and probable emotional baggage with the father.

The top card in the column: Four of Wands. The relationship has reached a stable point (fours), but pushing beyond this will require a lot more effort and will. There are obstacles ahead, implied by the next number, five, a number of tension. While stability may sound good it can also mean 'not going anywhere'. As the other cards have been pushing towards a negative reading of the relationship, the Four of Wands in the conclusion position suggests that even if the querent were to continue with the relationship for a while, he will eventually lose the will and want to leave. The woman's predicament is difficult, and he is probably not ready or willing to take it on.

A Quick start with the Rider Waite Smith Deck

1. Come up with a question.
2. Shuffle the cards.
3. Draw the cards into one of the spreads below.

Three-card spread

- The left card is the past.
- The middle card is the present.
- The right card is the future.

Question: My kid no longer goes to school or plays with his friends, what is going on?

Example:
Left Card: High Priestess. Your child is going through a time of deep inner experiences, which involve a mixture of imagination, emotion, dreams and depression. He doesn't have the language to explain his inner world to anyone else and this is making him feel alone and shut off.

Middle Card: Seven of Cups. Part of his loneliness is caused by not being interested in the same things as other kids. He strongly feels there must be more to life, and that most children's interests are distractions from something more important or more personally fulfilling. It is very possible that he has a latent ability, or a need to express himself, which has not yet found an outlet or a role model. When he discovers his passion, a higher purpose, it will help lift his depression, lethargy and his lack of meaning.

Right Card: King of Pentacles. The answer will come in the form of an older male role model. When he finds this role model, he will be shown a mixture of inner self-expression (the Priestess) and practical work done with the hands to a high standard of quality (The King of Pentacles). The male role model will be a craftsperson who makes things with his hands, a woodworker, metal worker, sculptor, artistic mechanic or something similar.

The querent should introduce their son to art galleries, museums, car shows, hobby shops, movie special effects, or other similar things with a male interest group. When he sees the thing that makes sense to him, and understands that it is possible for him to do that too, he will know quickly that it is 'his thing'.

Over time, grounding his identity and self-esteem in a craft will lift his isolation and improve his self-worth.

Six-card spread

- The top left card is what you think about the past.
- The bottom left card is an underlying reality about the past that you haven't considered.
- The top middle card is what you think about the present.
- The bottom middle card is an underlying reality about the present.
- The top right card is what you think about the future.
- The bottom right card is an underlying reality about the future.

Question: An old lady has a live-in tenant who is costing her money with electricity and food, how should she deal with the problem?

Top left card: King of Wands. An older male authority. The old lady has nostalgia and longing for her deceased husband, a charming and clever, but also dominating man. She decided to take in a young male tenant partly out of loneliness, and partly because she missed the interaction with a male personality. Because of this, she was very obliging and friendly to the young man, who was much less socially aware and communicative than her late husband. As a result, the young man has not fully understood her boundaries.

Top middle card: The Hanged Man. The old lady has not confronted the young man but instead has become withdrawn and resentful, feeling like a martyr and stewing on the problem without addressing it, even though she feels as though she is in the right.

Top right card: Ace of Swords. Rather than projecting her ideas about her late husband on the young man and resenting him for not living up to her standards, she should instead take on the forthright quality of her husband herself, and become more assertive for the first time since his death. She has misunderstood the power dynamic with the tenant. She is in fact the one in the power position, but she has been seeing herself instead, as the victim of his behaviour. She needs to set her boundaries and communicate them in a calm assertive, and 'rational' manner. If she is able to do this the young man will have to comply. She can achieve this by asking herself first 'What would my husband have said' and then acting this role out herself. This is both a good way for her to connect to her husband's memory and also to get what she wants.

Bottom left card: Queen of Wands. This card is the passive power in relation to the King of Wand's assertive power. In her nostalgia, the old lady has forgotten how much influence she had on her husband, who often behaved in accordance with her will, but acted as the spokesperson for the couple when they engaged with others. She may have forgotten how often her husband's actions were as a result of her own dominance, which she only exerted in private conversations with her husband. This suited them both. She saved him his male pride by not opposing him in public, and she saved herself from the unpleasant risk of looking like the 'bad guy' when she had difficulties with other people. Now that he is gone she will have to take on her late husband's role for herself which she sees as masculine. Because of the presence of Wands, (a phallic symbol) as Queen of Wands, she is actually very capable of this. The Queen of Wands is a female who has learnt to harness what is traditionally male, without necessarily losing her femininity.

Bottom middle card: Two of Pentacles. A balancing act. To have a successful discussion with the young man, she needs to show an understanding of his financial situation and ability to do his own housework and make his own food. She will have to have thought of a practical and clear compromise beforehand. It would serve her to first write her response down. She will also need to show she has listened to his concerns. A strong move to persuade him would be to 'compromise' on one term, making him feel like he has been listened to and preventing him from interpreting their interaction as one where she has forced his hand. On all other terms of the new agreement, she should be firm. This will work and be seen as 'fair' as long as the terms are within the abilities of the young man.

Bottom right card: The Hermit. The outcome will work in the short term if she sticks to this plan. However, the underlying emotional cause of her loneliness will come to the fore afterwards. The young man is not there to replace the memory of her husband. This is a projection of her own psychology, which is preventing her from addressing her sense of loss. She will need to find other avenues to address her loneliness.

Though the removal of this projection will initially feel like 'ripping off a band aid', it is necessary in the longer term. She will need to learn to take her own emotional well-being into her own hands. Wisdom lies in the future.

Cross (six cards)

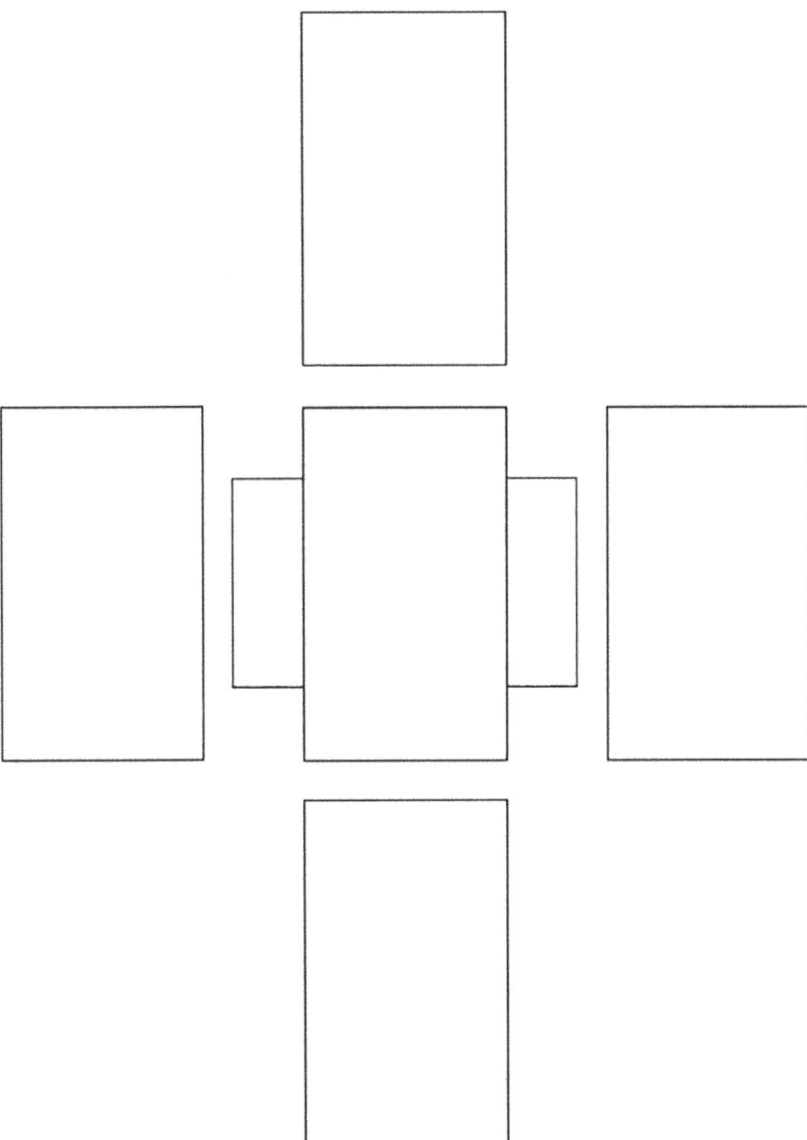

- The middle top card is what you think is going on.
- The middle underneath the card (which is crossing it) is an underlying reality.

- The left card is the past.
- The top card is what is helping the situation.
- The bottom card is what is not helping the situation.
- The right card is the future.

Question: The querent is a male around 20 years old, who has started writing songs, and would like to form a band to perform them. Where can he find band members?

Example:
The middle top card: Two of Swords. The querent has become very attached to his own songs. He needs to make a decision on whether he is a songwriting frontman with a backing band or a collaborator in a band that creates songs together. The former may turn off potential bandmates who also want to write. The latter means compromising the artistic vision of his songs. He has been playing this out in his head and this conundrum has caused him to hold back on playing with other people.

The middle underneath card: Ace of Pentacles. He may not realise that his songs and playing are good enough to start gigging as a solo musician. Once he plays a few solo gigs, he will be able to attract a backing band from people who hear him, as musicians often go to each other's gigs. If he wants to keep the integrity of his songs and lead the project, then this is a more powerful approach than joining an existing band or trying to place or answer 'Band Members Wanted' ads.

The left card: Knight of Swords. He is nervous about performing live due to previous attempts where he rushed in before he was ready, and got out of his depth. This affected his ego. In order to preserve the idea of himself as a good musician he pulled away from playing live for a time. Because of this, he thinks that performing with others may be a 'safer' option this time, but this conflicts with his drive to express his songs exactly the way he wants.

The top card: Five of Wands. This card is healthy competition amongst peers. A good approach has been to seek influence from his peers and from other musicians and to figure out what the competition is doing, i.e. other solo musicians or songwriters in bands. This will make him aware of the standard that a performing musician must live up to in his town. This is a better approach than the more self-centred 'Knight of Swords' approach where one has already decided that they are talented and then tries to make the rest of the world accept that too. In the Knight of Swords, he has all the motivation he needs. He can channel it through a healthy sense of competition with others who are already gigging, and this will push him to improve.

Although being competitive is often seen as a negative trait, it is highly motivating, and artists and musicians are often more motivated by competition than is often admitted. If the outcome is sharing music that other people enjoy, there is nothing wrong with this. A little ego and competitiveness can be a good thing.

The bottom card: Queen of Pentacles. The querent has felt pressure from a dominant female, probably his mother, to look for the monetary value (Pentacles) in the things he undertakes. She especially questioned the amount of time he spent on things that didn't produce a tangible value. This is a harmful mode of thinking at this stage in his musical career as he has not yet proven himself well enough in order to negotiate a price for his performances or to expect steady paid work from it. For now, he should be humble, not overcharge, and expect to have to play some shows for pocket money rather than for rent money.

The right card: Six of Swords. Following this advice, the querent will succeed in playing some shows and forming a band. In doing so, though he will progress in skill and he will eventually end up having to thoroughly re-evaluate his goals on what he wants to achieve as a musician. Until now, music has been a very personal, meditative and 'therapeutic' thing for him. He perhaps writes songs to counsel himself.

It will become clear when performing and playing music with others that, in order to achieve a higher level of success, he will have to find a way to play music that other people like, and relate to. This will be a difficult thing for a while, as it means compromising on playing the songs and singing the lyrics that he most relates to. To find stability means finding the music that both he and his audience enjoy.

Though playing live will be very beneficial in the long term, he will also become aware of how far he is from performing at the level of his most favourite musicians. Being a musician presents a lifetime journey, and those who are trying to 'make it' will find that there is never an objective point where one has completed this goal. (Learning to read Tarot cards is similar.)

Celtic Cross (ten cards)

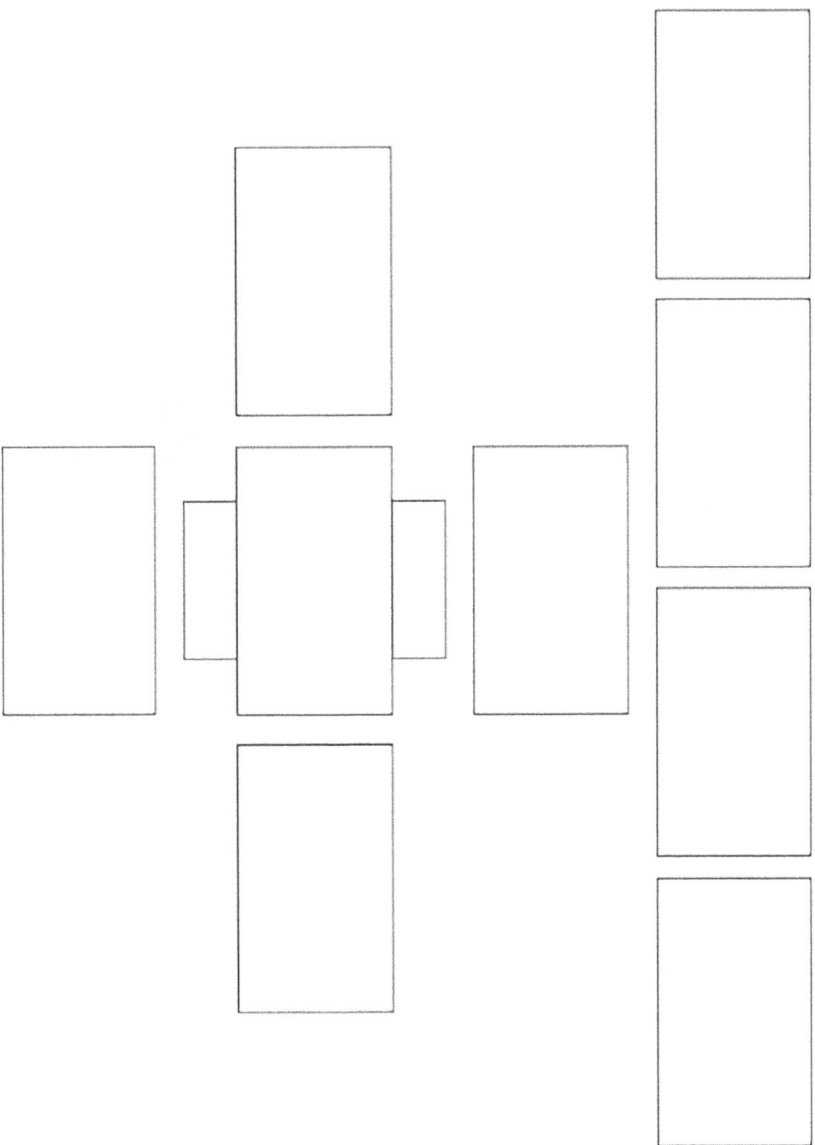

The first six cards are the same as for the cross, but four additional cards are placed to the right in a column.

The cross

- The middle top card is what you think is going on.
- The middle underneath card (which is crossing it) is an underlying reality.
- The left card is the past.
- The top card is what is helping the situation.
- The bottom card is what is not helping the situation.
- The right card is the future.

The column

- The bottom card of the column is what is motivating the querent.
- The next card up represents the behaviour of the people around the querent.
- The second card from the top represents the hopes and/or fears of the querent.
- The top card in the column is a finality, or conclusion card. What one can reasonably expect to play out.

TAROT READING 63

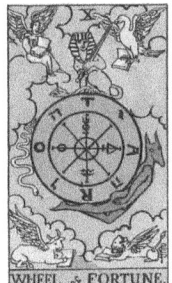

Question: A journalist has a job writing for a shoddy paper. He wants to do hard-hitting investigative journalism, but he is stuck writing copy for the automotive page. How can he find an opportunity to get the career he wants?

Example:
The middle top card: Page of Pentacles. A hardworking apprentice. Despite his aspirations, the querent is currently seen as a junior writer who has yet to prove himself to his employer.

The middle underneath card (which is crossing it): The World. To expand to the world stage requires expanding his own worldview. He is correct in thinking that the local paper does not have a wide enough readership to get him opportunities with international publications.

The left card: Five of Wands. When studying journalism, he felt inspired by competition with his fellow students, several of whom had great talent. At his current job, this feeling is no longer there. He doesn't find the writing of his colleagues to be inspiring or motivating.

The top card: The Devil. The great journalists who are his heroes all had a darker side that he has perhaps not considered. They all wrote initially for organisations that were perhaps in some way 'shady' but which allowed experimental approaches in their articles, for example, Hunter S. Thompson writing for *Playboy* magazine or publications that were in some way radical, communist, libertarian, pornographic or otherwise subversive, rebellious or 'fringe' to the mainstream.

The bottom card: The Knight of Wands. Even though all of these great writers had a powerful voice, in practice they were not the 'divas' that they might appear. They still played the game by the rules, met deadlines and wrote on the topics they were asked to report on. They all had to answer to bosses in some way or another. They found their voice despite these compromises, and not because they refused to compromise. It is easy to lose one's job in the highly competitive world of investigative reporting, and these writers played the game. The exciting 'risk-taking' approach of these writers didn't always come from their own ego, but often came out of desperation for trying to meet the competitive standards of the sometimes ruthless or demanding corporations (the Devil) to which they sold their work to.

The right card: The Queen of Cups. The querent's masculine, journalistic heroes of the past, actually reflect a mode of journalism which has fallen out of favour and may not actually even be the querent's own strength. Many of the bosses of news outlets are now women, and the querent should consider writing for a female audience, on female interest topics, or in a female 'inclusive' way. There are opportunities for this type of writing. Having an emotional, compassionate and perhaps, more feminist tone to his writing might give him an edge. Considering which stories fire women up is also advised.

The column

The bottom card: Nine of Cups. The querent is motivated by the idea of sharing emotional and human stories with a wide audience. This can actually give him an advantage over more 'edgy' writers. Nine of Cups is also hospitality. He may find stories in the hospitality industry.

The next card up: Wheel of Fortune. The querent has been holding back due to fear of failing. Getting his break will be a bit of a 'crap shoot', akin to the image of the roulette wheel which this card implies. Timing is everything. He needs to be aware of trends in current human interest stories and be ready with an article speedily written on an upcoming current event that will be of great interest to people. If he can get this article out at the right time to the right news agency he will have a foot in. He has to be ready to 'fail' several times before he ultimately gets this right.

The second card from the top: Nine of Wands. The current state of the institution of journalism is one of uncertainty and decline. Because of this, he is going to face many people in fear of losing their readership and their jobs. Journalism is a more difficult world now than in the 'risk-taking' days of the past. He will need patience to get a foot in. Sometimes it will feel like fighting a 'last stand'.

The top card: Three of Wands. When success comes, it will at first look like a compromise. Getting an opportunity in one thing requires a sacrifice of other ambitions. If he perseveres and is willing to do what it takes he will, after a struggle, find a way to be successful.

LEVEL 2

Advanced Tarot reading

A deeper dive into the cards

By now I hope you have a few Tarot readings under your belt, and that you have developed an understanding of how it works. Like many skills, but especially with magic, it is important to participate and do the thing in order to understand it. In my experiences with reading for sceptics, the nearly universal reaction is that they expected the experience to be some 'New Age nonsense' and that it ended up being something very different, and much more interesting than they expected. Something much more like a session with a very sharp counsellor. With very rare exceptions (only one that I can recall), all my sceptics have gone away excited with their heads buzzing, as if they have participated in a feat of illusionism that challenged what they thought was possible. In the most dramatic case, I read for a self-proclaimed 'rational materialist' who started the reading with the furrowed brow of a critic. By the end he was pacing up and down, too excited to sit, nervously saying to himself 'This can't be happening!'

Whatever your results, I suggest going into every reading with a kind of stoic reservation, ready to accept the results however they fall. Let the querent fully make up their own mind about what is happening.

The reading is for them. Don't be overly concerned about how they respond at the beginning of the reading. Some readings start a bit flat but end up with dramatic results. In some readings, my querents remain poker-faced throughout and only once the reading is done do they reveal that I have accurately described their situation in detail.

From your basic readings, the next step is to add more detail. From here you will start to note that the fairly specific meanings of the cards I have laid in the previous simple Tarot readings become more interpretive. From here on out, whatever you add to your Tarot readings should be in the service of telling better stories, and the measure of this, just like any performance art, is the response of your querent.

For this reason, we are leaving the realm of yes/no, wrong/right, and going into an area of nuance. If you talk to other experienced Tarot readers, you will start to find that there are many ways to skin a cat, many of which seem outright contradictory to each other.

Judge by the results. A guitarist's performance should not be measured by whether they play left-handed or right-handed, how they hold their pick, or what model of guitar they play, but rather by the effect of their performance on their audience. The same is true of magic and divination and specifically of Tarot reading.

Similarly, the purpose of this section, though we have gone up an order of magnitude in complexity, is not to overwhelm you with information. Instead, start taking notes on the card meanings that make the most sense to you, and add those onto the scaffold of your simple readings. It is not important that you add everything to your readings. More important is that your readings work.

My own approach was to write a manual as I went, which has eventuated in this book. This was contributed to by my good friend Ciaran MacConneach, who is an expert fortune-teller and scholar. For years I have carried a printout of this manual with my cards. This allowed me to show questioning querents the system I had learnt and had the added benefit of allowing me to train others who were interested in becoming Tarot readers. It also gave me a backup prompt at the times when I was stumped.

My recommendation is that you create your own notebook, recording the card meanings that you most connect with.

If you come across a card meaning that doesn't jive with you, there's nothing wrong with skipping over that point or even modifying it. Keep note of how these additions and subtractions affect your readings, especially how they affect the overall balance. If your readings always lead down the same road, then you need to diversify your understanding of the meanings of the cards.

Finally, note that sometimes the most useful definitions are the ones that jar at first. These get one outside of one's regular thought habits, and can be helpful in overcoming the main thing that can go wrong with readings, namely the tendency to project our own psychology onto other people. Anyone who has studied counselling, or has experienced a terrible counselling session will know what I mean.

As I expect you to refer back to the descriptions of the cards in this section over and over as a reference, there is information here, such as Kabbalistic and astrological correspondences, that will be properly explained in a second book. Do not be too concerned to try and understand everything on the first reading.

Crowley's Thoth and the Rider Waite Smith Decks

These are the two most commonly used decks for Tarot divination, and both present a higher density of information and symbolism in their imagery than the traditional Marseilles deck. There is nothing, in principle, wrong with starting on any of these three decks, and most in the English-speaking world start with the Rider Waite Smith as I did.

In retrospect, I now think that the easiest way into successful Tarot reading is to start with the Marseilles Deck, using the numerological approach that I have taught so far for the Minor Arcana, and then to progress to the Rider Waite Smith, having mastered the core structure by which it was designed. After that, it can be good to spend some time with the Crowley Thoth Deck, which has the most complex imagery and is more explicit in its use of occult systems such as astrology.

That is not to say that any of these decks is inferior or superior. They do, however, all give different styles of reading, and the Marseilles is the most straightforward. I personally read with all three and several other decks as well. I have found that the Rider Waite Smith Deck is one of the best decks for counselling and that Crowley's Thoth Deck is one of the best decks for questions of politics, philosophy and magic.

Many feel most attracted to the Rider Waite Smith Deck because of its Art Nouveau imagery, and the pictures on the Minor Arcana, instead of the 'pip' layout of Marseilles, and the hybrid layout of the Crowley Thoth Deck.

This has led many to view the Rider Waite Smith Deck as a deck for 'intuitive' readers. By that people usually mean that they think they can forgo learning the traditional meanings of each card and just improv the whole reading based on their own interpretations of the images.

In my experience, the readings I have had from these so-called 'intuitive' readers have been uniformly terrible. In the worst cases, people have used it as a licence to unload all their own internal thinking and prejudices on the querent, without stopping to consider how things look from the querent's point of view. This kind of reading is going to tell one more about the reader than the querent, and that is, in my opinion, at odds with the primary goals of fortune-telling.

If one finds oneself falling into this trap, learning to read with the Marseilles or Crowley Thoth Decks can help one get out of it. These are simply much harder to improvise with. I will cover the history of these decks and their designers in the history section later on. First, though, let's get reading.

The Major Arcana in depth

The Major Arcana present us with the overarching causes, cast, morals and themes in our story. They can be thought of as 'archetypes'—universal aspects of human narratives and the human psyche as proposed by the psychoanalyst Carl Jung (1875–1961).

I have discussed archetypes in my previous book, *Pragmatic Magical Thinking*:

> Archetypes can be symbolic, biological and social. They underlie the things people find important. So any story, including new reports, are necessarily going to draw from archetypes. They can be thought of as an ordering structure for roles.
>
> Depending on one's chosen framework, Archetypes can range from a few to numerous. As with most creative thinking, it's not so important whose structure we adopt, as what we do with that structure and the results it produces.
>
> Archetypes can be considered instinctual behaviours that we act out. Typical human experiences that may shape our lives consciously or unconsciously. Feeling like you are fated, is over identification with an archetype. Feeling like you are on a crusade is identification with the hero archetype. Feeling ostracised is identification with the outsider archetype. We can read about these types of characters and then use them to frame our own behaviour. Such is the many layered nature of the human condition.[13]

The Major Arcana cards that represent people are roles and relationships we play out in the world. Other cards depict or imply virtues and vices, generating the tension and release that are the most fundamental elements in all narratives. Others depict events which we are forced to react to. Finally are those which guide us in stages of our life, and there is very much a theme of self-improvement to the Tarot which has its roots in Christian religion and society.

---

[13] (Freeman 2023).

0 Fool

The Fool from the Marseilles, Rider Waite Smith and Crowley Thoth Decks.

Letter: Alef א ox.
Astrological attribution: The Primum Mobile.
Path: 11 Keter to Chokhmah.
Deities: Har-Pa-Khered, Horus the Child. Harpocrates, Pan, Dionysus, Bacchus, Loki, the Child Hermes.
Also known as: Le Mat, Le Fou, Joker.
Alchemical Substance: Prima Materia.

The Fool can be considered card XXII as well as the zero card. Beyond reason or logic, he is the beginning and the end. In the continental tradition, the Fool is often card XXI, with 'The World' being XXII. In most divination decks, however, the Fool is zero, as this card also represents the precondition for existence.

The Fool represents first actions, before definitions, knowledge or rules, unburdened by wisdom. As a concept, he relates to the first spark that created the universe, and with it the ongoing hidden cause behind reality that we never see directly but can only infer by witnessing manifestation. The Fool is always looking for new things, and never dwelling in one place.

As a character, he is the 'know nothing' who often achieves extraordinary things despite himself. This is a common archetype that appears in fairy tales: Jack from *Jack and the Beanstalk*, The Brave Little Tailor who starts off killing seven flies in one blow, and in his foolish self-confidence ends up defeating a giant, or the youth who goes forth to find out what fear is. The Fool is the outsider who steps into the game, and through misunderstanding the rules discovers the loophole that defeats the masters of the game.

In fairy tales, the fool is the black sheep of a family, a trickster or a weird young stranger who wins a trial or ordeal by finding a way around the face-value rules of the game. He then marries the king's daughter, or in some stories gains the kingship and breaks the land out of stale old ways into a new paradigm. He succeeds where the skilled and learned fail.

The fool gets one unstuck. He breaks down the rigid order that has restricted movement (the old order being represented by Saturn). For this reason, some associate the Fool with Uranus, a planet that heralds great change.

Negatively aspected, the fool is an idiot who unwittingly annoys all who are around him with no gain. They are the person who screws everything up and never understands why. The fool can also be the Jester who is ostensibly a figure for light relief, but is traditionally the only person in the court who can criticise a King or Tyrant, without being executed or imprisoned.

In Kabbalah, which has in turn influenced physics, the way to create something out of nothing is to notice a contradiction and then split it by its difference. Zero has no parts, yet $0 = (-1) + (+1)$ is mathematically sound. Now we have created a positive and a negative part of the equation, which can be split to produce one positive and one negative number. These can then be used to produce all other numbers. This is a 'Fool' manoeuvre.

In science, the Fool is the crazy theory that breaks the established model, for instance: The non-locality of photons, particle entanglement and the double-slit experiment in quantum physics. Hypnosis and the placebo effect are examples in medicine. Our current medical models are not sufficient to explain either, yet they work. Psi phenomena and parapsychology, especially when they give scientifically measurable results, are also relevant to the Fool. Divination, such as Tarot reading, looks like 'the Fool' to science, yet it keeps giving results to practitioners.

The Fool can represent the state of being intoxicated, and the inspiration that can sometimes arise from this. In the Greek pantheon, this holy intoxication was personified in Dionysus and Pan. Extensions of this concept in the real world are raves, wild rock concerts, ecstatic dance, and some psychedelic experiences.

In the Rider Waite Smith Deck, the Fool is depicted as a carefree youth teetering on the edge of a precarious cliff. Despite being in full sunlight, he notices nothing. He carries a phallic baton and a white rose, representing male and female puberty. Beside him is a harmless white dog representing innocence.

In some older decks, like that of Oswald Wirth, the Fool takes a darker, less romantic, image as a hideous village idiot, his trousers pulled down by an attacking cat. This represents someone without dignity who is oblivious to social graces. Something to keep in mind when the card takes on a negative aspect in a reading.

In Crowley's Thoth Deck, the image of the Fool is modelled on Harpo Marx, the silent comic character in the Marx Brothers' films, who Crowley took to be a play on Harpocrates, a Greco-Egyptian god who is the silent, child version of Horus.[14] The card's imagery in the Thoth Deck is flooded with symbols too numerous to completely describe here, but which can be slowly understood by deciphering the other Major Arcana first and then coming back to this card. I will describe a few of them:

A tiger bites his leg as he is unaware of the risks and dangers. Around him flies the caduceus, or rod of Hermes, a child God also associated with the Fool. Likewise a butterfly symbolising transformation and beauty and before it a dove, the herald of new life after the flood of Noah. Behind him are the grapes of the drunken god Dionysus, and on his head, Dionysus's beastly horns. Above him in his right hand is a flaming pine cone, another symbol of Dionysus, which is also the pineal gland, and the chakra Ajna, known as 'the third eye', which when mastered by the yogi, brings forth inner vision and a connection to Brahman, the all.

He holds a bag of unordered coins with astrological signs on them denoting great luck, but also an uncertain fate. He is coloured green like the 'green man', a 'Father Nature' deity of the British Isles. Between his feet are the two alchemical twins, lying dormant. Below him is the Egyptian crocodile deity Sobek, protector of the Nile.

---

[14] It is uncertain whether Harpo is based on Harpocrates, but Crowley's observation was apt. He fits the bill perfectly.

The Hebrew letter Aleph is either silent or denotes a glottal stop or the vowel sounds 'ah' or sometimes 'e'; for this reason it is associated with the breath and therefore the spirit. Symbolically it is the space that precedes a sound or a form.

On the Kabbalistic Tree of Life, the Fool corresponds to the path from Keter to Chokhmah, which is the first unseen spark of creation. This comes into play when things are acted upon before they are understood—pre-rational thought. The Fool is the first breaking through of a new paradigm. Chokhmah is like a blank page, ready to be drawn upon. The path from Keter to Chokhmah also represents the most abstract of divine experiences, as Keter cannot be experienced. Therefore the arrival of Keter's influence in Chokhmah is the first experience of creation.

Finally, the Fool is a leap of faith into the unknown, a place where rationality can't go.

Examples:

- Harpo Marx.
- Mr Magoo.
- Road Runner.
- Bugs Bunny.
- *The Youth Who Went Forth to Learn What Fear Was* (a German fairy tale).
- Ivan the Fool (a Russian fairy tale character).
- Rincewind from *The Colour of Magic*, by Terry Pratchett.
- Percival, a knight from the Arthurian Legends.
- Forrest Gump, from the movie of the same name.
- Stimpy from the cartoon *Ren and Stimpy*.
- Bilbo Baggins from *The Hobbit* by JRR Tolkien.
- Anansi the Spider (a fairy tale character of the Akan people of Ghana and West Africa).
- Brer Rabbit (a fairy tale character from the southern United States and the Caribbean).

I Magician

Letter: Bet ב house.
Planet: Mercury ☿.
Path: 12 Keter to Binah.
Deities: Thoth, Mercury, Hermes, Heka, Óðinn (after his stay on Yggdrasil).
Also known as: The Juggler, Le Bâteleur (the Baton Bearer), the Magus.
Alchemical substance: Mercury (alcohol created by fermentation of organic material).

The magician is the counterpart to the Fool. He is a knowledgeable master whereas the Fool is ignorant. The magician is aware of all, whereas the Fool is oblivious. He is articulate whereas the Fool is confused or nonsensical.

As the Fool is the first incomprehensible spark of creation, the magician is its first formation, the *Logos*. The *Logos* is an ancient Greek concept associated with Heraclitus (approximately 500 BCE). Most easily summed up, the *Logos* is the boundary that is drawn around things so that they can recognised as separate concepts. Without *Logos*, everything is everything else and nothing can be understood because there is no difference. The *Logos* has its precedent in the Egyptian concept of 'Heka', who was personified as a God of magic, as well as also being their word for magic. In some versions of the Egyptian creation myth, Heka is the first thing to be created at the beginning of the universe by the creator God Amun, and without whom nothing else can exist.

Any act of will first requires a conceptual act of separation between what is desired and what is not. This is at the core of all magic and all intention. The Magician represents will. He is the personification of decisive action, and everything he does he does on purpose. He has the power to explain and also to deceive. It is he who pulls concepts and order out of chaos, and in this way he is all geniuses who understand things before other people are able to. The Magician is a trickster archetype because he has the power to unsettle any established idea.

In alchemy, will and mind is associated with mercury, which in this connotation refers to alcohol rather than quicksilver, because of its evaporative nature. This is the same association that leads us to refer to alcohol as 'spirits', from *spiritus*, itself a very old word meaning 'breath'.

The Magician in Tarot has mastered the four elements of the four suits: Wands (fire, creativity and willpower), Cups: (water, emotion, desire and charm), Swords: (air, intellectual powers, rationalisation, and scepticism) and Pentacles: (Earth, resourcefulness and the body).

In the Rider Waite Smith Deck, he is depicted with an Ouroboros belt, depicting the eternal cycle of life and death. An infinity symbol (∞) above his head represents knowledge of the divine unity; Ein Soph/Brahman/the Monad. His wand points towards the heavens showing wisdom of the spiritual realm, which includes the world of concepts, and his other hand points to the earth, inferring manifestation. Together these two gestures refer to the alchemical adage from the Emerald Tablet of Hermes Trismegistus:[15] 'As above so below'. This is to say that, magically speaking, there is a mutual relationship between the macrocosm of the universe and the

---

[15] A mysterious single page alchemical text which first appears in the historical record in Arabic around the ninth century (though some think it is a translation of an older Greek text). It became somewhat of a spiritual manifesto for Arabic, Persian and later European alchemists. Hermes Trismegistus is a mythical figure who first appears in Egyptian writings around the second century CE. His name means 'Hermes thrice great'. This comes from the ancient Egyptian literary practice of repeating a title three times to emphasise excellence or superiority.

microcosm of the individual human experience. It also means that the realm of ideas, concepts and spirits affects the manifest realm of shared experience and physicality. In turn, the manifest realm influences the realm of ideas in a great cycle.

In Crowley's deck, the card is called the Magus, and depicts Hermes Trismegistus, a syncretism between the Greek god Hermes and Egyptian god Thoth, who became the central spiritual figure in the Hermetic movement which birthed alchemy and ultimately science. Behind him is Hermes' caduceus staff. Around him are the four suits, the cup, a sword, a bowl of fire (standing in for Wands) and a pentacle. Above his right hand is an arrow symbolising directed will. At his right hand is the Egyptian Was-sceptre of dominion, which was carried by some of the Pharaohs. To his left is the Orphic egg, which birthed the universe. Below him is the ape of Thoth, one of the forms in which that god appears. Above him to his left is a scroll representing the written word, as Thoth and Hermes are both gods of writing and information. Directly above him is a dove which to Crowley represented the Holy Spirit as well as Venus, who he connected to Mother Mary.

The Magus maps the path from Keter to Binah on the Kabbalistic Tree of Life. This is the thought that pops into the head already understood. 'Eureka' moments. Unlike the fool, distinctions are clear with the Magician's path. This path is more pragmatic, and decisive. It forms strong connections to higher truths. The letter Beth means house or home. This represents the safety that comes from a clear distinction between an inside controlled space and an outside world. Belonging and not belonging. The Magician represents the word written on the page or the stroke of the brush or pen (Wands). As Aleph is the breath, Binah is the word which the breath powers.

Finally, the Magician is the power of creativity at their best.

Examples:

- Merlin, the wizard of the Arthurian Legends.
- Gandalf of Tolkien's *The Hobbit* and *Lord of the Rings*.
- Dr House from the TV show of the same name.
- Hindu and Buddhist Gurus such as the Buddha himself, Siddhartha Gautama.

- Éliphas Lévi (1810–31 May 1875), the nineteenth-century occult writer.
- Aleister Crowley (1875–1947) (in relation to his readers).
- Harry Houdini (1874, 1926) was a famous stage magician, escape artist and debunker.

II Priestess

Letter: Gimel ג camel.
Planet: Moon ☽.
Path: 13 Keter to Tiferet.
Deities: Isis (as the Priestess), Nut (Nuit), Artemis, Diana, Luna, Selene, Hecate, Freyja.
Also known as: Papess or Popess.
Alchemical association: Consciousness.

The Priestess represents knowledge from hidden places—that which has to be experienced to be understood. She allows the divine to come into our present experience. She is the master of intuition and occult wisdom.

Where the magician is overt magic and action from the will, for instance, casting spells to get things done, the Priestess is magic from the soul and subtle forces. She represents states of consciousness on the verge of awareness such as hypnosis, lucid dreaming, meditation and trance as well as flow states. She is also communion with spirits, and of course divination, including the Tarot.

After the initial spark of creation represented by the Fool, its separation into concept through Logos into something we can understand, represented by the Magician, we now have the ability to interact with and 'feel' the concept. The guardian of this state is the Priestess.

The moon at her feet is the Tarot symbol for hidden things come to light, and the concept of cosmic and natural timing. In the Rider Waite

Smith image, she has the pillars Boaz (strength) and Jachin (unity)[16] behind her which represent judgement and mercy.

She is in a state of inspiration. The Goddess Nuit, Crowley's understanding of the Egyptian Goddess Nut, who is the space which precedes existence, and which grants the possibility of form. The Priestess is the midwife of the archetypical to the formative. Clothed in the veil of light which is the final veil that hides spirit. She is that which links the higher self, or 'Holy Guardian Angel', to the magical initiate. In Kabbalah, she is the 'camel' (the letter Gimel) which travels one through the desert 'the abyss', which separates the highest possible states of consciousness from common states.[17]

In older Tarot lore she is the 'Popess' a hidden female counterpart to the Catholic Pope, also known as 'Pope Joan', a legendary woman who disguised herself as a man and rose to the office of Pope. Her gender was occulted. The Priestess represents the secret tradition of the late mystery schools, who incorporated Tarot into their late teachings. The most famous being the Hermetic Order of the Golden Dawn.

In the Thoth Deck, the Priestess is Isis, who Crowley associated with initiation and spiritual experience. She is depicted in the act of unveiling herself, a representation of the spiritual experience that comes to light. Below her are a variety of objects of growth; fruit, seeds and a flower. A camel which is the meaning of the Hebrew letter Gimel. Also present are the Platonic solids, the mathematical secrets of matter and form.

In Kabbalah, she is the Shekhinah שְׁכִינָה ('dwelling'), a Jewish conception of God's Holy Spirit, which is always described as feminine. The path of Gimel on the Tree of Life represents the boundary between the conscious and unconscious realms, the connector between the transcendent and the human. This can be understood by the feeling of 'Frisson'.

Examples:

- Artemis, the Greek goddess, who is the huntress of the moon and who married herself and left the world of men.
- Isis, as the eternal virgin, is the template for the Virgin Mary.

---

[16] Symbols from the mythical Temple of Solomon, the wise Jewish King of the Old Testament, and an archetypical judge. This imagery, which is also used in freemasonry, is throughout the Tarot.
[17] These are central themes in Crowley's magic which we will explore later.

- Mary as the divine pathway for god to manifest as Jesus on Earth.
- Nut/Nuit, an Egyptian sky goddess of the void, from which all manifestation comes.
- Pope Joan.
- Galadriel in *Lord of the Rings*.
- Stevie Nicks from the band Fleetwood Mac, especially in her relationship with her fans through the archetype of the 'Gypsy Witch'. This image sold many Tarot cards.
- The fortune-teller in her role to her clients.
- A stripper, in her relationship with her audience, is an idealised, sexualised and idolised form of the feminine, who can be watched, but who can't be touched.

III Empress

Letter: Dalet ד door.
Planet: Venus ♀.
Path: 14 Chokhmah to Binah.
Deities: Isis (as the mother), Mut, Demeter and Persephone, Ceres, Venus, Juno, Hera, Frigg.
Alchemical substance: Salt (the ash of a burnt substance).

The Empress is Mother Earth and her connection to women and motherhood. She represents fertility, fruiting and the growing of crops. She is that which binds all nature together through a common origin and a continuity of life. She is the Anima, or feminine aspect of the soul, especially in relation to men. She can be an understanding sympathiser and a nurturing motherly figure. The Emperor is her consort and male counterpart, representing the animus. Together they are the idealised divine masculine and feminine.

In magic, the Empress is connected to the spirits of nature. For example elves, elementals and fairies. In alchemy, she is 'salt', the ash left over after burning substances such as organic matter. This is symbolic of the body, and lower consciousness, especially sensory awareness.

In the Rider Waite Smith image, the 12 stars on her crown are the zodiac, representing natural time cycles. A field of corn ripens in front of her, and her dress is covered in pomegranates both symbolising fecundity. Behind her is a life-giving waterfall. She holds a sceptre with a globe, representing the Earth. She represents Mother Mary in her interactions with mankind as the mother of God. She represents the Logos (the word) manifested. She carries the Word but not its interpretation (the interpretation, being the realm of the Magician).

In the Thoth tarot image, there is a depiction of Venus who is facing away from a stork of motherhood, towards a dove of spirit. This may have something to do with Crowley's idea of the role of women in his new 'Age of Horus'. Crowley was, in his own Victorian way, a feminist. He encouraged the women in his life to pursue magic, art and spirituality, and had his own idea of the divine feminine in Babalon, a sexually liberated goddess. He was also a contrarian, who dedicated his life to inverting or reconfiguring the strict values of the society around him. The world we now live in is very much a result of that wish carried out.

Venus holds a lotus, a natural symbol of feminine sexuality, being the same shape as a chalice (the womb). The lotus is also a symbol of Isis, as well as a symbol of the awakening of consciousness in yoga. The eagle on her shield is a traditional sign of rulership and is also in the Marseilles Tarot, but in this case it has two heads, one a pelican of tradition, feeding its young and the other, the white eagle of alchemy, a symbol of purification. The double-headed eagle is also used in Scottish rite freemasonry of which Crowley was a member. This symbol also appears on the Emperor card, this time in red. The belt around Venus is the zodiac.

Below her are two fleur-de-lis symbols, which are associated with Mother Mary, of traditional female virtue, the trinity and dynasties. These also appear on the Emperor card. The marriage of the Empress to the Emperor is the union of two dynasties via marriage and children.

The magician and writer Josephine McCarthy describes the Empress as a household's or nation's ability to feed itself. In relation to Kabbalah, the Empress is the balancing point and path between Chokhmah, inspiration, and Binah, understanding. These two Sefirot are associated with the two sides of the brain and corresponding aspects of mind: Pattern recognition on the right and reasoning on the left. In the human brain, the corpus callosum connects these two hemispheres and is larger, and more connected in females. The letter Daleth is the door. This is a symbol both of motherhood, the doorway by which we enter the world, as well as her role as the guardian of the upper realm of the world of concepts and therefore the custodian between the human realm and that of the highest spiritual connection to creation. The Empress can be thought of as the one at the gate, whereas the High Priestess, the previous card, is one who guides a secret diverting path into the upper realm.

The Empress can be considered a balance of all the four Queens, an archetypical ideal.

Examples:

- The 'motherland', all feminine symbols of nations, such as Mother Russia.
- Mother Nature as life-giver, and all the corresponding goddesses.
- Mary Mother of God.
- The Child-like Empress, or Moon Child in *the Never Ending Story*.

IV Emperor

Letter: Heh ה window (Crowley switches this to Tzaddi צ (fishhook/sword) in his Thoth Deck, and puts the Star in its place).
Sign: Aries ♈.
Path: 15 Chokhmah to Tiferet. (Crowley switches this to Netzach to Yesod).
Deities: Amun (A ram-horned God), Horus (as a sky god), Jupiter, Minerva, Athena.
Alchemical substance: Sulphur (oil).

The Emperor is the Animus or male part of the soul. He represents a stable kingdom. That which tames the wild by offering it the comforts of civilisation. A deal that can also be broken. He is humankind at its intellectual height. He symbolises order, determination, leadership, stable governance and great plans. The type of ego that allows one to be a leader. This is symbolised in the image by the four rams heads denoting Aries, leadership and the stability of the number four. The original association of the ram with the Emperor comes from Amun, an ancient Egyptian sun god whose symbol was the ram, and who was the primary god associated with Pharaohs during the Eighteenth Dynasty.

In the Rider Waite Smith image the Emperor holds the 'Crux ansata' (Christianified Ankh) in his right hand, which is originally an Egyptian hieroglyph representing life, and in this case, dominion over life. He holds the world-globe in his left hand.

Crowley associates the Emperor with the alchemical concept of 'sulphur', which in the spagyrics of Paracelsus refers not to the chemical element, but rather the essential oil which can be pressed from animal fats, plants and seeds. Oil is both fluid and flammable, a great source of energy and power, but it is also dangerous if not contained or disciplined. This hot-headedness is also applied to the sign of Aries in astrology (which we will explore in a later chapter). His image is similar to that in the Rider Waite Smith Deck, but Crowley includes a sheep and flag, representing loyal subjects and the nation, and a golden sun of Ra, with which the Egyptian emperors were associated. On his vestment is a bee, the 'masculine' correlates to the Empress' flower.

He is the consort to the Empress, the masculine ideal to which she responds. Where she is nature and its domestication, he is the world of thought, ideals and laws.

The Emperor is a man of vision. What he thinks is important is what will be enforced. When poorly aspected, that which he fails to notice or prioritise will degrade the empire. The letter Heh implies a frame of vision. That which is inside is seen, judged and valued, and that which is outside is disregarded or missed. That which is in the frame is the empire, over which the Emperor oversees. Heh, the window, can be considered a 'reality tunnel'.

The Emperor is a balance of all the four Kings, an ideal. In Kabbalah, the path of Heh connects Chokhmah and Tiferet on the Tree of Life. The connection between the active principle of wisdom and the harmonious balance of beauty.

The Emperor is the master of authority.

Examples:

- King Solomon.
- Emperor Augustus (in his idealised and deified form).
- Pharaohs of the Egyptians (as an ideal).
- Charlemagne, King of the Franks from 768, King of the Lombards from 774 and Holy Roman Emperor from 800 until his death in 814.

V Hierophant (Pope)

Letter: Vav ו a nail or a hook on which to hang things.
Sign: Taurus ♉.
Path: 16 Chokhmah to Chesed.
Deities: Osiris (as psychopomp), Charon, Kerubim, Legba, Freyr, Ma'at.
Also known as: The Pope (Le Pape).

The Hierophant is the leader of the flock. He represents membership and initiations into institutions with a group identity such as religions, schools and academia. The focus of this card is on groups rather than the individual, and on conservatism over liberalism and radicalism.

Previously called 'the Pope', the Hierophant holds the earthly office to the heavens. Where the Priestess represents personal and occult spiritual experience, the Hierophant represents public and orthodox spirituality and morality. He is wisdom through dogma rather than the High Priestesses' wisdom through direct experience (gnosis). He also represents the spirituality in human institutions whereas the Empress represents the spirituality in nature and sensuality.

In the Rider Waite Smith image, the crossed keys in the coat of arms of the Holy See (the jurisdiction of the Pope) symbolise the keys of heaven entrusted to Saint Peter.[18] The gold key alludes to the power in

---

[18] In the Gospel of Matthew 16:19, Jesus says to Peter, 'And I will give unto thee the keys of the kingdom of heaven: and whatsoever thou shalt bind on earth shall be bound in heaven: and whatsoever thou shalt loose on earth shall be loosed in heaven' (King James version).

the kingdom of the heavens and the silver key indicates the spiritual authority of the papacy on earth. The Hierophant holds a staff with the Papal triple cross, and with his other hand he gestures to and offers passage to Heaven. He wears the triple crown of the Trinity. He sits between the pillars of judgement Boaz and Jachin, of the Temple of Solomon, as seen previously in the Priestess card. This is because he acts as a spiritual judge.

He is the guide of the macrocosm and microcosm. The macrocosm is the universe, including the heavens and the microcosm is the world of human experience, and humans themselves; that is, universal powers in relationship to human individuality.

He relates to the Kerub, the carved guardian spirits who protect altars in the Jewish (and Babylonian) tradition. Like Hierophant they are the protectors of holy secrets.

In the Thoth Deck image, there are nine nails above the Hierophant's head, a number denoting wisdom. The Hebrew letter Vav, to which the card is assigned, means 'nail'. These hold in place a snake, perhaps a defeated Apophis or Typhon, both snake gods of disorder. He is suspended in front of a window depicting a five-petalled rose. This is the Rosicrucian symbol. The dove, in the image, is the Holy Spirit.

Around the Hierophant is a bull, Taurus, the astrological sign of the card. On either side of him are elephants, which Crowley also associates with Taurus. Around him are the four Cherubs the beasts of the Hayyot.[19] These are the guardians of every shrine and represent the four fixed signs of the zodiac, Taurus, Leo, Scorpio (as an eagle) and Aquarius: Earth, Fire, Water and Air, respectively. On his chest is the child Horus and below him is Isis his Priestess, who represents spiritual experience or revelation, on which religion is built. Crowley says she is the 'scarlet woman'.[20] His staff has three rings, Crowley says these are the three aeons of Isis, Osiris and Horus. We are supposedly at the beginning of or about to begin the age of Horus.

While the Hierophant can be associated with religion, it can equally, and for the same reasons, be associated with educational institutions. As many people in the twenty-first century no longer centre their social life around churches, temples or synagogues, other institutions such as schools and universities have increased in importance. In education,

---

[19] The 'living creatures' of Ezekiel 1:6–28.
[20] The incarnation of Crowley's sexually liberated goddess, Babalon.

lecturers, tutors and teachers are the 'priests and priestesses' and the path from initiation to graduation is even more overt than at church.

Likewise, many workplaces follow a similar structure. Entry-level jobs are followed by paths of promotion, with bosses taking the role of the Hierophant. As such, the Hierophant card has something to say about all human institutions.

The church is supposed to open the path to God's mercy. It offers a softer side than the Justice card, grace rather than punishment, and the two cards share some symbolism. The Devil card presents an inversion of these principles. In the Devil card, an authority or institution takes more than it gives. Interacting with such a corrupted institution becomes a gamble rather than a sanctuary. Taurus (♉) is ruled by Venus, who to Crowley has become a 'scarlet woman'.

The Hebrew letter Vav, which can mean a nail or hook on which to hang things, can be thought of, in relation to the Hierophant, as a 'skyhook'. A label for explanations that appeal to powers of a transcending or supernatural order. This term is sometimes used pejoratively by critics of religion. That is, concepts by which we 'hang' our meaning on or explain events, but in which the explanation doesn't play by the normal rules of rationality. A 'God said so' or 'God of the gaps' type rhetoric. However, this criticism itself is flawed when one compares other types of explanations to religious ones. Almost no human models of reality, philosophy or morality are complete in of themselves. Rather, leaps of faith are almost always necessary in order to get anything done. To a magician 'sky hooks' are not so much 'logical fallacies' to be completely avoided, but rather, useful tools in order to achieve pragmatic results. Put another way, don't judge by the explanation, but rather by what it allows us to do (pragmatism).

In mathematics, there are axioms which are held to be true by which all other emergent theories are judged to be truth. This is another way to conceptualise 'skyhooks'.

Nails bind things such as wooden buildings together. The word religion comes from the same Latin root as the word 'ligature', meaning 'to bind'. Religion is that which binds human groups in a common doctrine. The 'sky hook' (Vav) is the metaphysics on which the doctrine is hung.

In Kabbalah, The path of Vav connects Chokhmah and Chesed. It represents the connection between divine wisdom, Chokhmah, and

Chesed's compassionate mercy. Divine mercy and redemption was the currency, or 'skyhook' by which Christianity converted the pagans.

Examples:

- All high-ranking religious leaders.
- The Pope.
- The Dalai Lama.
- Obi-Wan Kenobi in *Star Wars: A New Hope* (1977). He initiates Luke into the Jedi.
- Yoda in *Star Wars: The Empire Strikes Back* further guides Luke into a higher order of power.
- High-ranking academics such as deans.

VI Lovers

Letter: Zayin ז sword.
Sign: Gemini ♊.
Path: 17 Binah to Tiferet.
Deities: Eros and Psyche, Orpheus and Eurydice, Castor and Pollux, Adam and Eve.
Also known as: The Lover.
Alchemical concept: The chemical wedding or synthesis.

The Lovers card represents the subjective experience of falling in love and of faith, the feeling of 'knowing' the unknowable. In philosophy, it is the synthesis that follows analysis (represented by swords in the Tarot). Put another way, it is the joining of ideas in relation to each other that can only happen after they are separately, carefully considered and understood. In this way the card can literally refer to a romantic relationship, or it can represent a 'love' or bonding experience in the abstract: A leap of faith.

In the Rider Waite Smith image, the Lovers are joined by the archangel Raphael. They are Adam and Eve in the Garden of Eden and therefore represent all romantic pairings. Other Tarot interpreters sometimes say that the Lovers are married to the Hermit. The lovers in the card are naked, representing their honesty. The Tree of Life is behind Adam and the Tree of Knowledge of Good and Evil, complete with a serpent, is behind Eve. They are innocence and love before the fall.

In alchemy, the pair are the 'chemical wedding', an allegory for the holy union of opposites, necessary for both personal enlightenment and for unlocking nature's secrets.

Crowley also associates the lovers with Cain and Abel. A tale of a failure to unite opposites, resulting in one extinguishing the other. This incorporates the Hebrew letter Zayin, which is symbolically, the sword. In the Bible, Cain is the first murderer and Abel his victim. This correlates to equal yet opposite reactions in alchemy and chemistry. The formulation of any idea creates its opposite at the same instant.

The Lovers are also the first manifest division in the creation of the world. Matter and antimatter pulled out of the void. Emptiness cloven in two. This is a trick used equally by modern astronomers and ancient astrologers in order to explain how something can come out of 'nothing'. $0 = (+1) + (-1)$.

In Crowley's Thoth Deck, there is a lot of added imagery in this card. The white and black children wield the sacred lance and Holy Grail, divine masculine and feminine symbols. The Orphic Egg, which births the universe, complete with its encircling snake stands before them.

In the Marseilles Deck, this card is 'the Lover', singular. Here a young man, rather than a couple, is being prepared for marriage by two women. This seems to be a quirk found neither in earlier nor later decks. In this case, it refers to the preparation for a love bond rather than the direct experience of it. Simply put, the Marseilles card depicts the scene before the marriage, while other versions depict the marriage itself.

When the married figures of the lovers card reach their full potential, they become the Emperor and Empress: Powers which join the powers of nature, and society, for the benefit of humankind, and their offspring. When most negatively aspected, the Lovers card, like in the story of Romeo and Juliet spells misfortune or destruction for both parties.

In Kabbalah, the Path of Zayin connects Tiferet (beauty or heart) and Binah (understanding). Tiferet represents beauty, harmony, and balance, while Binah represents understanding, intuition, and the ability to conceptualise and give birth to new ideas. The Lovers are the unification of the masculine and feminine energies embodied in Tiferet and Binah, respectively. Zayin is the sword, and the Lovers is all about dualities. Primordial concepts 'cloven' in two. The Lovers must learn to balance their personal needs and desires with their partners to achieve balance within their relationship.

Examples:

- Adam and Eve.
- Wesley and Buttercup in the film, Princess Bride.
- Negatively aspected: Romeo and Juliet, the lovers played out as a tragedy.
- Similarly: Tristan and Isolde.
- Pyramus and Thisbe.
- Orpheus and Eurydice.

VII Chariot

Letter: Chet ח boundary/fence.
Sign: Cancer ♋.
Path: 18 Binah to Gevurah.
Deities: Apollo (as the sun charioteer), Óðinn (as leader of the great hunt). Merkabah (God's angelic chariot), Horus (as the avenger of his father Osiris), Thor (as Charioteer).

The Chariot represents the resolve to achieve great things by unifying powers that normally oppose or cancel each other out towards a singular goal. It is the prowess of a great leader, such as Alexander the Great. An empire builder. It signifies hard-won victory and success.

While traditionally the card connotes a military victory, it is important to note that the imagery of the card, especially the two sphinxes pulling the chariot in the Rider Waite Smith version, represents a victory of the mind rather than a victory of physical force alone. Waite sums the card as 'the victory which creates kingship'. The figure in the card is on his way to becoming the Emperor.

In the Rider Waite Smith, the card depicts four pillars which are the Tetragrammaton YHWH. The sphinxes are two harnessed individual powers that have been convinced by the rider to work in cahoots. In Crowley's Thoth Deck, the chariot is pulled by four Kerubs, the 'Hayyot', or 'living creatures' of Ezekiel's vision in the Bible. The chariot therefore takes on heavenly connotations, becoming like God's chariot in heaven pulled by angels. Likewise, the charioteer bears the Holy

Grail, complete with the blood of Christ, representing a divine mission, in contrast to the Rider Waite Smith's more earthly mission.

When the Chariot card appears in readings it signals that it is the right time for the querent to set their plan in motion. The armour worn by the charioteer, like the Cancer crab's shell, signifies that part of the mission is to defend against opposition. The sign Cancer, the armoured crab, is ruled by the moon, so the drive to get the task done must draw from intuition, inspiration and instinct. Over-rationalisation in the face of opposition can cause one to lose resolve. Likewise, the Chariot is not a card of democracy, but rather of an individual's vision to achieve a task. It is the egocentric symbol of the visionary. Allowing others to talk one out of an ambition can spell failure. For this reason, the intuitive powers of the moon, are more important for this card than the rational powers of the sun.

In the Rider Waite Smith Deck, the chariot rider holds a staff of power and will. The square on his chest represents the four directions of the physical world. He has learnt the skills of the Magician, the High Priestess, the Empress, the Emperor, and the Hierophant. Now he rides out to be tested. He wears the crown of divinely inspired kingship with a star that represents the lofty goal (see the Star card). His shoulders hold two crescent moons, waxing and waning, which are a symbol of Venus seen also in the Priestess. In this case, the ability to lead others by charm. His canopy is decorated with the stars of the night sky, denoting the destiny of the zodiac, or 'one's stars being in line'. The winged disc on the chariot is the symbol of divinely ordained royalty and solar power. It has its origins in Ancient Egypt and Mesopotamia. The spindle on the front of the chariot is the spindle of the fates who weave our destiny. The two sphinxes are the powers of light and darkness, a similar concept to Jung's idea of individuation, the completion of the self by facing the dark 'shadow' parts of one's personality and bringing them under the power of one's will. On one side of the chariot is a city; on the other, ecclesiastical buildings, a balance of secular and spiritual institutional powers.

In the Thoth Tarot Deck, the card depicts an Arthurian knight who holds the Holy Grail. The card's sign is Cancer, which is the cardinal, or initiating water sign, which Crowley attributes to flows of water, and by symbolic comparison, our lifeblood, hence, the Holy Grail.

The scarlet wheels of the chariot are, for Crowley, Gevurah, which Hermetic magicians associate with Mars, and therefore war, power, action and force. In the Thoth deck, the original two horses of the Marseilles image have been replaced by four sphinxes, with the heads of the Hayyot, the four angels of the fixed signs of the zodiac. The meaning is that the rider has aligned with his destiny. On his armour are ten stars which Crowley calls the stars of assiah. Assiah is the Kabbalistic concept of the manifest world of action, where we share experiences. Some call this the material world, though while it includes our experience of the material world, it is also the place where we communicate through words and meaning. The ten stars are a reference to the ten Sefirot of the Kabbalistic Tree of Life. A map of how creation unfolds.

The Hebrew letter Chet is tied to enclosures and gateways. The chariot rider extends his enclosure, breaches the enclosures of his opponents, and encloses new lands. This concept aligns with a parable about Alexander the Great called 'the Gordian knot':

The Phrygians found themselves without a king. An oracle at Telmissus, the capital of Lycia, declared that the next man to enter the city driving an ox-cart should become their king. A peasant farmer named Gordias drove into town and was immediately declared king. Out of gratitude, his son Midas dedicated the ox-cart to the Phrygian god Sabazios (whom the Greeks identified with Zeus) and tied it to a post with a complex knot that no man could untie. It was said that anyone who could undo the knot would become the next king after Midas. Alexander the Great arrived and seeing that the knot was untieable, clove the rope in two with his sword, making him the next king.

The path of Cheth connects Gevurah (Strength) and Binah (Understanding), the balance between plan and action.

Examples:

- Napoleon (1769–1821) (on his rise).
- Alexander the Great.
- King David from the Old Testament.
- Genghis Khan (1162–1227).

VIII Strength (Lust XI)

In the Marseilles and Crowley's Thoth Deck this card is XI.

Letter: Tet ט serpent.
Sign: Leo ♌.
Path: 19 Chesed to Gevurah.
Deities: Hercules, Thor, Vesta, Hestia, Bastet, Sekhmet.
Also Known as: La Force, Lust.

The Strength card represents the resolve to tame one's own, or someone else's wild nature. Rather than exercising force or brutality, it is the act of bringing force under one's control so that one does not fight in the first place. Therefore it is a card of personal charm (Leo), and of personal discipline. It is represented by the Hebrew letter Tet which means 'serpent'. As the serpent plays the role of a critic or doubter (Ha Satan) in the Bible, the card denotes the overcoming of the doubts of oneself and of others. It is the conquering of one's devils and overcoming the test of morality.

On the Kabbalistic Tree of Life, the path of tet, from Chesed to Gevurah is the balance of power to get work done, symbolised in Chesed, and the discipline required to allocate that power, in Gevurah'. Think of the flow of a river (Chesed is also 'flow') and its containment (Gevurah) along a course, by its river banks which prevents a flood. One now has a powerful flowing force which can be used for travel or as a source of power by way of water wheels. In the modern world, this image can be reimagined by an electrical metaphor. The flow of voltage and current through the wire is contained by its conductive properties and its insulation covering the length of the wire, both allowing a containment of the energy which can flow from one place to another in order to do work for us, or transmit information over distances.

This path can also be considered the balance between compassion and discipline. The implication is one of self-mastery, fitting the image of the Strength card.

In the Rider Waite Smith Deck, the imagery of the card comes from the tale of Androcles: Androcles was a runaway slave of a former Roman consul administering a part of Africa. He took shelter in a cave, which turned out to be the den of a wounded lion, from whose paw he removed a large thorn. In gratitude, the lion becomes tame towards him and henceforward shares his meat with the slave.

After three years, Androcles craved a return to civilisation. Unfortunately on his return he was imprisoned as a fugitive slave and sent to Rome. There he was condemned to be devoured by wild animals in the Circus. The Emperor who was named in the account as Gaius Caesar, (presumably Caligula), was in attendance. The most imposing of the beasts unleashed upon Androcles turned out to be the same lion he cured, which displayed its affection toward him. Thus he was protected and saved from the punishment. After questioning him, the Emperor pardoned the slave in recognition of this testimony to the power of friendship. The tale was later adapted several times. In Catholicism, it was retold with St Jerome as its hero, and also as the older Biblical tale, of Daniel in the lion's den.

This card was swapped by the Hermetic Order of the Golden Dawn, from its original position as XI in the Marseilles Deck to VIII.[21] This alteration was retained by Waite. The Justice card was traditionally in position VIII. Crowley disagreed with this move and in his Thoth Deck he retained the original positions of VIII for Justice which he named 'adjustment', and XI for Strength, which he renamed 'Lust'. By this Crowley meant a kind of erotic life force which motivates all living things, and the universe itself.

---

[21] This was actually first done by Oswald Wirth who influenced Oswald 's ideas about the Tarot. The Golden Dawn in their own (secret) deck, designed by Mathers and his wife Moina, used the swapped places for the Justice and Strength cards, and Waite carried this over to the Rider Waite Smith Deck. Crowley therefore put the cards back to their traditional positions.

Crowley's version of the card depicts a woman in an erotic pose atop a lion with a serpent's tail, referring to the Hebrew letter Tet which means 'serpent'. The lion has seven heads[22] which he lists as the head of an Angel, the head of a saint, the head of a poet, the head of an adulterous woman, the head of a man of valour, the head of a satyr, and the head of a lion-serpent. This, along with the term 'lust' is supposed to describe a kind of drunken Dionysian ecstasy. In her left hand, the figure holds the reins, and in her right a stylised 'Holy Grail' which resembles a clitoris.

> Behind the figures of the Beast and his Bride are ten luminous rayed circles; they are the Sephiroth latent and not yet in order, for every new Aeon demands a new system of classification of the Universe. At the top of the card is shown an emblem of the new light, with ten horns of the Beast, which are serpents, sent forth in every direction to destroy and recreate the world.[23]

Negatively aspected, the card can be misplaced compassion, for instance, Stockholm syndrome. Where one is charmed by one's own captor.

Examples:

- Belle from *Beauty and the Beast*.
- Androcles and Daniel in the lions' den.
- Shamhat the woman who tames the wild man, Enkidu in the *Epic of Gilgamesh*.

---

[22] Also a reverence to the seven-headed beast in the book of Revelation 13:1.
[23] Page 96 (Crowley 1944).

IX Hermit

Letter: Yod ' hand.
Sign: Virgo ♍.
Path: 20 Chesed to Tiferet.
Deities: Atum (the god who creates himself), Óðinn (as 'Hárbarð'—Greybeard the wanderer), Persephone (as she who bridges life and death) and Anubis (as psychopomp).

The Hermit represents the type of learning that can only be done in solitude. The wisdom he craves is that which is provided by the Priestess, which is gained through 'gnosis'—direct experience. The Hermit can also represent facing adversity alone, but in quietude rather than in an overt struggle (which would be the Hanged Man). It is trust in one's own judgement.

The magician and writer Josephine McCarthy says:

> The card can also represent great learning that by its nature isolates you.[24]

The card refers then to long periods of isolation and patience.

In Jungian theory, the Hermit is the act of facing 'the shadow', the unpleasant or merely hidden aspects and drives of the personality that can cause mental illness, defences and complexes. The goal of facing

---

[24] Page 53 (McCarthy 2020).

and integrating one's shadow is called 'individuation', the act of aligning the whole personality under one will, rather than as many separate drives that can get in each other's way or cause self-destruction.

This is the same goal represented in the alchemical act of making 'gold' from lower elements. This is not only a chemistry experiment, but a metaphor for purifying and refining the soul. Likewise, this refinement of one's personality is the goal of Rosicrucian organisations including the Hermetic Order of the Golden Dawn. This act is formalised in the occult ritual of knowledge and communion with the 'Holy Guardian Angel', usually understood as either the highest part of the soul or one's personal guiding spirit. Aleister Crowley considered this the most important part of his magical system.

In the Rider Watie Smith Deck, the image depicts a robed traveller. His way is lit by the Star, a reference to that card, and he holds the staff or wand of a magician. In a sense, he is on his way to becoming the Magician card.

The Thoth Tarot card depicts a rather more psychedelic inner vision, and the wanderer is there in a more abstract form. A star is in a lamp in the shape of an eight-sided polygon, Crowley states that this is the sun, which in astrology is one's sense of self. It is held by the Hermit, and his hand is directly in the centre of the image, as the Hebrew letter Yod, assigned to the card, means 'hand'.

Below him to the right, is Cerberus the three-headed dog guardian of the underworld, symbolic of facing mortality and one's shadow. Below him to the left, is a staff, which is actually a stylised sperm, denoting a divine male force which like the Yod fertilises the universe. In the background are sheaves of wheat, of the astrological sign of Virgo, fertility. The Hermit is the male fertilising aspect of nature, who herself is Virgo. The Hermit contemplates the Orphic Egg, the mysteries of the universe and of its creation.

The Hermit can also be seen in the idea of a seed, for example, an acorn which is expected to become a tree. In a sense, the future tree is there in the acorn. The Hermit is the teleology of that seed, the inherent will of the seed to become a plant. The seed is willing to wait until the time is right to sprout, just like the Hermit waits for wisdom before he returns to society. In astrology, Virgos are also said to have this tendency. They are ready when they are ready.

In the divine name YHVH (יהוי), the first letter Yod is symbolic of the initial will before action. The Hermit embodies this. In Kabbalah, the path of Yod connects Chesed (Mercy), and Tiferet (Beauty). This represents the balance between inner wisdom and outer action. Trusting one's inner guidance.

Examples:

- Radagast in *The Hobbit*.
- Gandalf the Grey as the wandering wizard in *The Hobbit* and *Lord of the Rings*.
- Obi-Wan Kenobi as a desert hermit in *Star Wars Episode IV* (1977), who watches in secret over Luke until he is ready to be trained as a Jedi.
- The desert fathers, ascetics who were the first Christian monks.
- John the Baptist, a biblical wild-man preacher of the desert, who baptised Jesus.
- Siddhartha Gautama (sixth or fifth century BCE), the Buddha, when he is waiting under the tree for the wisdom of enlightenment.

X Wheel of Fortune

Letter: Kaf כ palm of the hand, a spoon, and the state of being bent in submission.
Planet: Jupiter ♃.
Path: 21 Chesed to Netzach.
Deities: Sphinx/Hermanubis/Typhon, or Sphinx/Set/Typhon. The Hayyot. Fortuna, Tyche. The Fates, the Norns, Shai.

The Wheel of Fortune represents transcendental cycles, especially the understanding that good fortune and bad fortune are temporary. When it comes up in a reading, it signals that one cycle is reaching completion and another will start. It also represents the types of big changes that are outside of our control. The events that take one's life into a new stage.

In the Rider Waite Smith Deck, the image is a central wheel containing a sigil made of the alchemical symbols for sulphur (oil), mercury (alcohol) and salt (ash). These are the three components of spagyric medicine as put forth by the alchemist Paracelsus. Together they are a symbol for purifying, strengthening and unifying the spirit. The fourth symbol is Aquarius, the zodiac sign which heralds great change. Around the sigil are the words ROTA (meaning 'wheel' in Latin), TARO (Tarot), and the Tetragrammaton, YHVH, symbolising god's will manifested, and sometimes understood to be symbolically a wheel.

Atop the wheel is a sphinx denoting the mystery of fortune, the serpent, Apep/Apophis/Typhon denoting disorder and chaos, and

Hermanubis, a Jackal-headed syncretic god of Roman Egypt combining Hermes and Anubis, both psychopomps who conduct the dead to the underworld. Chaos is something that ordinary people fear, but which magicians understand offers an opportunity to rebalance the scales.

In the four corners outside of the wheel are the Hayyot, or 'living creatures', four of the angels of Ezekiel's vision in the Bible. A bull, a lion, an eagle and a man. They are associated with the four fixed astrological signs Taurus (Earth), Leo (Fire), Scorpio (Water), and Aquarius (Air). A balance of the elements and a reference to our fortune being affected by great cycles 'in the stars'. Together they make the structure of 'God's chariot'. The wheel itself could be understood to portray an Ophan, a wheel-shaped angel.

Crowley's Thoth Deck has a similar image but includes a ten-spoked wheel denoting the Sefirot, the Kabbalistic Tree of Life. Crowley also brought in some Hindu symbolism with the three 'Gunas': Tamas, Rajas and Sattvas. These are three qualities which are said to be found in different proportions in all things. Tamas is the darkness of ignorance and sloth. Rajas is energy, brilliance, restlessness and excitement. Sattvas is calm, intelligent, lucid and balanced. These Gunas revolve, never remaining in one state, represented respectively by Typhon (Tamas), Hermanubis (Rajas), and the Sphinx (Sattvas).

In Kabbalah, the path of Kaf connects Chesed (Mercy) and Netzach (Victory). In this case, Tiferet is harmony and Netzach is endurance and eternal time cycles. In this sense the Wheel of Fortune is the hand that gives and takes and an eternal pattern of interaction between order and chaos, resulting in an overall balance.

The letter Kaf represents the palm of the hand, and also 'grip'. It is also a spoon ready to receive.

Examples:

- Wyrd, the Anglo-Saxon concept of duty and fate. In Old Norse, the same concept is called Urðr.
- Saṃsāra, the Hindu wheel of karma and reincarnation
- The roulette table and by extension all gambling.
- The four seasons, and the 'luck of the weather'.
- The zodiac, and the luck of the stars.

XI Justice/(VIII) Adjustment

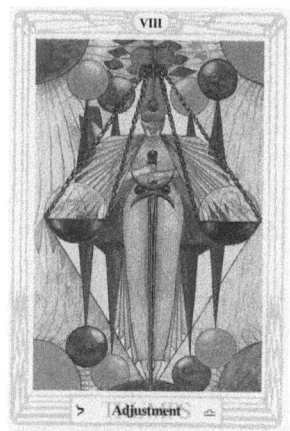

In Crowley's Thoth Deck, this is 'Adjustment' and assigned to VIII; this was a return to the traditional placement which it shares with the Marseilles Tarot Deck.

Letter: Lamed ל ox goad (or yoke).
Sign: Libra ♎.
Path: 22 Gevurah to Tiferet.
Deities: Themis (divine justice), Justitia, Dike (goddess of moral order) Athena (as the judge), Raguel (Kabbalsitic angel of justice), Forseti. Ma'at (as Goddess of universal balance), Mithra (law and order).

The Justice card represents objectivity, balance, doing the right thing, the settling of accounts, court proceedings and conflict resolution. Implicit in it is a reminder to accept a pragmatic victory, rather than a wrathful, self-righteous or idealised one. One is almost never fully compensated for wrongdoings and we must be satisfied with vindication and, hopefully a partial compensation. Likewise, being compensated may require accepting partial responsibility, as well as allowing the offending party room to change. This implies the possibility of forgiveness.

If someone has come around to your way of thinking or has changed their behaviour from that which was aggravating, then that is a win, it is usually too much to also expect them to be happy about it. This type of acceptance is implied by the Justice card. Often the roles may be reversed and the Justice card can mean comeuppance or punishment for the querent.

In the Rider Waite Smith Deck, the image is rather simpler than some of the others. A crowned judge, suggesting King Solomon, sits on a throne. The two pillars Boaz and Jachin, (mercy and punishment), make their return. He holds scales, as his job is to maintain balance and order, and he has the sword of rationality, that which cuts away untruth.

In the Thoth Deck, this card is 'Adjustment' and is assigned to VIII, which is the traditional position for Justice in older decks. Crowley renamed the card as he wanted to discuss a more universal, cosmic, natural concept, as is the theme of his deck. 'Adjustment' to Crowley meant a balance that nature upholds. He felt that the term 'justice' had a connotation that was too human, or perhaps too Judeo-Christian. The Goddess of the sign of Libra (Crowley's sun sign) is depicted and in her scale are the Alpha, and Omega, the first and last letters of the Greek alphabet which symbolise a containment of all. She holds a sword of truth, in a dormant position of mercy. Ready to be wielded should she be challenged.

In the Thoth image the figure is crowned with the plumes of Ma'at, the Egyptian goddess of moral order, and on her forehead is the Uraeus serpent, an Egyptian symbol of divine authority. Above her are four orbs and below her four more. Four is the number of stability which in the card is balanced above and below.

On the Tree of Life, the path of Lamed connects Gevurah (Strength) and Tiferet (Beauty). Gevurah represents forceful and decisive action, while Tiferet represents harmony, beauty and balance. Enforcement of the law in the name of order. Justice represents the connection between strength and balance.

The letter lamed, which means a 'yoke' is the discipline of tying yourself to a responsibility. A judge has to embody the letter of the law, and a punishment, such as a jail sentence, is a yoke to this law. Lamed is also a goad, the subjects or citizens are goaded towards certain behaviour by the law.

In Norse mythology, the god Forseti is the son of Baldr and Nanna. A god of courts. All those who come before him leave are said to leave reconciled. In Greek Mythology we have the Goddess Dike in this role, who is similar to the Egyptian Ma'at, a goddess of cosmic order. Related are the Greek Goddess Themis and Roman Goddess Justitia who are more in the human sphere of justice.

Reversed or negatively aspected the Justice card represents the inefficiency of the court system or bureaucracy that is supposed to work for fairness, but either rewards the wrong people due to corruption or ineptitude and entraps one in an ongoing case without end.

Examples:

- The court system.
- The Wizard from *The Wizard of Oz*.
- Solomon judging the two mothers in the Old Testament: 1 Kings 3:16–28.
- Judge Judy, from the reality television show of the same name.
- Franz Kafka's *The Trial* (negatively aspected).

XII Hanged Man

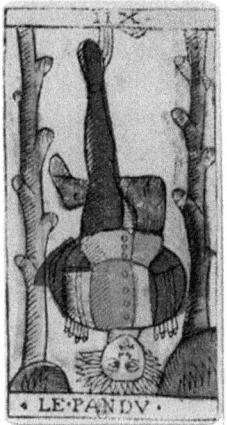  

Letter: Mem מ water.
Planet: Neptune ♆.
Path: 23 Gevurah to Hod.
Deities: Óðinn (as a sacrifice to himself), Jesus on the cross (God incarnate sacrificed to God the creator), Neptune and Poseidon (as the god/s of the unconscious), Prometheus. Negatively aspected; Loki.
Also known as: Le Pendu or Le Pandu.

The hanged man represents a self-sacrifice for wisdom or going against orthodox thinking in order to gain experiences that are not had by most people. Being hung by one foot was at one time the traditional punishment for traitors, so the hanged man has ideals in opposition to those who judge him. He can be a martyr, a self-martyr or viewed from the outside, a heretic. The card can also correspond to a time of internal focus, and a struggle with no clear end. In this case, unlike the Hermit, wisdom is not a sure outcome.

On a grander scale, the card represents a self-sacrifice in order to bring a paradigm shift. In Norse mythology, the god Óðinn hung himself, half dead, on the world tree, Yggdrasil, for nine days, and in a vision discovered the runes on the last day. This gave him the technology of writing and the magic of divination. Unlike other sacrificed gods, his was a self-inflicted sacrifice. An offering made to himself, reminiscent of the psychedelic experience, and especially 'ego death'.

This myth has echoes in the history of science with the legend that Francis Crick discovered the DNA molecule and the implications of its code while high on LSD. Similar are the self-confessed mystical visions of Nicola Tesla to which he attributed many of his inventions in the field of electronics and electrical engineering.

As the letter Mem represents water, the hanged man also suggests a baptism. Perhaps pertaining more to the type of adult baptism given by a figure like John the Baptist, than a baptism by an orthodox church.

Mem can also be the waters of the womb, from which the hanged man's position is like a spiritual rebirth akin to the symbolism of the baptism; a ritualised death and rebirth. A womb is also a 'waiting room', the meditative quiet state that allows the hanged man to transform himself. Or like the chrysalis of a butterfly. It might be worth noting that most children are born head first.

On the Tree of Life, Gevurah is the Sefirah of punishment, the man's hanging, and Hod is the Sefirah of hard work, intellectual understanding and ritual, and it is associated with meditation and the act of magic. This is the path marked by the letter Mem. This suggests a stripping down of the self and the cutting off of one's personal attachments in order to gain self-mastery. The hanged man archetype, like Óðinn hanging on Yggdrasil, represents suffering and endurance before becoming transformed into a higher or more useful form.

Magically it is the situation where the magician withdraws in order to face the inner world of spirits or perhaps their own psychology. This is the operation prescribed by the infamous Abramelin ritual, a 6 or 18-month ordeal (depending on the translation) in order to gain knowledge of, and communication with one's 'Holy Guardian Angel'. This is variously understood to be the highest part of the self that defines one's life purpose, or a literal spirit being assigned to each person in order to guide us through life. Perhaps these are two ways of understanding the same thing with one no less true than the other.[25]

A similar experiment was run by John Dee and Edward Kelley, locking themselves in Dee's chambers where they communed with the angels who, as legend had it, imparted Dee the idea and logistic plan for the British Empire.

---

[25] I explore this dichotomy and its implications in my first book *Pragmatic Magical Thinking*, in a chapter called: 'Outside voices vs inner voices' (Freeman 2023).

When negatively aspected, the card can represent resentment that despite one's sacrifice, one's genius is not recognised. In this, the card is more like Loki than Óðinn. While both gods brought new useful ideas out of chaos, in Loki's case the end result is not glory but punishment and ostracisation by the other gods. In this way, it can represent a 'martyr-complex' rather than a true martyrdom. It is important to remember that one cannot declare oneself a martyr and expect to be taken seriously by others. A true martyr is decided by those who survive them. Also important is that a self-sacrifice that nobody asked of you, might not be seen as heroic by other people. Take note if the hanged man appears in readings along with the Fool.

Crowley suggests that the card is one of inversion, as the man is symbolically upside down. That is, the knowledge is that which is gained as a result of subverting society's values: sex, drugs, magic, and perhaps rock'n'roll. The symbol is the wisdom of heretics. In his Thoth Deck image, the figure hangs from an upside-down Ankh, a life symbol inverted. This is life dipping into death. Behind him is the square of the material realm through which he descends.

> The legs are crossed so that the right leg forms a right angle with the left leg, and the arms are stretched out at an angle of 60° so as to form an equilateral triangle; this gives the symbol of the Triangle surmounted by the Cross, which represents the descent of the light into the darkness in order to redeem it.[26]

Above him is the holy light of Keter, the origin of all things, and below him is an underworld plane with a serpent (Apophis or Typhon), the destroying force without which nothing can be created. Finally, the hanged man alludes to God incarnating himself as Jesus and then letting himself be hanged by the Romans. This is perhaps the most extreme case of one-upmanship ever performed by a deity. Even so, the card depicts Jesus as the Jewish and Roman heretic, not the Jesus of orthodoxy.

In modern astrology, the planet Neptune, which is assigned to the card, is the realm of dreams from which new paradigms and understandings can be pulled. Negatively aspected or reversed one still goes

---

[26] Page 96 (Crowley 1944).

through the martyrdom but comes out without the wisdom. As previously discussed it can also mean ostracisation by others.

Examples:

- Óðinn hanging from Yggdrasil.
- Jesus on the cross, especially his crisis of faith.
- Altered states of consciousness, 'ego death' trips on psychedelic drugs.
- The 'Walkabout' of the Australian Aborigines and other solitary initiations and spirit quests.
- Prometheus' punishment by the Olympian gods for having brought fire and technology to humans.
- The psychedelic experience, especially the 'heroic dose' and 'ego-death' experiences as championed by the ethnobotanist, psychonaut and counter-culture icon Terrence McKenna.
- Negatively aspected: Loki's punishment by the Aesir for murdering Baldur.

XIII Death

Letter: Nun נ fish.
Sign: Scorpio ♏.
Path: 24 Tiferet to Netzach.
Deities: Mars (as a bringer of death), the grim reaper, Osiris (as the slain god resurrected, and as a psychopomp), Christ (slain and resurrected), Kali (as the destroyer who allows rebirth). Hel, Hades (when he interacts with the human realm).

This card represents a range of emotions in the face of death. It can represent physical death, but it is much more often about conceptual death or a dramatic and emotional change which brings about an ending. Something happens that makes one reconsider one's relationship to death, or which causes grief. In balance, the card is just as much about the precursor to rebirth as it is about final endings. It is a return to the most primal, sometimes brutal, laws of the universe: The Kali force; necessary destruction.

It symbolises the often-painful ending that must occur in order for new things may grow or regenerate. The passing of responsibility and authority from one generation to the next. A culling of animals, or a weeding of a garden. The selling of a house that one grew up in, in order that a new household may begin.

Scorpio is the sign of the Death card. It signifies the middle of autumn. A cycle of death that leads into winter, before the rebirth of spring. It is also associated with fermentation, the death and breakdown of one substance to form another: Alcohol, bread, yoghurt, cheese, etc. As such, this card could possibly come up for a brewer, without the traditionally morbid association.

In classical astrology, Scorpio is ruled by the planet Mars. Martial thinking, without restraint, leads to death. In modern astrology, Scorpio is instead assigned to Pluto, who is Hades, the god of the Dead and of the underworld.

In the Rider Waite Smith image, a warlike skeletal knight leaves behind a dead King. He faces a bishop, who is the caretaker of souls entering the afterlife. The skeleton carries a banner with a white rose, a symbol of new beginnings. Beside the bishop are a morning wife, and a child who is the heir to the kingship. In the background are the pillars of mercy and punishment which are present on several other cards, but especially the Justice card. In a sense, the king has already been judged and punished. In the background, there is a sunrise or sunset, a life/death cycle seen in the metaphor of day and night.

In the Marseilles, and similar traditional decks, the card, which has the 'unlucky' number of 13 (XIII) often doesn't have the number printed. Normally there is a rather simple image of a grim reaper skeleton with a scythe, also a symbol of Cronus, who eats his children, or Cronos the god of time, with whom he is often conflated. These are the destructive sides of 'Father Nature', in a sense they are the male expression of the Hindu Goddess Kali. They also can be thought to represent the scientific concept of entropy. The skeleton is sowing the body parts of the dead king and queen in a field. Even given the macabre image, a memento mori (remembrance of death), the implication is that new life will return. The sown bodies will sprout into new life.

In Crowley's Thoth Deck the grim reaper figure is in a more abstract form, with a Typhonian serpent standing for the destructive force, a scorpion and eagle which are symbols of Scorpio, a fish representing the element water and the letter Nun, a dead lily and an opium seed pod (although some say it is a swamp lotus) perhaps indicative of Crowley's addiction to heroin, a drug he was prescribed and almost certainly exploited for magical visions.

Climbing up an abstract ladder to the heavens are a number of spectres. This is almost certainly indicative of the soul's journey up the Sefirot, or Tree of Life, from the bodily and sensory world up to union with the godhead (Keter), a world of pure will.

In the Marseilles Deck, the death card is said by some traditional readers to be the skeleton of the fool.

The path of Nun connects Tiferet (Beauty) and Netzach (Victory). Understanding this correspondence is more difficult than most. Tiferet, the heart centre which is ruled by the sun (in the Golden Dawn interpretation), is also the seat of the ego and selfhood. Netzach is tied to eternity. The only way that eternity can be truly achieved by the individual is by dissolution of the self. Likewise, beauty in nature is nearly always temporary, youth, childhood, and new growth must eventually grow old, wilt and die.

Examples:

- Hel, the Norse goddess and the realm of the afterlife.
- Hades, the Greek god and the realm of the afterlife.
- Pluto, the Roman version of Hades.
- The grim reaper.
- Winter, as a death cycle of nature.
- A culling of beasts.
- Weeding a garden in order that new plants may be sown.
- Fermentation, the destruction and decay of one substance in order for it to be transformed into another. Life feeding on life.

XIV Temperance/Art

Letter: Samekh ס support/pillar/prop, or medicine.
Planet: Sagittarius ♐.
Path: 25 Tiferet to Yesod.
Deities: Michael, Aphroditus, Hermaphroditus, Holy Guardian Angel (Crowley says: Diana the huntress, Artemis).

Temperance is a card of rebalancing. It advises the avoidance of extremes. It is equilibrium, moderation, and reconciliation of opposing viewpoints. This card may come up symbolising mediation after an argument, abstinence after an addiction or a necessity to understand the view of one's opponents, without necessarily taking on their beliefs. Implicit is an avoidance of extremes, and separation from one's passions.

In the Rider Waite Smith image it is an androgynous angel, balancing masculine and feminine aspects. This is usually interpreted as either the archangel Michael or one's Holy Guardian Angel, the highest communicable aspect of one's self and a being who is aligned to the concept of one's 'true will'. The angel has one foot on land, symbolising consciousness, and one foot in the waters of subconsciousness. The two cups are similar but indicate an active rebalancing of emotional energies. The imagery symbolises rising from a lower, material, plane to a higher, more idealistic one. This fits well with its astrological sign of Sagittarius.

The angel has the sun on their forehead and an alchemical fire symbol on their chest. Fire in this case is the will, and the sun is things brought to light, and out in the open. This is a card of confession and facing one's vices with the intent to fully change. The sun in astrology is also the self.

Crowley takes a more alchemical approach, calling the card 'art', and depicting a chemical experiment where water and fire are combined in a basin. Where the Rider Waite Smith image focuses on the origin of its path, Tiferet, the heart centre of the Sefirot which is associated with the sun, Crowley focuses on its destination, Yesod, associated with the moon: An uncovering of spiritual mysteries. Crowley says the card is the fulfilment of VI, the Lovers: An 'alchemical marriage' (the union of opposites). The female figure represents several possible goddesses. Diana the huntress also known as the virgin Artemis, who is also paradoxically, a great mother of fertility, Diana the many-breasted goddess of the Ephesians, and Isis (relating to the Empress, and High Priestess cards). One of the goals of alchemy is the mingling of previously contradictory elements into unity. For instance, Fire and Water combine in the form of the sun and rain, allowing life on Earth. In this sense, the card represents the final stage of the 'Great Work' (Magnum Opus) and considered psychologically, contradictory emotions or wills are combined peacefully. For instance, as is the case in Carl Jung's psychological concept of individuation, a healing of the self into a common willpower. Like Crowley, Jung was also influenced by alchemy. In the background of his card is a long path up a holy mountain towards a shining golden crown, the godhead (Keter). Compared with the Lovers card, which depicts an earlier stage in the same operation, the lion and eagle have switched colours. The motto on the card is '*Visita Interiora Terrae Rectificando Invenies Occultum Lapidem*' translated as 'visit the interior parts of the Earth: By rectification, thou shalt find the hidden stone'. VITRIOL. In alchemy, this is the universal solvent, later associated with sulphuric acid. The hidden stone is the Philosopher's Stone, the universal medicine which grants eternal life, cures all ailments and turns lead into Gold, an allegory for self-improvement. The card presents a balanced combination of the three alchemical principles according to Paracelsus: Sulphur (oil, I Magus), Mercury (alcohol, II Empress) and Salt (ash, III Emperor).

The path of Samekh connects Tiferet to Yesod; it is in the balanced 'middle pillar', the prop which is the literal meaning of the letter. In Kabbalah, Tiferet is the seat of the ego, or the overt self, and Yesod is the seat of the hidden self, or subconscious. Yesod is also the sphere of communication and magic, especially magic of words and oratory. Samekh also has the meaning 'medicine'. Which is in this case about rebalancing the mind and body.

Examples:

- The temperance movement and its association with early feminism.
- A teetotaler.
- The 'straight edge' movement in punk rock.
- Zen Buddhist retreats.
- The stance of being apolitical.
- Gandhi and Martin Luther King Junior's non-violent protests.
- The political 'centre'.
- Homeostasis in biology.

XV Devil

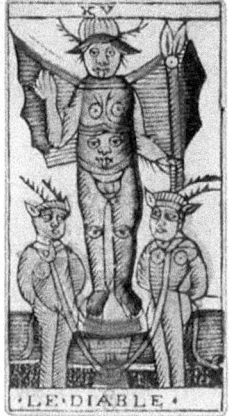  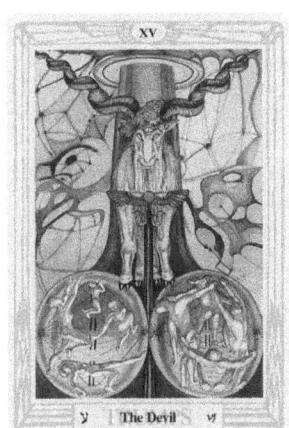

Letter: Ayin ע eye.
Sign: Capricorn ♑.
Path: 26 Tiferet to Hod.
Deities: Satyr, the Devil, Satan, Baphomet, Loki (as a fall into corruption from resentment), Set, Pan (hedonism, and submission to a wild nature), Dionysus/Bacchus (as gods of intoxification).

This is a card of chaining oneself to negativity. It is chosen slavery be it via addiction, vice or obsession. The two chained figures are Adam and Eve after the Fall. They have tails, and horns or antlers, indicative of their lower animal drives and carnal instincts.

The devil can represent a powerful person, or institution, who is hard to resist, with carnal influence. It can also be an unhealthy co-dependency, commonly referred to as a 'toxic relationship', sometimes by people who are trying to distance themselves from their own responsibility for the relationship, itself a 'devil' attribute.

In the Rider Waite Smith imagery, the card is a parody of the Hierophant, as the devil figure stands at an altar instead of a Pope. It is also a parody of the Lovers card, as the idyllic relationship has turned negative. The image of the devil has his right hand is raised and extended, the reverse of the gesture which is given by the Hierophant in the fifth card. In his left hand, there is a great flaming torch, inverted towards the earth. The lovers are chained, albeit loosely, with the ability to escape if they wished to. Éliphas Lévi, who influenced the magical theory of both the Golden Dawn and Crowley, attributes this card to Baphomet the divine androgyne. Ever the contrarian, Crowley says, given a better knowledge of the history of Baphomet since Lévi's time, that Baphomet is better understood as the Fool.

I see the Devil card as the 'pop-culture Baphomet', a scapegoat originally derived from the Catholic scapegoating of the Knights Templar. Where, if we are to agree with Crowley, the Thoth Fool card can be a more esoteric understanding of Baphomet. A divine androgyne.

The idea of the devil being a hermaphrodite is apparently nothing new, as he is depicted as such in some, but not all, of the Marseilles Decks. As such, the Devil can be understood as a third, rebel category, which challenges a stable dichotomy. This third figure emerging every generation or so is eventually incorporated, only to re-emerge once again, and is always reconfigured to shock the status quo. In Crowley's day, the shocking rebellion was homosexuality, especially between men. Later it was the gender-benders of rock'n'roll, Bowie, himself a Crowley fan, being a figurehead. There are always those who play the Devil's rebellion against the conservative part of society, and this is a story as old as time, and one that is perhaps a necessary tension forcing a stale society to change.

The Devil card is the symbol of corruption. A cult personality trespassing the rules of engagement in leadership. The corruption is allowed to exist because it is unpleasant to confront, and thus we avoid looking at it. The only way to defeat the Devil, the shadow nature of human psychology, is to face him, deny him his indulgences, and then incorporate him into the rest of the personality. The Devil is misapplied energy to get stuff done, or the tendency to waste energy on short-term pleasures. When incorporated, rather than fighting the rest of the self, he can add power to one's drive.

Inherent is a self-delusion which controls you and a submission to brainwashing, especially in matters where one is trying to avoid responsibility. A focus on the material over the spiritual and especially repurposing spiritual approaches for material gain. The solution is not to blame the corrupt force but rather to come into one's own will and accept the responsibility of one's own choices.

My favourite summary of the card is 'inversion without liberation', a phrase offered to me by my friend and fellow magician Aurora, during a conversation about rebellion. I was teasing out the idea that reversing the morality with which one was raised when taken to extremes, will rarely, if ever, truly set one free. Put perversely, the card is a belief in 'everything that was bad is now good'. A rebellion for the sake of rebellion.

The card represents the corruption of morality in people and institutions that is the precursor to the Tower card, the downfall. The material plane becomes elevated to a reverence that only rightly belongs to the spiritual. Magical orders that have tried this approach are Anton LaVey's Church of Satan and at times the teachings of Crowley himself, especially his sex magic. There is an initial freedom granted by this approach, but it never amounts to a stable new order that truly fixes the deeper problems of the old. True freedom comes from starting a new game with new rules, rather than merely playing the same old game, this time on the team of the enemy.

In Hebrew, the letter Ayin (ע) means 'eye'. On the Tree of Life, this path connects Tiferet, which is usually described as beauty and balance but is also the seat of the ego, with Hod, which many take as the intellect, but which has also been interpreted as the individual. Tiferet experiences are either an experience of a fire-like energy in the ego, where one feels oneself enlarged and powerful or it can be an experience of one's sense of self, merging or touching another's, such as during sex. Both sensations are generally very pleasurable.

Like some of the other Tarot paths, this is not a perfect fit with the traditional Jewish teachings of the Kabbalah. However, in relation to the Devil card, I understand it as follows: If the Sefirot of the Tree of Life is to be understood as a state of consciousness, akin to the Chakra systems of Yoga, then Tiferet, similar to the heart chakra Anahata, offers a blissful type of consciousness that is often described by people as feeling like a 'mini-enlightenment'. In this state, one's ego becomes merged with another. This can be reached during sex, with 'love drugs' such as MDMA, as well as through group spiritual experiences. The sensation is one of being filled with light in connection to one or more people. The issue with this state is that while the experience is blissful and radiant, it does nothing to fix the pathologies of the ego. The ability to produce this experience in others has often been exploited by spiritual cult leaders, who can create bliss in their followers. It is not however a true removal from the ego, and thus a strong personality can use this experience to impose their will on another. While a beautiful experience, the bliss experience is not a direct connection to divinity, but rather, one person affecting another.

The more balanced path is for this experience to be channelled through Netzach, attributed to Venus. This offers a group experience and one of love and connection. Instead, the Devil card's path of Ayin, goes straight from the Tiferet experience to Hod, the individual, without the balance of group connection, group morality or social graces. For this reason, though it can be a positive thing in balanced healthy people, it has the danger of becoming addictive and diverting one's attention from the things that keep on the straight and narrow. It can also be the full and unhealthy submission of one person to another.

Hod, is tied to the intellect and also to Mercury, the god of ideas and information. As such it is the home of the 'doubter' or sceptical part of the mind. The term 'satan' especially in the Old Testament means the same thing, a doubter or opposer.

The Devil card is symmetrically placed on the Sefirot with card XIII, Death. The association of the letter Ayin, and the Devil card with the eye, is similarly complex. There is the idea of an 'evil eye', used as a magical curse. This is an inversion of the 'Eye of Horus', a symbol for the sun (Tiferet) used as a protective symbol, especially on amulets.

According to Thelema, Crowley's religious system, the 'eye' is the meatus or hole of the penis. A one-way system. This gives a secondary meaning to the Devil card as a divine masculine force of nature, associated more with Pan than the Christian devil. The name Pan means 'all' and implicit is the idea of the 'Pangenetor' the 'all begetter', the masculine conception of nature's creative force. As one of Crowley's missions was to invert the values of his Christian upbringing, he sought some positivity in the Devil archetype.

Finally the 'eye' can be associated with Capricorn, the sign assigned to this card, in the idea of being 'one-eyed', or of a fixed opinion, as well as having one's 'eye on the prize', stereotypical Capricorn traits.[27] Crowley said the card portrays 'the divine madness of spring. The Goat leaping in "lust"', a primal and creative drive that Crowley considered fundamental to the universe, and focused towards material experiences. He related it to a state of consciousness where one is especially creative

---

[27] If you feel that some of these associations are sometimes a little stretched, I'm right there with you. While many of these systems are beautifully aligned, the Tarot is not always a perfect fit to the Kabbalah. Rather than smashing our toy castle because of one broken Lego block, I prefer to accept esoteric Tarot on its own terms, even when it is imperfect. Where most writers just avoid explaining the paths on the Tree of Life, for me 'making it work' is part of the game.

but not focused on an outcome. This could equally be the play of a child, or the often self-destructive 'experimentation' of an adolescent. He saw a freedom from repression in the archetype of the Devil and lust, almost certainly because he was raised in the Plymouth Brethren a very puritanical Christian sect.

In the Thoth image, the Capricorn goat is in the centre. This is also Pan, a god of frightful ecstatic states, as well as the scapegoat, who takes on society's sinful debts so that they may themselves be cleansed.

The goat has his third eye, the chakra Ajna, opened, meaning that he has achieved a spiritual sight that most lack. This is Crowley's take on the Hebrew letter Ayin, meaning 'eye'. As the word 'Pan' is also Greek for 'all' Crowley considers him the experience of integration with the 'all' through the 'ego-death' experience.[28] For some people, this is blissful, while for others it is panic-inducing.

Before the goat is the wand of the 'Chief Adept' a rank of the Hermetic Order of the Golden Dawn in which Crowley was initiated. It is crowned with the winged globe and the twin serpents of Horus and Osiris. The goat has a crown of lotuses, perhaps representing the opening of chakras or of spiritual awakenings.

Behind the goat, is a giant phallus and testicles, simultaneously a tree trunk and two seeds. Representative of the divine male sexual force. The trunk pierces a circle or cosmic vagina. On the left testicle are four female figures and on the right are four male figures, the next generation of people.

Negatively aspected the Devil implies cowardice; an unwillingness to face up to wrongdoing, a negative influence, or a short-term gain with a long-term cost. A negation of responsibility; blaming others or playing the victim. It is also the draining feeling of giving power to someone, or an institution who doesn't care about you.

Positively aspected, the Devil card offers temporary liberation and pleasure. A great cathartic blowing off of steam and a release of moral tension. As long as one doesn't stay here all the time this can be a lot of fun.

---

[28] As I have described above, I argue that the experience of Tiferet or Anahata, the heart Chakra is not a true 'ego death' but a temporary merging of consciousness with others. This has been informed by my personal experiences. True 'ego-death' is a much stranger experience, which I associate with the Sefirah Keter, or the crown Chakra Sahasrara, which in Tarot is the Fool card.

Examples:

- The '27 club' of young deaths in rock and roll history, often the result of addictions, hedonism, or succumbing to mental illness (one's devils).
- The film *Trainspotting* (1996), which is about Scottish heroin addicts, can be thought of as an allegory for the Devil card.
- Organised crime such as the Mafia (*The Godfather*, *Goodfellas* and *The Sopranos*).
- Drug use (especially dependency).
- Hedonism.
- The writings of the Marquis de Sade, can be thought of as a fascination with all the things that the Devil card represents.
- Darth Vader's allegiance to the 'dark side of the force' in *Star Wars*.

XVI Tower

Letter: Peh פ mouth.
Planet: Mars ♂.
Path: 27 Netzach to Hod.
Deities: Mars/Ares (defeat in war), Montu, Shiva (the destroyer).

If the Devil card is a deal made with corruption, then the Tower is the fall from grace that usually follows. It symbolises a sudden loss of faith in institutions and authority, especially at a societal level.

For example, security breaches, the collapse of banks, organised crime in national institutions, sexual abuse scandals in religious or educational institutions, large-scale fraud in institutions and mass-produced products that turn out to be dangerous to consumers.

In history, the 9/11 New York Trade Center Tower collapse of 2001 was a perfect example of this symbol materialised. A sudden breach of America's national security resulted in a collapse of faith from which the nation has never fully recovered. Many have called it the death of the 'American Dream'.

As the Tower is ruled by Mars, the card can represent a devastating attack in war, the most extreme example being the atomic bombings of Hiroshima and Nagasaki. An act which struck terror not only into the hearts of the Japanese but also America's own citizens, who were shocked at the unholy power unleashed by their own side. This was an act that has forever changed geopolitics and war.

On a more personal level, the Tower is the shock of being faced by one's sins. The 'rock bottom' moment of the addict or the alcoholic. It can be considered a kind of spiritual 'immune response', an expulsion of that which would result in death if one continued to do it.

Mythologically, the Tower is, of course, the Tower of Babel. Man's prideful ambition to reach the heavens by material and intellectual means. The story is a reminder that truly experiencing the highest spiritual 'heaven' first requires a dissolution of the ego. Something that many people find to be scary and difficult. Without this step, the experience can be harrowing instead of enlightening.

In the Rider Waite Smith image there is a tower struck by lightning: Punishment by the gods, reminiscent of Zeus' thunderbolt. Around the tower are 22 golden Yods, a letter of the Hebrew alphabet, conceptualised as the brush stroke out of which all the other letters can be formed. These are the 22 paths that connect the Sefirot on the kabbalistic Tree of Life. That they have all collapsed into yods is symbolic of the structure breaking into its core parts. Yod is also the first letter of the holy name YHVH, signifying the idea that all comes from God; the core creativity of the universe. These yods are split into a group of ten, referring to each Sefirah and another group of 12, symbolising the zodiac. Two figures fall from the tower. They are perhaps the two figures initiated earlier by the Hierophant.

In Crowley's Thoth Deck, the symbolism is similar. Above we have the eye of Shiva or Horus, the opening of which is supposed to bring the destruction of the world (or at least herald the destruction of one cycle and the rebirth into a new age). The dove, from the story of Noah's ark, and the serpent, Apophis, represent the Schopenhauerian[29] 'will to live' and 'will to die', two contradictory forces that drive the behaviour of human beings.

Crowley considered the scene to be a precursor to the judgement card XX, a necessary destruction of the current (patriarchal) age of Osiris in order to usher in a New Aeon of Horus the Child, for which he considered himself the prophet.

Below are 'the jaws of Dis'. 'Dis Pater' is a Roman rendering of Hades complete with the fires of hell. The jaws are the letter Peh, which means mouth. Crowley, though a religious rebel, remained fond of the imagery of the Book of Revelation in the King James Bible. It is important to note

---

[29] (Schopenhauer 1818).

that Crowley's deck, while excellent for divination, was not primarily constructed for that purpose, but rather as a vehicle for magic and his teachings.

While the Tower is at face value a negative card, it brings a purge of a failed system. What follows, if one resets one's values, is a chance of redemption which we will see in the next card, the Star. For those who are already outside of the system, this can feel like a moment of justice.

Peh means the mouth, which is tied to speech. This connects to the splitting of languages as punishment for the Tower of Babel. It is also the mouth of the archetypical beast, waiting to eat those who trespass the natural order. Think 'there be dragons' on the edges of old maps.

The card is assigned to the path connecting Netzach and Hod which are tied to the story of Job. Netzach represents perseverance and faith. Hod is the individual, an individual's understanding, and hard work. In this instance, the Tower card explores the negative side of this equation, the loss of faith and its effect on the individual.

The Tower card teaches us that sometimes, to grow and evolve, we must experience sudden and unexpected events that shake the foundations of our lives.

Examples:

- The September 11 attacks on the Twin Towers of the New York World Trade Center, and the Pentagon in 2001.
- The Jewish Holocaust at the hands of the Nazis during World War II, which murdered 39 per cent of all Jewish people.
- The COVID-19 pandemic in 2020.
- The 2008 banking crash.
- The Tower of Babel from the Bible.
- The plagues of disease that killed most of the first nations of the Americas were estimated at more than 56 million deaths.
- The 1346 to 1353 CE 'Black Death' pandemic of bubonic plague in Eurasia and North Africa which killed between 75–200 million people.
- The Irish potato famine, which caused the deaths of around one million, and which were affected by the colonial policies of the British.
- The freeing of the slaves in 1865 CE, which destroyed the economy of the Southern States of America, was a 'Tower Moment' for the

slave owners, and an example of a positive outcome of the Tower archetype for the American Blacks.
- All large-scale acts of war, especially bombings such as Dresden by the Allies (1945), the Blitzkrieg of the UK by the Germans, and of Hiroshima and Nagasaki by the US (1945).

XVII Star

Letter: Tzaddi צ fish hook (Crowley assigns this card the letter and path Heh, exchanging it with the Emperor).
Sign: Aquarius ♒.
Path: 28 Netzach to Yesod (Crowley assigns it instead to the path from Chokhmah to Tiferet).
Deities: Ishtar, Venus (as the morning star), Lucifer (as the morning star who sheds light on what was hidden), Nuit (as 'mother heaven'), Babalon, Sirius/Sopdet/Sothis (the star that precedes the flooding of the Nile), Juventas/Hebe (goddess of youth), Ganymede/Ganymeda.

After the loss of faith represented by the Tower card, the only path forward out of nihilism is to build a new faith in something better. The Star represents a lofty goal and an orientation point. Stars were universally used for navigation by our ancestors and as focus points for deities. As an ideal, the goal of the Star will never be truly reached in a human lifetime, however, because of this, it will never cease to inspire one to improve. It provides the goal but not the destination.

The Rider Waite Smith image has some similarities to the Temperance card, only now the figure is a naked earthly human female rather than the angel. She nourishes the earth and the body of water with the water of life from two jugs, carefully balancing the pragmatism of the element of earth with the emotional world of the element of water. Behind her is a tree, perhaps the tree of knowledge of good and evil. This symbolises the moral path, and pictured is an ibis bird, a symbol of Thoth, the god of intellect, words and magic. Josephine McCarthy, says that the birth in the tree is the Benu bird featured in the *Egyptian Book of the Dead*, a symbol of renewal. The bird is said to appear in the depths of darkness just before a journey towards the light.[30] The number 17 (XVII) of the card can, by the rules of numerology discussed earlier in this book, be broken down to 1 + 7 = 8. Above the maiden are eight, eight-pointed stars. The seven smaller stars are the chakras, the Pleiades or 'seven sisters', and perhaps the seven classical planets. One could further make assertions regarding the seven notes of the major scale in music, representing order and harmony. In any case, the seven smaller stars represent perfection in perfect balance. The eighth golden star can be considered an octave, a new beginning on a higher plane. It is the star of Ishtar who is also associated with Venus, the morning star, the 'light bringer'.

Waite considers the female figure to be Binah, the Sefirah of divine understanding, who pours her inspiration down to the lower Sefirot. In this case, the water can be considered the Shekhinah, or feminine flow of the 'Holy Spirit' in Kabbalah.

The path of Tzaddi, which means 'fishhook', connects Netzach to Yesod. Tzaddi as an abbreviation is tied to tsafon (צָפוֹן), meaning, 'north', of which it is the first letter (Hebrew is read right to left). This implies orientation, like the navigating star. The hook can be considered like the hook of a celestial tow rope. One 'hooks' one's attention onto the orientating star and that allows one to navigate. This relates to the 'skyhook' idea discussed for the Hierophant card. In this case, however, the inspiration is personal, rather than being prescribed by an institution such as a religion.

In Tarot readings the navigation at play is more often moral than geographical. Hooking into a higher principle or ideal in order to keep on the righteous path. In this sense, the card is a redemption from the Devil card, where one has had a deal with destructive forces and the Tower card where one has experienced a moral comeuppance.

In Crowley's version of the card, the imagery is a little simpler, though the figure is now the Goddess 'Nuit',[31] his spelling of the Egyptian Goddess Nut, who is the cosmic void from which all creation

---

[30] (McCarthy 2015).

[31] It is my guess that Crowley who was a polyglot and a lover of languages sought to align the Egyptian 'Nut' to the French 'nuit' meaning 'night'. While the etymology is false, the two languages being unrelated, they both connote 'night'. Crowley was fond of this kind of coincidence.

springs forth. Above her to the left is the seven-pointed star of Venus, which Crowley also associates with Babalon, his conception of a rebellious and liberated female divinity. Some people also call the seven-pointed star, or heptagram, 'the fairy star'. Crowley switches the corresponding path with the Emperor, making the Emperor Tzaddi and the Star Heh. His explanation for this is to align the word 'Tzaddi' with the word 'Tsar' which sounds similar but is a false etymology. Crowley took it as a magical link nonetheless.

In both versions of the card, the cup-bearing figure represents a feminine version of Aquarius, the change bringer. Waite and de Gébelin say that the Star card represents Sirius, the dog-star (part of the constellation Canis Majoris). The rising of Sirius marked the precursor to the flooding of the Nile in Ancient Egypt, a time of fertility and regrowth.

The letter Tzaddi is assigned to the Path from Netzach to Yesod. Netzach is associated with Venus. It is the inspiration to action, an overcoming of fears and an allegiance to our moral faculties. Yesod is the Sefirah of communication, of the hidden forces of the subconscious (the Moon) and also of magic. The implication is one of renewed faith, without rationalisation (which would be the Sefirah Hod).

Examples:

- The star of Bethlehem.
- A lighthouse which aids in navigation.
- A 'higher calling', the star as a symbol for one's spiritual path.
- Negatively expressed, the Star is the 'White Whale' from Moby Dick. Captain Ahab's self-destructive futile request which he believes will offer him redemption.
- The belief in Utopias.
- Idealism in politics.
- The Enlightenment (beginning in 1715 CE with the death of Louis XV of France), or 'the Age of Reason', where faith in moral rationality, and a rational universe replaced faith in religions.
- The Renaissance of the fifteenth and sixteenth centuries.
- Communism and Marxism as idealised movements.

XVIII Moon

Letter: Qof ק back of the head.
Sign: Pisces ♓.
Path: 29 Netzach to Malkut.
Deities: Kephra, Selene, Luna, Diana/Artemis (as night huntress), Hecate, Khonsu, Legba.

My favourite association with the Moon card is the plot of *The Wizard of Oz*. Depicted in the Rider Waite Smith version is a 'yellow brick road' leading into a landscape past the, now familiar, towers of judgement. This implies a personal trial. Just like in the film (and the book), there are three male characters, in this case an armoured crayfish climbing out of the waters of the subconscious, representing man's primordial drives, a wild wolf, representing an untameable, uncivilised nature, and a tame dog, representing the part of us that fits in with our society. Implicit in the card is a fourth, female character, our Dorothy, who is mysterious to the men and is coming into womanhood and her own individuality and willpower. This is her trial. For our purposes, she is becoming like Artemis, a heroine in a strange land, and she must solve her problems using a feminine charm, intelligence, mysterious luck, and her own sense of right and wrong. In a way, she is the full personality in comparison to the 'sub-personalities' that are the three male characters.

Together these parts of the psyche are tasked to travel along a magical and metaphorical road towards finding their true nature, to meet a Wizard (the Hermit), represented by the two pillars in the background, who will judge if they are worthy.

Like with the Priestess, the Moon card represents the knowledge and wisdom gained through direct experience. Only this time, the journey is harder and the knowledge can only be gained after an ordeal. The implication of the Moon is that it brings to light that which was hidden, or 'occulted', by darkness. With a small amount of light, via the Moon, the secrets are now uncovered for those who look carefully. These are the things 'hidden under one's nose'.

In a very Jungian sense, the journey depicted in the card is one of 'individuation', the attempt to bring all of one's separate drives, complexes and sub-personalities under one unified will and common purpose. When Dorothy and her party finally meet the Wizard of Oz, they are presented not with a supernatural sorcerer, but with 'the man behind the curtain', the 'shadow'. Carl Jung wisely understood that this 'shadow' must first be confronted. In particular, Dorothy must face her wicked witch, a feminine shadow character, and then the shadow must be incorporated (she is called a witch herself by other characters). Misapplied, the witch is cruelty and resentment. However, becoming a witch is also an opportunity for Dorothy to learn to defend herself and come into her own power. If one fails to incorporate the shadow then it will always exert some control, often preventing us from getting stuff done or leading us to self-destructive behaviours.

The alternative to 'facing the shadow', the wishing away, or burying of unpleasantries, can be very dangerous. Every positive thinking movement, like the flower-power scene of the hippies, will, given enough time, produce its Charles Manson. A violent person who takes advantage of the love and goodwill of others. This is why Artemis, the heroic feminine figure and moon goddess, has a bow to protect herself.

Another implication of the card, like the land of Oz, is liminality. Being between two worlds. The road can also be understood as the crossroads, a cross-cultural symbol with a triple meaning: The first is a crossroads between what is expected by one's upbringing and society, staying at home, and a desire to leave for adventure and travel, a decision that all of us face many times, but which particularly faces young people.

A second implication is that of rebellion against the norms of society. One has met the devil at the crossroads, and taken his offer of fame, sex, drugs, hedonism and partying, as depicted in the blues and rock'n'roll. At its best, this path is a liberation. At its worst, it is a self-sacrifice.

A third implication is the crossroads between the lighted world of the living and the dim hidden world of spirits and the dead. The Devil at the

Crossroads is also a psychopomp, for instance, Papa Legba, a Voudou deity, who can put one in touch with the dead, or with other gods.

Somewhat ironically, the Moon card is not attributed to the astrological moon (which is assigned instead to the Priestess). Instead, the card is associated with Pisces, a very liminal sign where the subconscious meets the conscious. Pisces is associated with psychedelia, drugs, and the breaking of boundaries and dreams.

Also in the Rider Waite Smith image is a moon with 32 rays representing the 22 paths between the Sefirot plus the ten Sefirot themselves, together these are referred to as the 32 paths in the Kabbalah. Below are 15 rays, which are Yods, the Hebrew letter from which all the others can be formed. The exact meaning of 15 here is not easy to find, though some assume it refers to card XV, the Devil, which fits the crossroads concept perfectly.

The Thoth Tarot card depicts a scarab beetle holding the sun just under the horizon, this is Kephra, the god of the dawn, whose name was written with a scarab hieroglyph, and who is depicted either as a scarab or a scarab-headed man. The obvious symbolism is of hidden things just below the surface, about to come to light. Alternatively, the ability, like the dung beetle to turn shit into something useful that grows. Above are the two towers of judgement, and Anubis the judge of souls, here in double form. Crowley says the card represents resurrection, symbolised by the resurrection of the sun from night, and implied, from winter. The moon card itself is midnight.

> The Moon, partaking as she does of the highest and the lowest, and filling all the space between, is the most universal of the Planets. In her higher aspect, she occupies the place of the Link between the human and divine, as shown in Atu II. [the Priestess] In this Trump, her lowest avatar, she joins the earthy sphere of Netzach with Malkut, the culmination in matter of all superior forms. This is the waning moon, the moon of witchcraft and abominable deeds. She is the poisoned darkness which is the condition of the rebirth of light. This path is guarded by Tabu.[32,33]

---

[32] From the Māori word 'Tapu', which gave us the English word 'taboo' or as Crowley spells it, 'tabu'. Originally this is the Māori concept of ritual restriction. It is similar to the Muslim concept 'haram', and the Hebrew concept 'trefah'.
[33] Page 112 (Crowley 1944).

Above and below in the background are sine wave-like patterns being the time cycles that the moon describes, and also strangely, pre-empting the discovery of the brainwaves during consciousness and unconsciousness. From the moon descend nine drops of blood in the shape of Yods, the Hebrew letter of initiation of will. Crowley says the card can be symbolic of depression, the dark night of the soul.

The letter Qof means the back of the head and is symbolic of the unconscious, inspiration from the liminal parts of the mind, and from dreams. The card is assigned to the path from Netzach to Malkut. Malkut is our base instincts such as our will to survive. Netzach is lust for power, charm, to inspire and to be inspired (ruled by Venus, the charming one). When these two are in an unhealthy relationship it can result in complexes, self-defence mechanisms and manifestations of our Jungian 'shadow'. These can be present in our actions (Malkut) and also in the realm of our Psychology (Netzach). This can result in a pathological need to be loved by people, to charm them, to chase after approval, and to yearn for sex and attention.

Until these issues are faced one risks these shadowy sub-wills running the show.

Examples:

- Carl Jung's (1875–1961) individuation process.
- *The Wizard of Oz*.
- The road taken after meeting the devil at the crossroads.
- The journey from childhood to adulthood.
- Entry to the underworld such as in the story of Orpheus and Eurydice.

XIX Sun

Letter: Resh ר head.
Planet: Sol ☉.
Path: 30 Hod to Yesod.
Deities: Apollo, Helios, Baldr, Adam and Eve (in the garden), Heru-Ra-Ha (Thelemic mix of Horus of the Horizon, and Harpocrates), Ra, Aten, Horus and many other Egyptian sun gods.

The sun is one of the simplest cards in Tarot. It depicts the innocence of a child's day in the sun. It represents being present in the moment, without cares or worries. It alludes to Eden, the walled garden, and the innocent state of Adam and Eve before their fall.

Positively aspected, it is the joy of the moment. Negatively aspected, it is 'rose-coloured spectacles', a failure to notice the negative in the situation, or even the tendency to look away from anything unpleasant.

Unlike the reflected light of the moon, the light of the sun is direct and shows things exactly as they are. All is overt, honest and upfront. Nothing else is noticed. In the Rider Waite Smith image, there is a naked child, representing innocence, riding a horse. The horse is our animal nature in good times, bodily well-being, and pleasure. It is not controlled by force, as it is saddleless, and so the child and horse interact instead by intuition. There is no force used. The four sunflowers are the four elements. As they are in harmony, they all look the same. The red flag is the blood of renewal, perhaps the regrowth after the death card.

In the Marseilles Deck, there are two figures under the sun, perhaps Adam and Eve, though one could also interpret them as the twins, Gemini. In Crowley's Thoth Tarot, there are two winged fairy children. The sun radiates 12 rays of the zodiac and the 12 signs are depicted around the outside. The secondary rays split each of the signs into three decans,[34] which we will apply to the Tarot in the minor arcana section. The children dance above two scarabs, the symbol of the god Khepri of the morning sun. In the background is a walled peak of a holy mountain. In Biblical symbolism Eden is atop a mountain, and Crowley was himself a mountaineer. The mountain could also be interpreted as Mount Meru, an axis mundi,[35] which in Hindu cosmology, is the centre of all possible universes, and, like Olympus to the Greeks, the home of the Gods.

The letter Resh ר is the head, representing that which goes into our senses directly and doesn't need to be implied or interpreted (unlike the Moon which is Qof, the back of the head, which must be taken in through interaction with the subconscious).

Finally, the Sun represents those experiences that are described as coming from Tiferet, the heart/sun centre of the Sefirot, which correlates to Anahata the heart chakra. People who have control over this centre are said to be able to radiate or tap into pure bliss. This is also accessible through sexual contact with a loving partner or through euphoric drugs such as MDMA. The experience can feel like a mini-enlightenment; with accompanying 'all is love' feelings. However, despite its pleasures, it doesn't solve any of the problems of the ego. These people who can radiate 'Sun' charm can be found as the 'golden boys' of mythology, for example, Baldur, and Apollo, or goddesses of beauty and love such as Freyja and Aphrodite.

Despite the association with Tiferet and the Heart chakra Anahata, the Sun card is somewhat awkwardly attributed to the path from Hod to Yesod. Applying knowledge (Hod) to direct subjective experience

---

[34] In astrology the decans are 36 divisions of the ecliptic, each being 10°. They split each sign into three sections, and are each assigned one of the classical planets. This creates three types for each sign of the zodiac.

[35] In the geocentric model of the universe the Axis Mundi was the point of rotation of the 'celestial sphere', the layer of sky that holds the 'fixed stars' as opposed to the planets, or 'wandering stars'. Symbolically the *axis mundi* is the focal point for our relationship to the universe and our fate, as written in the stars.

(Yesod). Resh. So the experience is one of living in the moment. Learning and knowledge via direct experience.[36]

Examples:

- Baldur, the most beloved of the Norse gods. A golden god of beauty and charm. He is murdered via trickery by the jealous Loki, the god of our shadow nature.
- Apollo the Greek god of the sun, and of analytical thinking.
- *Here Comes the Sun* by the Beatles. The lyrics call us to cheer up and live in the moment, just as the card depicts.
- Summer pop hits such as *Surfing USA* by the Beach Boys.
- The Garden of Eden before the fall.
- Heaven.
- The movements naturism and nudism. Both tend to attribute time spent in the sun, and sun tans with good health.
- Negatively aspected: 'Lovebomb' cults.

---

[36] Another attribution to the Tree of life which I find to be a little forced.

XX Judgement/Aeon

Known as 'Aeon' in the Thoth deck.

Letter: Shin ש tooth.
Planet: Sometimes assigned to Pluto ♇.
Path: 31 Hod to Malkut.
Deities: Anubis (as weigher of souls), Jesus resurrected, Osiris resurrected, Gabriel, Fenrir, Hephaestus/Vulcan (surviving his fall).

This card signifies the moral judgement of a cycle of the Wheel of Fortune, an apocalypse in the true sense of the word; an 'unveiling'. Sins and problems of the past are brought to the fore so they can be properly faced and put to rest. A great levelling occurs, where debts are settled or forgiven. Some people will lose and some people will gain. Compared with the Justice card, Judgement can either be seen as the next frame, where the verdict is reached, or the Justice card can be considered the personal level with Judgement being at the societal level.

Great court cases of institutions fit the bill, such as the Catholic Church child abuse scandals of the early 2000s. In therapy, judgement is the act of facing trauma, especially one's own wrongs or the wrongs of one's family members. It is the necessary scene before achieving catharsis. In Jungian analysis, it is the direct interaction with the 'shadow' before integration can be achieved. Things that have gone unsaid are said, and the long-buried past is brought to bear and assessed.

In the Rider Waite Smith image, which is based on a scene from the book of Revelation, the archangel Gabriel (or in some versions, Israfil) blows his trumpet to herald God's grand judgement. The Red Cross is the flag of order. The dead are raised in order to receive justice. A metaphor for the past coming back to affect the present.

In the Thoth deck, the card is named 'Aeon', and it focuses less on the apocalypse and more on the new age that follows it. Crowley was obsessed with the book of Revelation and he shared the Victorian era fascination with Ancient Egypt, considering himself the prophet of the coming 'age of Horus'.

The image in his Thoth Deck is based on the Stele of Ankh-ef-en-Khonsu, also known as the 'Stele of revealing'.[37] Nuit, goddess of the void and of the sky is at the top as a blue figure, representing limitless possibility, referred to in Kabbalah as *ain soph aur* (limitless light). Hadit,[38] a god envisioned by Crowley to represent a singularity, is the red dot in the centre. He is the 'point of view' reality as it is experienced by a single individual. The marriage of these two deities produces 'Horus the child', depicted in transparent blue, and holding his finger to his mouth. Crowley called him Heru-Ra-Ha, his mix of the Egyptian 'Horus of the horizon', and Harpocrates, understood by the Ptolemaic Greeks to be the god of secrets and mysteries.[39] The letter Shin burns in flaming yellow below, suggesting both fire and a flower. In the letter Shin, are three yods, with three human figures representing a new generation of people for the coming new age.

The letter Shin in Judaism often refers to the Shekhinah or God's Holy Spirit. It is always expressed as feminine. Shin is also the element of fire, as well as the teeth, both attributed to judgement.

The path of Shin connects Hod (Splendour) and Malkut in Kabbalah. Hod represents the energy of intellectual insight, analysis, individuality and the ability to understand complex ideas. Malkut is the manifest realm and the body. So here is pure reason, rationality and judgement manifested without concern for emotion, mercy or kindness.

---

[37] Stele: A stone slab monument bearing a carving, often from a tomb.
[38] There is no ancient Egyptian god known as Hadit, Crowley either invented this deity, or 'channelled' him, likely through his wife Rose.
[39] Actually derived from a misunderstood hieroglyph meaning 'child'.

Examples:

- Armageddon and the apocalypse from the Bible.
- Ragnarök and the Götterdamerung from Norse and German mythology.
- Large historical court cases of institutions such as the Catholic sexual abuse scandal.
- All judgements by a judge or committee.
- Old trauma brought up before one can heal.
- Anubis weighing a soul against a feather in order to judge the dead in Egyptian mythology.
- The saying, 'skeletons in the closet'.
- The seizing up of a culture before a new age.
- The act of forgiveness of wrongdoings.

XXI World/Universe

Known as 'The Universe' in the Thoth deck.

Letter: Tav ת, a cross, or mark.
Planet: Saturn ♄.
Path: 32 Yesod to Malkut.
Deities: Saturn, Chronos, Gaea, Brahma, Ptah, Geb, Ophion and Eurynome.

The World card represents the expansion of one's worldview after a great realisation or change of awareness. It is the ability to see the whole instead of only the parts. Spiritually, it is the connection of one's consciousness to the 'axis mundi', or centre of the universe. It is also the grand completion of a long time cycle.

In Yoga and Kabbalah, as meditation systems, it is the ability to see the full flow of all possible conscious states as one big unified moving system. In Kabbalah, this is referred to as Da'at and represents a major achievement in conscious awareness. In Tantra, this is known as 'chakra samādhāna' (चक्र समाधान), the balancing of the chakra energies.

In a reading, the World card represents coming out of an experience with a true sense of perspective. It especially relates to the understanding that one is a small part of a whole system of will and action, rather than a separate, individual actor. Therefore it signifies engagement with a 'higher purpose', one's contribution to humanity or the world. The act of looking outward rather than inward.

Travel or international communication can be the cause of this, and many readers will use the card to mean the querent will go on or has been on a trip. It can however be applied to the querent being affected by global world events. In this card, there is usually a sense of completion.

In the Rider Waite Smith image, there is a dancer with two wands. Around her is a wreath of achievement and around that are the four 'Hayyot', or 'living creatures' of Ezekiels' vision[40] which are a bull (Taurus), a lion (Leo), an eagle (Scorpio) and a man (Aquarius) representing the four fixed astrological signs. These, as a shorthand, refer to the complete zodiac as a system for understanding fate.

In the Thoth Deck, this card is called 'the Universe'. Crowley was trying to update magic for his Victorian age. Astronomy, even in his time, had expanded the scientific worldview far beyond the geocentric universe of our ancestors to a realisation that our solar system is one of many. Even so, since Crowley's death, we now understand the universe to be an order of magnitude bigger than was even understood at the time.

The snake and maiden in his image are Ophion and Eurynome who from their union create the 'Orphic Egg' from which the world hatches. Around them is the firmament of stars symbolising fate. This is drawn from the Orphic mysteries of Ancient Greece.

Crowley's version of the card relates to the Fool, which Crowley and the Golden Dawn before him, related to the first action that created the universe. The universe card is then that creation competed and functioning as a system.

The fish hook is the letter Tzaddi, meaning hook or sword, which Crowley assigns to the Emperor, a representation of the divine masculine power. It has caught the serpent, perhaps symbolically the triumph of order over chaos, the serpent being Apophis. The sun in the image is the source of life and perhaps an allusion to the concept of alchemical 'Gold', a symbol for the goal of the journey of the soul in the Magnum Opus, or 'Great Work' in alchemy where the magician's consciousness has found its true purpose and its true relationship with creation.

Tav is the final letter of the Hebrew alphabet. It means 'cross' or 'mark' and in particular it refers to the balanced T cross. The World card is the end of a story where a new balance is found. Its numerical value

---

[40] Ezekiel 1 in the Bible.

is 400, representing a larger manifestation of four, associated with the Tetragrammaton YHVH, a power word, that sets all creation in motion. In Jewish Kabbalah Tav stands for the three essential acts of the soul and their result: Teshuvah (repentance), Tefillah (prayer) and Torah (wisdom of the Holy texts). The result of careful adherence to these is 'Tikkun', redemption.

The card is attributed to the path from Yesod to Malkut on the Tree of Life. This defines the final process of the Sefirot. A cycle is complete, manifest and is now beyond your control. Any further action requires setting in action a brand new process. A new story.

Ultimately the World card expresses a connection to the all.

Examples:

- The foundation of the internet, the 'World Wide Web' and the 'global village'.
- Global politics, especially geopolitics.
- The telescope's view of the universe.
- The Alpha and Omega. A metaphor taken from the first and last letters of the Greek alphabet, referring to the totality of God's power.[41]
- Field theories in physics.
- The Dao. A conception of the universal order of all things in the Chinese philosophy of Taoism
- Macrocosm/microcosm. The idea that the actions of the universe (Macrocosm) are reflected in the human (microcosm) and the human sphere of awareness just as the human affects the universe in turn. This idea was central to Western and Islamic Alchemy and originated with the Ancient Greek Philosopher Anaximander (c. 610–c. 546 BCE). Implicit in this idea is that the universe is alive, that it can be reasoned with and that it has a mind and thoughts.
- Karmic cycles and Samsara. In Hinduism, Buddhism and Yoga, Karma is the great wave of action of the universe which has an effect on the moral undertakings of humankind. Samsara is the great of life death and reincarnation. Both could be understood via the World card in Tarot.

---

[41] From the Book of Revelation 1:8, 21:6 and 22:13.

The Minor Arcana in depth

The minor arcana represent plot points, events and interactions in our narrative. Each card uses one of the four elements: Fire, Water, Air and Earth, and one aspect of numerology of the numbers from one to ten.

Since the popularity of the Rider Waite Smith Deck, many decks have images and specific meanings for each of the minor arcana cards. The numerology of the Marseilles style of decks still applies to the Rider Waite Smith however. Some RWS derivative decks, have been designed by artists rather than magicians and their images have strayed from the underlying numerology. Learning with these decks may make it harder to understand the logic of traditional decks, and while some 'artist decks' are also well thought out for reading, some, especially themed decks, can be quite unbalanced in their symbolism. Unbalanced decks can push the reader towards particular outcomes in their readings. For instance, decks that have only female characters depicted are going to make it harder to tell male stories.

This may push the reader towards an outcome they want, for instance, an enhancement of female stories, but ultimately they are ill-suited for general readings. The same goes for decks which are entirely cat pictures!

Learning from images rather than 'pip' cards, in some ways makes it easier to learn to read the Tarot, in other ways however, it narrows the scope of interpretation. There is something to be said for eventually learning both systems, but either will deliver results.

For instance, in the Rider Waite Smith Deck, the Three of Swords depict heartbreak. Numerologically it expresses the end of the first act in an interaction of ideas with other people, which frequently manifest as arguments. The outcome of this may be heartbreak, but equally it may be something more positive such as an understanding reached by the two parties after a struggle for ideas, and the continuation of that relationship to a new level of understanding. As one can see, the Rider Waite Smith chooses for us a negative expression of the Three of Swords, and the Marseilles or other 'pip' decks leave the interpretation more open to the reader.

In the following, we will continue our exploration of the imagery of the Rider Waite Smith and Aleister Crowley's 'Thoth' decks. For a simple reading with 'pip' decks such as the Marseilles, refer back to the chapter 'Simple Tarot numerology'. If you don't have a 'pip' deck, you can still apply the numerological method to the Rider Waite Smith Deck, and as you become more familiar with Tarot it can be useful to cross-pollinate different systems of interpretation.

Aces

The Aces represent causal powers that have not yet been manifested. They are core elements from beyond our perception which have just popped through into our minds, or that we have been made aware of. They associate with the connection to the force of creation that is just beyond the threshold of human awareness.

On the Kabbalistic Tree of Life, the first Sefirah is Keter, the first cause. It represents the undifferentiated all, from which all things emerge.

Ace of Wands/Batons

Fire in Keter

The Ace of Wands represents a new inspiration or breakthrough that opens up a new way to express yourself. It is the first will to act. Metaphorically, it is a phallus, the masculine force in all of us that purposely creates new things. In modern slang, it is a 'just do it' attitude.

Reversed or negatively aspected, it would either be a blocked path, or something new being forced upon the querent. In another context, it may also mean that the querent has radically misunderstood the amount of effort or practice that is required to master the new aspiration and may embarrass themselves by attempting to perform it too early. They may, for instance, imagine themselves to have the voice of a nightingale, while actually sounding like a strangled cat.

In the Rider Waite Smith image, there is a hand, representing the will (the Hebrew letter Yod means 'hand' and the ability to act), appearing out of a cloud representing thought. It is holding a wand representing a new concept that can be 'held' in thought.

In the Thoth Tarot, is a flaming staff. Each of the ten flames is a 'Yod' representing will, the causal powers and the ten Sefirot of the Tree of Life. The implication is of high 'energy' to get work done. In Kabbalah, spirit is associated with fire.

Astrologically, the Ace of Wands associates to fire signs. Aries the instigator, Leo the performer, and Sagittarius the goal-shooter. Mythologically, the Ace of Wands is the first appearance of any new concept or thing. For instance, Adam the first man. It can also be associated with Prometheus' gift of fire to man, which granted us technology.

In readings that require a location, Crowley wrote that the Ace of Wands represents Asia. Alchemically, the Ace of Wands is fire (or spirit) in abstract, or primordial form.

Ace of Cups

Water in Keter

This card shows us a new emotional experience or potential for a relationship, the promise of romance, and the idea of emotional fulfilment. It is the feminine, receptive, quality in all of us that wants to receive emotional attention from others, and is therefore the harmonious 'other half' to the active (masculine) Ace of Wands.

Where the Ace of Wands is the will to act, the Ace of Cups is the will to receive. In Catholic symbolism, it is the receptive rite of the Holy Communion where the Holy Spirit is first contained, then transmitted. For this reason, the imagery in many decks, including the Rider Waite Smith Deck, is of a communion chalice, or 'ciborium' (a container for wafers). Often depicted is a wafer being delivered by the dove representing the Holy Spirit. The chalice is held by a hand appearing from the cloud of thought or mind. This shows that, in the card, we are still in the pre-manifest world of concepts. Pouring forth are four fountains. These are the four rivers of paradise, which are said to flow from the garden of Eden in Genesis 2:10–14: They are the Euphrates, the Tigris, the Gihon and the Pishon. They were said to flow towards the four corners of the Earth in an orientating compass.

In the Thoth Tarot, the Ace of Cups instead depicts the Holy Grail, penetrated or filled by a lance of golden light, or spirit, triggering an awakening of consciousness or emotional pleasure. Reversed or negatively aspected the Ace of Cups is the tendency to seek emotional validation in the wrong places, or from someone who will not reciprocate. For instance, having feelings for a celebrity crush, falling in love with a fictional character, or with someone for whom you are not their type, i.e. a straight woman falling for a gay man or a straight man falling for a lesbian. The emotion is powerful and affecting, but it has no chance to manifest.

Astrologically Ace of Cups stands for the water signs. Cancer, the armoured emoter, Scorpio the seeker of depth, and Pisces the flowing personality.

In readings that require a location, it is said by Crowley to represent the Pacific Ocean and its islands.

Alchemically, it is water in primordial form.

Ace of Swords

Air in Keter

The Ace of Swords is a new decision first rationalised, the exposure of a deception or a new power play. It appeals to that part of us that likes to debate, argue, spar or judge; anything with the potential for victory. It can be taking up a 'sword' to fight 'the good fight'. Or it can be less noble, the first engagement with those competitive interactions which are affirming to the ego.

Negatively aspected or reversed, it is engagement in a battle which one can't win or which will diminish one's reputation. In the Rider Waite Smith image, the hand of 'will' emerges from the cloud of 'mind' holding a sword which is crowned by Keter, the Sefirah of the divine first concept. Around it are six golden 'Yods'. There is speculation as to the significance of the number six (VI) on this card. I presume it is six the 'number of Man' in Biblical numerology, as man is said to have been created on the sixth day.

In the Thoth deck, the image is of a green sword penetrating the cloud of mind into the celestial and crowned with Keter the divine will. The implication being the channelling of a divine purpose. For Crowley, green represents the New Aeon of Horus the Child, a mythical springtime, after what he considered to be an age of winter, the patriarchal age of Osiris. He also describes the sword as being the sword of the Magus. The implication is that the Magus (magician) has access to all the primordial elements.

Astrologically the Ace of Swords represent the Air signs: Gemini the thinker, Libra the balancer, and Virgo the organiser. Swords denote, logic, strategy, numbers, law, the military, and the intellect. They suggest a potential for victory and idealism. At their worst, they are fighting for the sake of fighting, for instance, the attitude of sophistry in debate, arguing to score points, rather than arguing on the side of truth.

Crowley says the location for this card is the Americas. The US is a secular nation founded on Enlightenment values. This fits the swords theme well.

Alchemically the card is air in abstract or primordial form.

Ace of Pentacles/Coins/Discs

Earth in Keter

This is a new opportunity to act in the world. It could be a new job or career. Investments that yield future gains, or the planting of a garden. In the Rider Waite Smith Deck, the image is simple, a hand emerges from the cloud holding a coin above a garden. In the Thoth Deck, there is a golden disc inscribed with *To Meta Ophion* Crowley's seal for the Thoth deck. Ophion is the serpent and divine male power that encircles the feminine Orphic egg. Together these powers birth the universe. As discs or pentacles represent manifestation, this can be understood as the will to manifest. Around it are the six wings of a Seraph, a Biblical angel which are said to surround God's throne in heaven and who are associated with serpents.

Crowley says its location is in Europe and Africa.

Alchemically, the Ace of Pentacles is Earth in its abstract, or primordial form. Earth is often considered its own element, but in Kabbalah it is the combination of fire, water and Air. It represents solidity, weight, dependability, and our resources; time, food, employment, energy to do work, and money. Negatively aspected or reversed, one fails to get a new job or access to resources. Or something you wanted fails to manifest.

Twos

In order for us to be able to perceive the universe, we must first divide it into parts. This act of separation creates difference, where one thing starts and another ends. This is the esoteric meaning of the number two. This brings us many dualities: Active/passive, male/female, light/dark, background/foreground, good/bad, etc. Likewise, in order to get anything done one must sacrifice all the other things that one could have been doing in that moment so that one choice may be acted upon. A difference is made between doing and not doing.

Two is therefore a number of judgements and a number of first actions. All the two cards represent a definite decision to be made.

On the Kabbalistic Tree of Life, the second Sefirah is Chokhmah, usually defined in English as wisdom. It can be thought of as the ability to experience, as well as the ability to discern and differentiate. It can be associated with the right side of the brain and pattern recognition. In Kabbalah, this is considered male.

Two of Wands/Batons

Decan: Mars in Aries.
Timing: 21 to 30 March.
Sefirah: Fire in Chokhmah.

In the Rider Waite Smith image, the two wands depict a man in a state of privilege or comfort, with the world of possibilities in his right hand. Behind him is a strong staff of support, the world he is familiar with, but also one that he finds limiting. In his left hand is another staff which promises novelty and adventure.

This idea fits the crossroads myth. One comes to a fork in the road. One path leads home, where there is limited opportunity for growth but one is taken care of, and the other path leads to a gamble, between fortune and ruin. Nothing significant can be gained without leaving comfort behind and taking a risk. This archetypical story of decision is something that every young person experiences when they leave home. It can also be the act of moving to a new city or country, taking employment in a new field of work, or any other decisive big change.

Negatively aspected or reversed, this card is the temptation to make a decision which is doomed from the start. Alternatively, it is the state of being frozen between two decisions to one's detriment.

In Crowley's Thoth Deck, the card has a very different meaning. He calls the card 'Dominion'. It is a card of empire building and of affirmation of ambition. The decision is still made, but rather than leaving behind what one has, here one tries to expand one's hoard and one's power. His reasons are astrological. The card is assigned to be the first decan of Aries, ruled by Mars, the god of war, and of the element of fire, which is will and ambition.

Two of Cups

Decan: Venus in Cancer.
Timing: 21 June to 1 July.
Sefirah: Water in Chokhmah.

Here we have a meeting of two in a partnership. This may be two parties deciding to pursue a romance, a friendship, or a mutually beneficial deal. All of these require 'feeling out' the situation, taking an emotional risk, making oneself vulnerable to the other and compromise.

In the Rider Waite Smith image, the male and female figures face each other. They are about to share their cups in a ceremony. Above them is the Caduceus staff of Hermes, referring to communication and the union of two (the two coiled snakes) aligned to a common purpose. Above that is a winged lion's head, an alchemical symbol for the transformation of one chemical into another, and the transformation of matter into spirit. The lion is also a symbol of courage.

In the Thoth deck, the key word is 'love'. Astrologically, it is Venus in Cancer. Crowley's focus is on the conceptual completion that comes from the love of opposites. Implicit in the idea of Venus in Cancer, is the idea of letting another person inside of one's 'armour'. Cancer is a sign that is either very guarded or very vulnerable. Cancers present an outer image to the world to hide a private self-image.

In the image is a lotus fountain, a symbol of life and rebirth, spilling water through two 'fish', which Crowley confusingly says are dolphins. In the tradition of heraldry, dolphins are often drawn to resemble fish, and they symbolise charity and affection towards kin. The left fish has a five-pointed fin, alluding to the Emperor card V, and the right has a four-pointed fin which is the Empress IV. These are the male and female aspects in their idealised human form.

If this card is negatively aspected or reversed, one is rejected by a potential partner. A relationship, especially a fresh one, breaks down, or never gets beyond the first 'spark'.

Two of Swords

  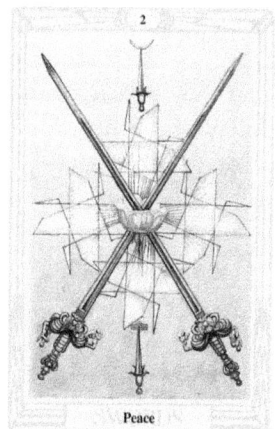

Decan: Moon in Libra.
Timing: 23 September to 3 October.
Sefirah: Air in Chokhmah.

This card represents the weighing up, and rationalisation of two equal options. Positively expressed, it can be the willingness to understand two opposing points of view perhaps with an end to bridging the gap between them, or else remaining impartial. For instance, a person deciding which of two major political parties to vote for in a national election. Or having listened to both sides of an argument between two friends, weighing up how a compromise might be made. It is a good card for diplomacy and negotiations between equals.

Negatively aspected, or reversed, it can signal fence-sitting or hedging one's bets.

Crowley named the card 'Peace'. A partnership between two parties who previously competed. He implies that it is the settling of matters after a shake-up or argument. The moon depicted at the top of both the Rider Waite Smith and the Thoth cards symbolises change, but it is softened by the balancing power of Libra which creates a new stability, albeit one that everyone has to, perhaps begrudgingly, get used to.

Two of Pentacles/Coins/Discs

Decan: Jupiter in Capricorn.
Timing: 22 to 31 December.
Sefirah: Earth in Chokhmah.

This card represents the juggling of time and resources. While it can be a card denoting stress, it is important to note that it is usually a positive thing to have resources to juggle in the first place. This often manifests in the modern age as personal issues such as the 'work/life balance': Free time, and relationships versus a higher bank balance. It can also be the decision to put money away for the future, saving for a large purchase. For example, the decision between buying a car or having a holiday. Blatantly put, it is a 'first-world problem'.

Negatively aspected or reversed it is a difficulty with self-discipline when it comes to time and money.

In the Thoth deck, the card is called 'change'. Crowley is rather vague on the meaning of the card except to state that it is the idea of change as the support to stability. Think perhaps of the necessity of a bicycle to keep moving in order to stay upright. On the astrology of the card, he says that the normal good fortune of Jupiter is limited by being in the sign of Capricorn (which is ruled by Jupiter's opposite, Saturn). Perhaps Crowley was a bit too tired that day to carefully explain the card, but hopefully my bicycle metaphor is sufficient. A plane needs a certain amount of speed to stay in the air. A house needs repainting now and then, a garden needs weeding etc. Simply put, if you stop moving, you will lose your stability.

Crowley's image depicts the Ouroboros serpent, which normally symbolises the endless cycle of life and death, but in this case it is twisted into an infinity symbol, with two Yin–Yangs, the Chinese sign of duality.

Threes

Threes symbolise progression. The fruit of the union of opposites, such as the child produced of the union of a male and female. Three also denotes harmony, for instance, in music, the major or minor chords, (triads) which are the foundations of Western harmony. Threes also suggest the parts of time: Past, present and future.

On the Kabbalistic Tree of Life, the third Sefirah is Binah, associated with the left brain, where things are compared and understood in relation to other things. In Kabbalah, this is female, as it is receptive. The right side gathers information and the left side considers it.

Three of Wands/Batons

Decan: Sun in Aries.
Timing: 31 March to 9 April.
Sefirah: Fire in Binah.

A careful decision is made to act upon one decision out of a number of possible decisions. A previously idealised large goal must be pared down, or broken into parts in order that something is to be achieved. At this stage, the only wrong decision is no decision. The temptation to procrastinate or be a perfectionist must be overcome. For many people, this will also manifest as struggling with, and then overcoming anxiety.

Negatively aspected, or reversed, this card focuses on the anxiety; being unwilling to make a decision and holding oneself back. Or being blocked or dissuaded from making a decision. Many readers also associate this card with a decision to travel. In any case, the card shows a desire to broaden one's horizons.

In the Thoth Tarot, the key word is virtue. The implication is to ask yourself 'What is the right thing to do?' Then to act upon that. Its astrological attribution, the Sun in Aries, denotes springtime in full force when life is re-awoken and active.

Three of Cups

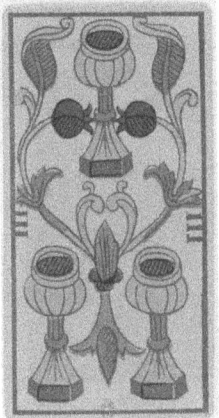  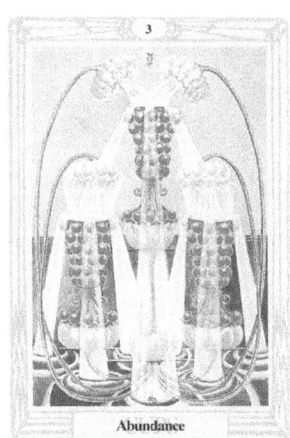

Decan: Mercury in Cancer.
Timing: 2 to 12 July.
Sefirah: Water in Binah.

This card expresses communication of the emotions. The scene depicts a close positive emotional experience between friends. The armour of Cancer is taken off and they are free to express themselves with a feeling of safety.

When negatively aspected or reversed, the feeling is short-lived, found to be shallow, or one observes a connection between other people but is emotionally blocked from taking part oneself.

Crowley calls this card 'Abundance' and associates it with Demeter and Persephone. It is high summer, and resources are plentiful. Presumably at this point of the story, Persephone has not yet been taken into Hades bringing winter to the Earth.

In the Thoth image, the cups are pomegranates being watered by lotuses, one symbol of life feeding another.

Three of Swords

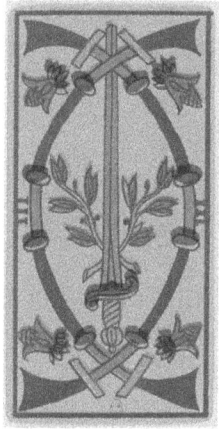 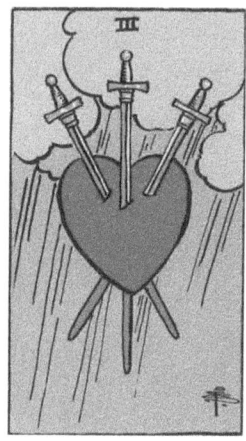 

Decan: Saturn in Libra.
Timing: 4 to 13 October.
Sefirah: Air in Binah.

In the Rider Waite Smith Deck, this is one of the more negative cards. It denotes heartbreak, betrayal or grief especially when over-rationalised. It is the power of negative thoughts to affect the emotions. An over-reliance on black-and-white thinking is challenged causing a third 'grey' state which causes cognitive dissonance. Psychologically it can be Post-Traumatic Stress Disorder caused by a broken narrative. An oath between two is broken (e.g. adultery) and a lover becomes an enemy.

The image for the card was taken directly from the Sola Busca Tarot, the earliest existing deck with a full 78 cards. It is also the earliest deck with full images for each card rather than 'pips'. Before painting the Rider Waite Smith decks, the artist and magician Pamela Colman Smith (and perhaps A.E. Waite), visited the Sola Busca deck in 1907, where it was displayed at the British Museum. She used a couple of its images as inspiration for her own artworks.

In the Thoth Deck, this card is called 'Sorrow'. The malefic Saturn, a difficult planet, has disrupted the balance of Libra causing restriction. The image is of storm clouds and bad weather preventing action. A yellow rose is destroyed by the points of the three swords signalling a period of depression. The intellect is in conflict with the emotions.

Negatively aspected or reversed, one has broken the heart of another or is about to. Alternatively (if it better fits the position in a spread), heartbreak can be narrowly avoided.

Three of Pentacles/Discs

Decan: Mars in Capricorn.
Timing: 1 to 10 January.
Sefirah: Earth in Binah.

This card presents the achievement of a new mastery in a craft, skill or trade. One's talents begin to be recognised by others. One's creativity and ambitions in a craft have begun to produce manifest results which can finally be enjoyed by other people. If this comes up in a spread about work, then the querent is applying for a job or a position and it is likely that they will get the job (unless the cards around it throw tension into the situation).

In astrology, Mars is exhalted in Capricorn, giving a power of ambition and energy to create this very pragmatic sign. This is the line of reasoning that Crowley takes in the Thoth Deck for this card. He calls it 'works'. Here 'works' are produced, and here things 'work'.

Negatively aspected or reversed, one fails the test, and one's product or produce is deemed unworthy.

Fours

Four is a number of stability. The four wheels of a car, the four legs of a quadruped or the four legs of a table or chair. It is also a number of orientation. The four cardinal directions are north, east, south and west. As such, it is very positive if one wants to stay in one place, but very restrictive if one wants to move on to new things. This is the number of Chesed, which is love, attention and flow.

Four of Wands/Batons

Decan: Venus in Aries.
Timing: 10 to 19 April.
Sefirah: Fire in Chesed.

Good results from hard work. A small celebration. A minor triumph. Plans have become realities. Crowley calls this card 'completion' and describes it as the manifestation of active power. In the Jewish Kabbalah, Chesed is flow, which implies expansion and activity. Think of a work of plumbing tested for the first time, and allowing the flow of water from one place to another. Or an empire, having taken a new territory, installs a new government, which is inaugurated allowing the generals to move on to new things. In any case, a plan which became a project, is completed and can now run by itself.

In the Thoth image, there are four crossed wands with the Aries ram's head at one end and the dove of the Holy Spirit at the other. The implication is of cosmic order in accordance with individual will. The Circle behind the wands is a symbol of completion and containment, ready to receive the Chesed flow energy without it spilling over.

Negatively aspected or reversed, the achievement is about to collapse or be halted. Counting one's chickens before they are hatched.

Four of Cups

Decan: Moon in Cancer.
Timing: 13 to 22 July.
Sefirah: Water in Chesed.

Like with the Four of Wands, something has reached completion. In this case, the recipient has received exactly what they have asked for, but now that they can see the results, they wish they had asked for something else. The Four of Cups represents a dissatisfaction with, or distraction from what one has in front of them. The manifestation doesn't live up to the idealised form. The 'having' was not as satisfying as the 'wishing for'. Love and friendship is taken for granted.

The solution of course is for the recipient to take more responsibility for what they ask for next time. Many times we might fall into the trap of blaming others or feeling resentment over something we could have taken care of ourselves.

Crowley calls the card 'Luxury'. The implication is that luxury is rarely fulfilling if it is indulged too often. The moon in Cancer implies a moodiness and a change of desire. The fourth Sefirah Chesed means 'kindness' or 'mercy'. For kindness to be meaningful in a relationship it must be bound by Gevurah, which is the restriction which allows order. Faith in a spouse's love is only possible if that love is exclusive. A cheating partner causes pain because the restricting, or containing order of

Gevurah has been lost. Gevurah is also discipline, which is lacking here in the Four of Cups. Consider the dissatisfaction of a spoiled child with his own parents. Love without restriction is the dissolution of true love. It creates insecurity and uncertainty and is spread too thin to be meaningful. Another idea is that of undivided attention. Attention given to a single person is rare, deep and valuable. The attempt to spread one's attention to many people causes it to be less valuable to each of those people.

When this card is negatively aspected or reversed, one has fallen into a cynical bad habit. The solution is to seek counsel, readjust one's expectations, and to engage with people who are optimistic.

Four of Swords

Decan: Jupiter in Libra.
Timing: 14 to 23 October.
Sefirah: Air in Chesed.

Blessed is he who is armed with a sword but who keeps it sheathed. In the Rider Waite Smith image, there is a knight at rest. The implication is both of taking time out to restore one's energy, but also of mercy, having the power and ability to win by the sword or take things by force, but staying one's hand in the spirit of long-term order. It is the realisation that winning a short game, may cause one to lose the long game and deciding to wait instead means a better outcome in the future. Jupiter, the expansive power is balanced here by Libra.

Crowley calls the card 'truce'. A realisation that a battle isn't worth the losses. One might have genuine reasons to act out in anger but one remains restrained in order to preserve stability. It is the situation of waiting for the storm to blow over.

Negatively aspected or reversed, one has no time to rest, and may soon suffer from exhaustion.

Four of Pentacles/Discs

  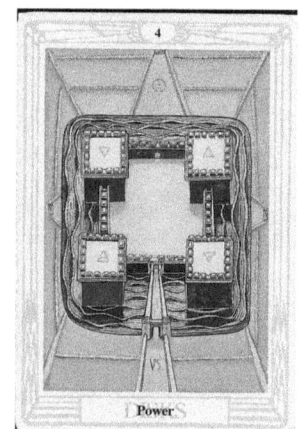

Decan: Sun in Capricorn.
Timing: 11 to 20 January.
Sefirah: Earth in Chesed.

This card depicts a miser saving for a rainy day that never comes. In this case, the four is not so much a stability, as a blockage in the system. Like a blocked sink, no movement will be achieved until one risks a small amount of wastage.

Crowley takes a different line of interpretation than Rider Waite Smith, and calls this card 'Power'. The image depicts a fortress with an element at each of its four corners. Alchemically this can be considered 'crystallisation'. Solidity has been achieved but all flow has stopped. One's material belongings are protected but not able to be used in the outside world. It is the stronghold so well built that there is no way to expand or repurpose it into any larger or more useful form.

Negatively aspected or reversed, one has become so risk-averse that one misses out on a lucrative opportunity.

Fives

Where fours are stability, fives are disruptions and change. A rearrangement is often upsetting, but without which, no long-term progress can be made. Something which has always worked until now has stopped working, the temptation is to double down, but instead one should change one's approach. Fives align with the Sefirah Gevurah which is discipline, restriction, punishment and retaliation.

Five of Wands/Batons

Decan: Saturn in Leo.
Timing: 23 July to 1 August.
Sefirah: Fire in Gevurah.

In the Rider Waite Smith image, there is a group of youths, all equal, fighting with quarterstaff. The implication is that of 'every man for himself'. While a card of tension, this is the type of competition that is generally positive, where one grows in confidence and expands one's skillset. All solo sporting competitions, against other competitors, such as sprints fit the bill. The winner will be initiated into the hierarchy and be given an opportunity to work towards a position of status. This card often comes up for job interviews, or for students competing in their studies.

Crowley calls the card 'strife'. He suggests that Leo, a sign that is generally responsible, balances out the element of fire which could otherwise be more dangerous, but that Saturn 'weighs it down' and embitters it implying an impending volcanic eruption. The symbols imply the power wielded by an underling, imparted by his superiors. Without the restriction of authority, the underling could be very dangerous, but they are restrained by the fact that they don't want to lose their position. Think of the rookie cop who is keen to interrogate you for a minor misdemeanour, but who would rather you didn't involve his superiors.

Negatively aspected or reversed, the underling or underlings are about to be reprimanded by their superiors for stepping out of line. Alternatively, the competition is futile, a mere squabble, and there is no reward for continuing.

Five of Cups

Decan: Mars in Scorpio.
Timing: 24 October to 1 November.
Sefirah: Water in Gevurah.

My key phrase for this card is 'crying over spilt milk'. In the Rider Waite Smith image, three cups are overturned, and a mourning figure is bent over in sorrow. Two neglected cups behind them represent a failure to see what they still have left. This is a card which represents the addictive nature of pessimism. The allegiance to a narrative where one feigns powerlessness in order to avoid responsibility. For example, the idea that the world is going to hell in a hand-basket, so one might as well do whatever one wants.

This is the sign Scorpio at their most impish. An attention-seeking display of negative emotion in order to rope in the attention of others. It is the card of a depressive drama-queen.

Crowley calls the card 'Disappointment'. The card is ruled by Gevurah, associated with Mars in the suit of Water. Because Gevurah is fiery and cups are watery one suppresses the other. The implication is that of active forces, such as the drive to get what one wants, being frustrated by opposing passive forces. The fiery drive gets cooled by the watery emotion. So this is a card about the frustration of not getting what one wants. The answer in this case is to change one's expectations rather than to continue trying to 'set water on fire'.

Negatively aspected or reversed, the whole emotional exercise is redundant, premature, or misunderstood and can only result in others being appalled and pulling away. Positively aspected, the play for attention works. Sympathies are won and a way to move on is found.

Five of Swords

  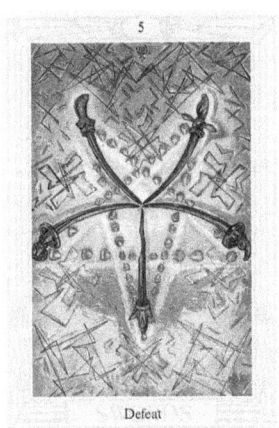
Defeat

Decan: Venus in Aquarius.
Timing: 21 to 29 January.
Sefirah: Air in Gevurah.

Someone wins a game, a debate or a challenge through a loophole or other sneaky means, that while not necessarily strictly against the rules, is deemed unsportsmanlike by the losers. A common occurrence in our time is debates on internet forums where one is playing to 'score points' rather than to learn anything. The game may be 'won' (usually because the other player gives up or moves on), but the others probably won't play with you again, so the victor has lost more than they have gained.

Oftentimes, when an egotistical sparring match has taken place, both parties can go away thinking it is they who have been wronged. This is a Five of Swords type of situation. If negatively aspected or reversed, then one is tricked or goaded into a battle that can have no beneficial outcome for either party. Often the argument will have started with two other people who try and draw in their friends.

Crowley calls this card 'Defeat'. Where the Four of Swords is a fortress well protected, the Five of Swords is the fortress breached. A gap in the armour was found, and the protective sword was not drawn in time. In his terms, it is a defeat due to pacifism. The loser was not aggressive enough to launch a defence. While this may be the case, it might be worth noting that Crowley went through life having many arguments and falling out with many people. Perhaps he was a bit too worried about not being aggressive enough. In any case, he had many dealings with people that played out like a Five of Swords situation. He was however also a master of controversy, and in part, because of this, we are still talking about him. In this sense, he also knew how to play the Five of Swords to his advantage.

Aquarius is the sign of rebellious ideas; Venus, however, being a passive power does not have the impetus to see these ideas through. It is a bold idea, without the force of charm to convince others. Put another way, it is an argument held by emotion that doesn't stand up to the rationalising swords of others.

Five of Pentacles/Discs

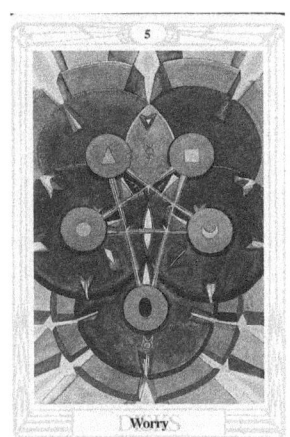

Decan: Mercury in Taurus.
Timing: 20 to 29 April.
Sefirah: Earth in Gevurah.

In the Rider Waite Smith Deck, this card shows us a loss of resources along with a reluctance to accept charity. It could be because of an economic downturn, heavy bills, a drop in business or a loss of employment. The subject remains proud and is not yet ready to accept defeat. Put positively, it can be sticking by one's partner in hard times. Negatively it can be the 'sunken cost fallacy', a tendency to fight harder to keep something that one has already lost time and money on. In gambling, this would be doubling down on a losing streak when one should be acknowledging the loss and walking away. As one of the two figures in the picture is injured, it is also often interpreted as an injury that sets one back.

Crowley calls the card 'worry'. He says this in the sense 'like dogs worry the sheep', which means to seize or shake by the throat. 'The economic system has broken down; there is no more balance between the social orders'.[42] Earth in Gevurah suggests something stationary where there should be movement. The river of Chesed has become congested and the waters are now still and will become stagnant. The martial hand of Gevurah cannot extract any more spoils through discipline,

---
[42] Page 181 (Crowley 1944).

fight or punishment. One needs to pull back and find a different territory to work upon.

Mercury in Taurus is also a stalemate, the ideas and intellectual charm of Mercury fail to move the stubborn bull. He is waiting to be charmed by Venus, and Mercury, who normally gets what he wants by talking can only become frustrated.

Sixes

Where fives are a frustration of progress or a loss of ground, sixes are an adaption and a re-correction. Through perseverance in a new direction or approach, obstacles are overcome. Sixes are a journey back towards harmony. They correspond to Tiferet, which is the heart centre, associated with the Sun and the seat of the ego.

Six of Wands/Batons

  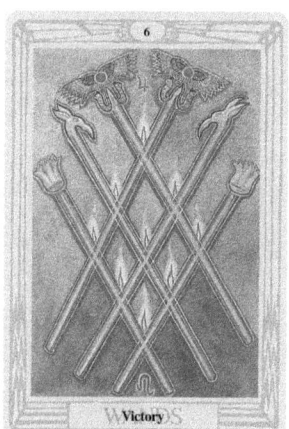

Decan: Jupiter in Leo.
Timing: 2 to 12 August.
Sefirah: Fire in Tiferet.

In the Rider Waite Smith Deck, this card depicts a parade. Under successful leadership, an attribute of Leo, a group has had success. Jupiter is a planet of good fortune. 'A king in a good mood'.[43]

Negatively aspected or reversed, the card could be a failure in leadership before the group is able to succeed. Somehow the drive to complete a project fizzles out.

Crowley calls the card 'victory'. The outburst and tension of five have created a temporary peaceful resolution in the number six, but this will fall if the energy is removed or depleted.

Tiferet is the heart centre, the centre of the sense of self, and personal identification. While it is associated with blissful experiences, it is also the type of charm where one might temporarily submit one's personal identity to another person or a group. This can be quite normal, participating in a crowd, dancing or playing music in a group, playing sports in a team etc. This can be used by people with strong leadership charm to motivate a team or a crowd. Fire radiates a lot of energy. A perfect manifestation of fire in Tiferet is a bunch of hippies in a drum circle around a bonfire an hour into a jam.

---

[43] Explained to me by the philosopher John David Ebert while he was giving me an astrology reading. Where Jupiter is 'the king in a good mood', Saturn its opposite is 'the king in a bad mood'.

Six of Cups

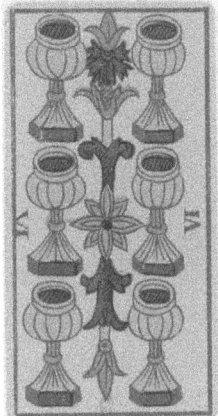  

Decan: Sun in Scorpio.
Timing: 2 and 11 November.
Sefirah: Water in Tiferet.

In the Rider Waite Smith image, there is a scene of nostalgia or reunion. A want to return to happier times of the past. If negatively aspected, or reversed, then the querent is avoiding the present. Astrologically, this card is the sun in Scorpio. Scorpios revel in intense experiences, and enjoy reliving good times; days in the sun. Likewise, Water (Cups), which is the element of the emotions, intuition and dreams has engaged Tiferet in the 'heart centre'. One feels filled with love and emotional connection.

Crowley calls the card 'pleasure'. He writes that this is to be understood in its highest sense: It is ease, the harmony of natural forces, without effort.

Scorpio is a water sign and denotes a type of deep intensity. With the sun in this sign, we are seeing Scorpio in her best mood. The result is one of deep connection.

Positively aspected, this card is comfort drawn from remembering the best of times. Negatively aspected, it is an unrequited sense of longing, wishing to return to the past, perhaps in order to avoid the present. It may also be homesickness. The issue with nostalgia is that one may remember the past as being better than it actually was at the time. In the worst, too much focus on the 'better' times of the past can be the precursor to despair.

When this card is in the future position of the spread, it may mean that what is happening now will be fondly remembered in the future.

Six of Swords

Decan: Mercury in Aquarius.
Timing: 30 January to 8 February.
Sefirah: Air in Tiferet.

This card may represent a journey or rite of passage. It is the power of the rational mind over emotion and intuition (Tiferet). In the Rider Waite Smith image, it is taking one's problems with one. To me this card summarises the attempt to leave town in order to 'start afresh', only to find that all of one's worries and traumas have made the journey too.

Though this can be upsetting, it presents an important emotional realisation without which, no psychological healing can take place. Whether this presents us with a positive or negative story has more to do with the querent's reaction to this situation. If positive, then they accept the situation and begin working on themselves, a path towards healing. If negative then they are prone to avoiding the issues and will seek distractions that may turn into addictions, complexes, or bad habits. This card is the element of Air in Tiferet, the heart centre, meaning that this card is ideas about matters of the heart. In this case, the intellect tries to guide and repair the emotions. The ideas can also be worries and overthinking. Mercury is the planet of the intellect and communication, and Aquarius is a sign of trying to push through to new ideas, novelty and higher ideals. It is often called the 'humanitarian sign'. Implicit is a desire to start afresh and to experience new things.

In the Thoth Deck, this card is the positive inversion of the Rider Waite Smith card. Crowley calls it 'Science', and he means this in the esoteric sense of the word, the achievement of spiritual knowledge.[44] With Mercury in Aquarius, the God of ideas and communication has acted on the sign that seeks new paths. Intelligence has won the goal. Implied is the idea of a personal intellectual and spiritual breakthrough, which allows one control over matters of the heart. The spiritual seeker gains an understanding that gives them much encouragement, even though it may first require acceptance of the pain of the past. In the end, a state of gnosis is reached.

Reversed or negatively aspected, it can be indicative of an impending emotional breakdown which one cannot run from. One becomes overwhelmed by their worries and feels there is no escape. Though unpleasant, even this is often a necessary stage in turning one's life around.

---

[44] Though we use the word science now almost exclusively for enquiry centring around the scientific method, it was often a more general term in the past, referring to a high ideal of knowledge. Many religions and mysticisms called their teachings 'science'. In fact the word 'scientist' was first coined only in 1833 by William Whewell. Before that time, scientists were normally referred to as 'natural philosophers'. Crowley being born in 1875 was only a couple of generations after this.

Six of Pentacles/Coins/Discs

Decan: Moon in Taurus.
Timing: 30 April and 10 May.
Sefirah: Earth in Tiferet.

Here, a level of abundance has been reached and the querent or subject feels charitable. This card signals a newfound financial security and balance. One feels positively affirmed by one's resources. The card can signal a windfall in relation to one's career or work. This situation will often be temporary if one doesn't put some money away for a rainy day.

The Moon in this case refers to our emotions, our direct experience, and hidden knowledge coming to light. Taurus is a sign of comfort and home. So here is an intuition that things are right at home.

Earth is the element of manifestation, and Tiferet is the heart centre and the centre of the self. So this card signals an emotional satisfaction with one's resources, especially belongings, career, money, time and energy.

Crowley calls this card 'success'. With the Moon in Taurus, a positive change has swayed the stubborn bull. 'The Moon is exhalted[45] in Taurus,

---

[45] While it is beyond the scope of this book to explain fully, in astrology a planet can be in 'rulership' or 'exhaltation', in the signs that strengthen or positively express their powers, or in 'fall' or 'detriment' in signs that weaken or turn their expression to the negative. These four expressions are an important part of reading astrological charts, and Crowley was an expert astrologer for his age.

therefore in her highest form'.[46] He describes this as Tiferet fully realised on Earth, a temporary balance of resources and a brief 'halt upon the path of labour'.

Negatively aspected or reversed, one may be taken for a ride or scammed in the name of a charity, or otherwise be misinterpreting a need for charity where none is needed. Otherwise, it can be a generosity of spending beyond one's means.

---

[46] Page 216 (Crowley 1944).

Sevens

In Tarot, sevens bring complication and an abundance of details. They are a push to a higher resolution. The romance of idealism that inspired the planning stage has now gone, and we are in the nitty-gritty of getting the job done. This is the realm of Netzach, the Sefirah ruled by Venus. A process of patience, negotiation, charm, leadership and encouragement is required to see through an ordeal or difficult task (Hod). Here Venus expresses herself as grace, etiquette and charm rather than romance or sex. In order to weather an ordeal one must keep the goal in mind. Crowley sees seven in a more negative light and this is reflected in his interpretation of the cards. He considers it a number of weakness or of futility.

Seven of Wands/Batons

Decan: Mars in Leo.
Timing: 13 to 22 August.
Sefirah: Fire in Netzach.

This is the situation of keeping your ground in an outnumbered attack. It is a defence against an offensive. In this card, there is a sense of consensual suffering. One stands one's ground 'on principle', in order to show a brave face when one could be using a more subtle strategy to one's advantage. It brings to mind the phrase: 'Kicking against the pricks', from Acts 9:5 of the Bible and it fits both in the traditional meaning of an unsubtle, direct attack that harms the attacker as well as the enemy, as well as the colloquial meaning: To desire to pain those who have angered you. Leo is a sign of the self, and Mars in Leo symbolises a reaction against an affront to the ego. It is a dramatic move, a resounding shout that you demand satisfaction!

Fire in Netzach is the rallying cry. One thinks of political movements such as 'cancel culture' and the equally idealistic libertarian backlash crying for the right to 'free speech', (though this often means the right to offend).

Crowley calls the card 'Valour' and attributes it to a defective Mars. For him, it is 'patriotism in the negative'. Because the battle is not well-focused, it will result in exhaustion even if considered a win. The army is disorganised and any win will now be down to individual valour.

When negatively aspected, or reversed, one is doubling down on a battle of principle that one cannot win, and which will only result in one being ostracised, or losing face. Despite feeling fired up, one should disengage before one loses. When positively aspected, one achieves a victory in the fight, though at the cost of near exhaustion.

Seven of Cups

Decan: Venus in Scorpio.
Timing: 12 to 21 November.
Sefirah: Water in Netzach.

This card means that one faces a luxurious selection of choices, with the implication that none of them will be fulfilling in the long term, or worse, that they all represent temptations that will lead one away from the path one should be on. It is hedonism in relation to 'sin'.

In the Rider Waite Smith Deck, the image for this card is especially symbolic. Before the figure is a choice of seven cups each containing a desire attached to one of the seven classical planets and one of the cards of the Major arcana. From top left are:

> Venus: Lust after beauty. The Empress.
> Moon: The enticement of the mysterious. The Priestess.
> Mercury: The Ouroboros snake. The danger of being lost in an infinite regress in an attempt to find order. Or alternatively the path of the 'doubter' like the serpent in the Garden of Eden: The magician.
> Mars: The Tower: Representing a building up of pride before a fall.
> Jupiter: Desire for riches. The Wheel of Fortune.
> Saturn: Desire for accolades and worldly prestige. The World.
> Sun: Facing a dragon. Desire for bravado. Strength.

These obviously also suggest the seven deadly sins: Pride, greed, wrath, envy, lust, gluttony and sloth. Crowley calls the card 'debauch', and he writes

> This is one of the worst ideas that one can have; its mode is poison, its goal madness. It represents the delusion of Delirium Tremens and drug addiction; it represents the sinking into the mire of false pleasure. There is something almost suicidal in this card.[47]

Crowley was famous for periods of his life when he engaged in hedonism. Perhaps he warns us here from personal experience. Water in Netzach implies too much emotionality when one should be reasoned, or perhaps too little form when one ought to have a clearly defined goal.

Venus in Scorpio suggests full submission to seduction. A drug-like high that comes from pursuing pleasure without self-control. Negatively aspected or reversed, one is given a chance to pull out of one's own addictive behaviour or a chance to disengage with a friend who is an addict before it becomes a huge problem. In the best-case scenario, it could represent the blowing off of a little steam after a long period of austerity.

---

[47] Page 183 (Crowley 1944).

Seven of Swords

Decan: Moon in Aquarius.
Timing: 9 to 18 February.
Sefirah: Air in Netzach.

In the Rider Waite Smith image, this card represents a thief stealing swords that are unguarded. The swords often represent someone's ideas, and the theft is often one of intellectual property. Someone is taking credit for something that was started by someone else. Looked at in a slightly different way, it is the loss of things left unguarded. Sometimes it will represent an actual burglary, other times it will be a warning.

Crowley calls this card 'futility' and his take is quite different to the Rider Waite Smith Deck. His description is a little more obtuse than the others. The implication is that too many ideas, or second-guessing, at this stage can destroy the goal. 'There is vacillation, a wish to compromise, a certain toleration. But, in certain circumstances, the results may be more disastrous than ever'. In short, stick to the plan and see it through with patience.

The moon suggests changeability and Aquarius is the sign of big new ideas. This could denote a time where the querent has need of a cause but hasn't found one, but more likely, where they should be sticking to one thing but keep second-guessing it.

Negatively aspected or reversed, a betrayal or theft dashes one's sense of security. For some readers, this card comes up after the querent has suffered a burglary. Positively aspected, the subject gets away with something sneaky or finds a 'hack' or a 'cheat code' that gives them a sudden shortcut or advantage.

Seven of Pentacles/Coins/Discs

Decan: Saturn in Taurus.
Timing: 11 and 20 May.
Sefirah: Earth in in Netzach.

This card is dissatisfaction with one's work and impatience for outcomes. The Rider Waite Smith image correlates to 'a watched pot never boils'. The advice to the querent should be to find something else to do while they wait for the outcome. Saturn here is interpreted as a seizing up, or slowing of time. Taurus is the stubborn Bull who responds best to either beauty or pragmatic results and here he is receiving neither.

Again Crowley sees it somewhat differently, calling the card 'failure'. Here it is the subject who has become seized up, slow and lazy. 'There is no effort here; not even dream; the stake has been thrown down, and it is lost. That is all. Labour itself is abandoned; everything is sunk in sloth'.[48] One thinks of those people whose response to a difficult life is to give up and coast, expending the bare minimum effort to sustain themselves.

Negatively aspected or reversed, the crop fails and dies in the earth.

---

[48] Page 184 (Crowley 1944).

Eights

Eight, relating to the Sefirah Hod, denotes perseverance. Here the message has been received. The task is clear but now the person or team either does the work or not. This is often a time which calls for endurance. Crowley says that eights come as a remedy for the error of the Sevens.

Eight of Wands/Batons

 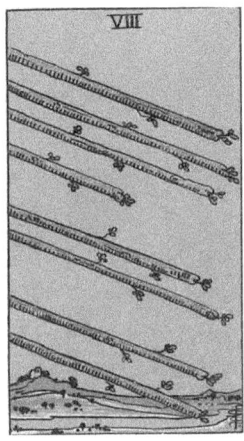 

Decan: Mercury in Sagittarius.
Timing: 23 November to 2 December.
Sefirah: Fire in Hod.

In the Rider Waite Smith image, this card symbolises action, speedy delivery or rapid change. The work ethic is strong and the job is done within or ahead of schedule, or the message gets through and is clear and understood. There is an implication of electricity which is apt in the modern age of emails and instant messaging. It can also represent a 'meme' or 'viral' message on the internet, a piece of information that gets away with itself.

Crowley calls the card 'swiftness' and the wands are depicted in the form of lightning bolts shooting in every direction. Mercury is the god of communication, and Sagittarius is the archer, sending his will through the arrow, far-reaching ideas. Hod is the Sefirah of hard work, and often that which is done in groups. It is also a Sefirah of the intellect and rationalisation. Here the implication is of eureka moments. One suddenly gets the message. Fire adds motivation and a clarity of will to the exercise.

Negatively aspected or reversed, the information or change, shoots past the querent and they feel left out and bewildered by what just happened. They are like a surfer who failed to catch the wave.

Eight of Cups

Decan: Saturn in Pisces.
Timing: 19 to 29 February.
Sefirah: Water in Hod.

In the Rider Waite Smith image, we see a figure walking away from their passions. These passions might be relationships, but just as likely, they are vices, bad habits or addictions. The figure is leaving comfort behind, in order to reach something better. The planet Saturn in this case is like a dam in a river, the water, symbolising emotional energy, and associated with Pisces, has ceased to flow. The Sefirah Chesed can be understood as 'flow'. In this case the property of Chesed, flow, is missing. The path of the river is well defined and well contained, attributes of Hod, but there is no energy or 'Chesed' to get the job done. In this sense, this card can be the realisation of emotional burnout.

Crowley calls the card indolence, with similar implications. The subject has run out of steam. Time and sorrow have descended on pleasure. 'A party where all preparations are made but the host has forgotten to invite the guests'.[49] In relationship readings, one partner will have become distant.

Negatively aspected or reversed, this card is a tendency to give up and 'throw one's cards'. Or the burning of one's bridges when it isn't actually necessary. In modern parlance: 'Rage quitting'.

---

[49] Page 184 (Crowley 1944).

Eight of Swords

  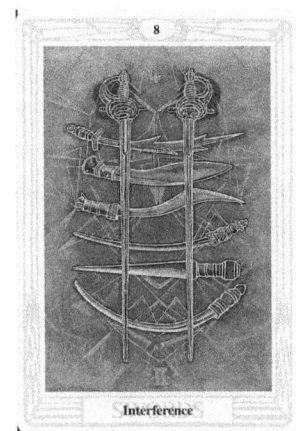

Decan: Jupiter in Gemini.
Timing: 21 to 31 May.
Sefirah: Air in Hod.

In the Rider Waite Smith image, a blindfolded woman with her arms loosely tied walks a perilous path between swords. As always, the swords are ideas, and in this case the one who has blindfolded and tied her, is herself. The implication is of one making things harder for oneself than they need be, or even self-sabotage. It is fear, not of failure, but the more ironic and perverse fear of actually achieving one's ambitions. A person holding themselves back.

Jupiter would like things to be straight forward, but Gemini has a tendency to over complicate the issue. Crowley calls it 'Interference', and suggests that the situation is one of trying to come over as a good or optimistic person in the face of fierce competition. His advice is that a more ruthless attitude would be more successful. 'In the world of Swords; if one must hit at all, a knock-out blow is best'.[50] Crowley was well known for burning bridges with people.

Negatively aspected or reversed, the querent is shown their folly before it comes a problem, or recognises the ruthless behaviour of another before being sucked in.

---

[50] Page 185 (Crowley 1944).

Eight of Pentacles/Coins/Discs

Decan: Sun in Virgo.
Timing: 23 August and 2 September.
Sefirah: Earth in Hod.

For this card, the blocks of flow that have affected the others are not present, so the hard work is fruitful. Virgo can be a stressy sign, focused on details. At it's worst, Virgo is prone to perfectionism, but in this case the sun brightens the issue and the subject is able to keep their optimism. So we are presented with a productive time working towards one's goals.

Crowley calls the card 'prudence', and interprets it more as a card of putting something away for a rainy day. It is a good omen for investors, or those saving or working towards a material goal. Intelligence is applied to material matters and comes to fruition. Hod is the Sefirah of hard work, especially work done in or for a group. The element of Earth shows manifestation, showing us that the hard work produces real-world results and success.

Negatively aspected or reversed, the card shows a workaholic. One who is avoiding emotional problems at home, by spending all their time at, or engaged in work.

Nines

Nines are a rebalancing of the previous tensions, towards the positive or the negative. The pendulum swinging back the other way. In Kabbalah, nine is the number of the Sefirah Yesod, which is the realm of mystery, magic, communication, writing, public speaking and performance.

Nine of Wands/Batons

Decan: Moon in Sagittarius.
Timing: 3 to 12 December.
Sefirah: Fire in Yesod.

The Rider Waite Smith image shows a figure facing adversity with bravery. It is the difficulty that comes from facing one's problems head on, with force, or a force of will. Negatively aspected or reversed, it can spell delays, exhaustion and failure. In the positive, the subject pulls through. A narrow success.

Crowley calls the card 'Strength'. In the Thoth image, the central wand stretches from a sun, to a moon symbol. The sun represents Tiferet, the heart centre, and the moon is Yesod, the second lowest Sefirah. Yesod combines, balances and communicates between the higher worlds of ideas, spirituality and concepts, and the lower manifest realm of Malkut. Fire gives Yesod energy and motivation. The other wands depicted are the arrows of Sagittarius, the zodiacal sign of far-reaching goals. Crowley says this card is the balancing point of change and stability. It is equilibrium after tension. Similarly it is the movement and change that keeps a situation stable. The example given is of the bicycle, which is stable as long as it keeps moving forward, but becomes wobbly and awkward when its momentum falters.

The Rider Waite Smith version accentuates the achievement (or failure) of the goal, whereas the Thoth Tarot describes the journey that led up to that point.

Nine of Cups

  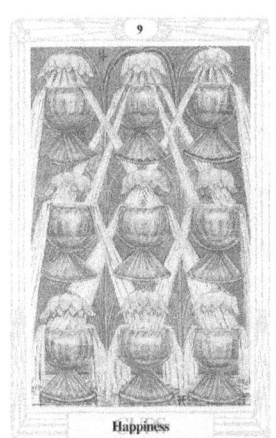

Decan: Jupiter in Pisces.
Timing: 1 to 10 March.
Sefirah: Water in Yesod.

The Rider Waite Smith image depicts a host who has prepared for a celebration with friends. This can literally foretell a party, or a performance, that the subject is to attend or hold, or it can symbolise generosity and camaraderie. It is the enjoyment of providing joy for others. Jupiter in this case is good fortune and optimism, and Pisces is group-focused emotionality. Yesod here stands for communication, and the water is relationships. It shows us a clear and fruitful connection with friends and family. Also implied is a time of well-being, health and security.

If negatively aspected or reversed, then either the energies of this card are not obtained, or one is so focused on good times with friends that one neglects and misses opportunities elsewhere in one's life. Crowley calls the card 'happiness'. The instability of the seven (Netzach) and eight (Hod) of cups has been fixed by Yesod. He says that nine is the number of the moon so emotionality is balanced here.

Nine of Swords

Decan: Mars in Gemini.
Timing: 1 to 10 June.
Sefirah: Air in Yesod.

This is a difficult card of anguish, grief, disturbed thoughts, despair, anxiety and worry. The only solution is to 'wake up' and engage with reality in the moment. The cause of the concern either no longer matches the outcome, or the outcome has become inevitable and therefore the anxiety no longer serves any benefit. Whatever the case, the situation is never as bad as it is in one's mind.

Mars is a powerful energy of force and battle, and Gemini is the sign of diverse ideas and intellect. Together they build a multitude of ideas that attack the sufferer. However bad the situation is, not all of these ideas can come true at once, so the answer is to get out of one's head and focus on what is in front of one in the moment.

Yesod is the Sefirah ruled by the Moon. Here there should be a flow of intuition, but it is interrupted by the intellectual over thinking of the element Air. Reversed, the card pre-warns us of a mental breakdown that hasn't happened yet. One is given the chance to redirect the anxious energy.

Crowley calls the sign 'Cruelty'. 'The Swords no longer represent pure intellect so much as the automatic stirring of heartless passions.

Consciousness has fallen into a realm unenlightened by reason. This is the world of the unconscious primitive instincts, of the psychopath, of the fanatic'.[51]

This would fit the worldview of the emotional conspiracy theorist, or paranoid thinker. The intelligence has stopped being of service and is now self-destructive.

---

[51] Page 209 (Crowley 1944).

Nine of Pentacles/Discs

Decan: Venus in Virgo.
Timing: 3 and 12 September.
Sefirah: Earth in Yesod.

This is a card of abundance and material gain. Venus is a passive power and Virgo is a sign of details and fertility, so one is the receiver of good fortune and is in control of one's environment. It represents general period of improvement in multiple aspects of one's life and financial security. The Earth in Yesod, is the manifestation of one's intuitive desires.

If negatively aspected or reversed, then one is living above one's means. In the Rider Waite Smith image, the feminine figure, presumably the matriarch of her household is holding a falcon. This is a powerful, far-seeing and precise bird of prey. Through her Venusian charm, she has the creature entirely under her control. Importantly the bird is not anxious or struggling. It is completely at peace on the hand. Behind the woman are the fruits and coins (pentacles) of her estate. Crowley calls the card 'Gain' and says that through the Venusian powers that 'everything is for the best in the best of all possible worlds'.[52]

---

[52] Page 188 (Crowley 1944).

Tens

Ten is a finality. A story that has reached its conclusion. The only further possible action is to start a new narrative or quest.

Ten is the number of manifestation. In Kabbalah, it is Malkut, which is traditionally described as the physical realm. In the alchemical age the physical was generally thought to be the lowest level, and the realm of the mind was 'above' it.[53]

Because our modern science has discovered and described a 'physical' realm that is much harder to grasp and understand, a world of information fields, energy and super-locality. I prefer to describe Malkuth as the 'sensory realm' or the 'manifest realm'. In any case Malkuth is world of objects, outcomes, realisation, and solidity.

One thing that both modern physics and alchemy agree upon, is that matter is, in a sense, condensed information (energy). In this way, the only way to continue the process of turning information into matter is to first turn the matter back into information. This move takes us back up the Tree of Life, and backwards in out number series: 10, 9, 8 ...

More typical of human nature however is to move onto a new story, starting the process back from 1, 2, 3 ...

Solvé et Coagula, Coagula et Solvé.

---

[53] In modern physics we now know that the human level is really the 'middle'. The human body is roughly the size of the cosmos to a 'Planck length', as the size of the cosmos is to a human body.

Ten of Wands/Batons

Decan: Saturn in Sagittarius.
Timing: 3 to 12 December.
Sefirah: Fire in Malkut.

The key phrase for this cards is 'the burden of success'. One has succeeded in achieving what one wants, and in having it, one now feels overwhelmed by the responsibility. It is the card of the workaholic and the precursor to burnout. As such, it is the result of an imbalance of energies. One has focused all ones ambitions towards material gain, or status, when a certain amount of that energy should have been put towards emotional well-being or relationships. We are reminded of Sisyphus pushing the boulder uphill only to have it always roll back to the bottom before he has reached the top. The solution is to be happy with the boulder at the bottom of the hill, and to direct one's drive somewhere else (if only Sisyphus was not compelled by Hades, or perhaps his own obsessions). There is a futility to the Ten of Wands. One is trying to press the world into a shape that it won't hold.

Crowley calls the card 'Oppression'. It is the outcome of only ever using force to get what one wants. With Saturn in Sagittarius, the very idealism and goal setting that ought to set one free has become restricting and the path is blocked by the slow-moving Saturn. The implication here is less personal that in the Rider Waite Smith version, and here one might be oppressed by society, an institution, an authority, or a relationship. It represents a dictatorship of force. An idealistic government, once good, has become a tyranny. Idealism has been taken further than its ability to achieve its goals. Alternatively, like in the Dune novels by Frank Herbert, the idealism that lead a successful rebellion has now, by the same values, become a brutal tyranny.

As Sagittarius is ruled by Jupiter, Saturn's optimistic opposite, Saturn is especially negative in this sign. Fire in Malkuth suggest the ambition and drive to do work in a place where the Earth won't move. One thinks of trying to dig into bedrock using only a spade. It is scissors versus rock.

Negatively aspected or reversed one is given a chance to alter course before becoming locked in.

Ten of Cups

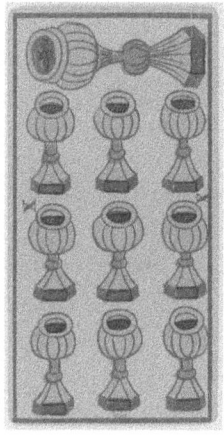  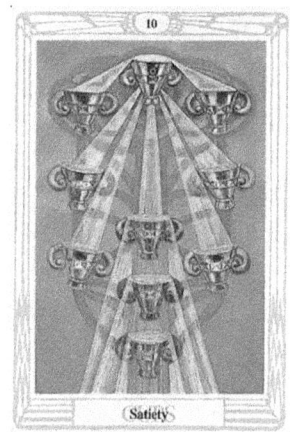

Decan: Mars in Pisces.
Timing: 1 to 10 March.
Sefirah: Water in Malkut.

This card represents emotional fulfilment and satisfaction. The feeling that one couldn't ask for more. It especially refers to relationships and family. The normally self serving power of Mars has had its boundaries opened, an attribute of Pisces, and now serves one's family and friends with fervour. It is an appropriate meeting between Mars' masculine power, and Pisces' feminine reception. Pisces is the final sign in the Zodiac, and it ushers in a new era. Implied in this is a new generation; children. When family doesn't apply, it is the feeling of being part of a 'tribe', for instance having fought for a cause and won. Consider a fan of a sports team after their team wins a major game.

Crowley takes a more general approach calling it 'Satiety'. Where Rider Waite Smith focuses on the positive, Crowley points out that while we are at peace, the only direction from here is towards a worse situation. He suggests that the active and fiery nature of Mars can not help but disrupt the watery passivity of Pisces. When the moment is broken it will be due to somebody's Martian ego. While he is probably right, it pays to have one's joys while one can.

Negatively aspected or reversed, it is feeling left out or not fitting in. The black sheep. Alternatively one is unsatisfied despite seeming to have everything. Perhaps feeling guilty and trapped.

An interesting case astrologically speaking would be Kurt Cobain, a Pisces Sun Sign, performing from a place of Piscean vulnerability through the fiery Martian energy of Punk rock. He would often perform, violently screaming and smashing his guitar while wearing a dress and makeup. This strange meeting of masculine and feminine imagery stirred up something in his audience.

However, just as Crowley predicts, after stardom, he struggled with the tension between his ego, his public image, and his inner emotional turmoil. The very same qualities and tension that fuelled his success when in accord, later brought about a fall.

Ten of Swords

 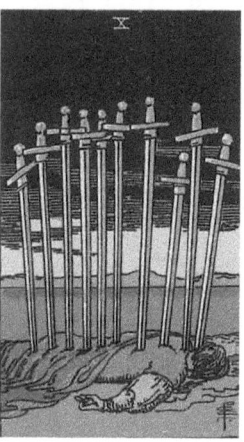 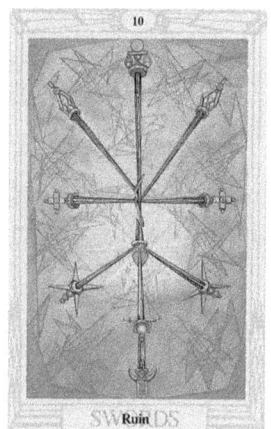

Decan: Sun in Gemini.
Timing: 11 to 20 June.
Sefirah: Air in Malkut.

The image of this card in the Rider Waite Smith is the most brutal and dramatic in the entire deck. Many people unfamiliar with Tarot symbols misinterpret it as violence. However, the swords here are ideas, not literal weapons. It represents, not death, but despair. The effect is always psychological, and rarely physical. Though it is the lowest of lows, the only possible pathway is upwards. It is the 'rock bottom' moment that recovered addicts credit with saving their lives.

My key phrase for the card is 'flogging a dead horse'. The sooner one accepts defeat and moves on, the better.

Crowley calls the card 'Ruin'.

> If one goes on fighting long enough, all ends in destruction. Yet this card is not entirely without hope. The Solar influence rules; ruin can never be complete, because disaster is a sthenic[54] disease. As soon as things are bad enough, one begins to build up again. When all the Governments have smashed each other, there still remains the peasant. Gemini never fully runs out of ideas, and if one feels defeated then the solution is to change teams to one that is on the rise.

---

[54] Having an excess of strength or energy.

The negativity of this card is attributed to the worst quality of Gemini. They take the unified rays of the Sun and scatter them into a million weak signals. This is the type of failure that was certain because one took on too many ideas for any of them to succeed.[55]

Because ten is the number of completions and swords are ideas and the intellect, the intellectual energies here have come to a dead end. Further rationalisation will produce no movement, benefit or opportunity. It is the type of madness that is the realm of the unhinged genius. To use my own term it is the 'smart person trap'.[56] A field of intellectual enquiry, that, while being endlessly interesting to those obsessed with it, produces no real-world results. An intellectual trap that only the smart fall into and which can be dismantled by simply asking 'but what is it good for'?

The astrology of the card, the Sun in Gemini can be hard to understand unless one remembers that the Sun is also the ego. Here ideas (Swords) are in dissonance with the ego. The result is a total loss of faith in oneself.

Negatively aspected or reversed, the querent is one step ahead and can avoid ruin if they act immediately to change their course.

---

[55] Page 209 (Crowley 1944).
[56] See the final chapter of my first book Pragmatic Magical Thinking (Freeman 2023).

Ten of Pentacles/Discs

  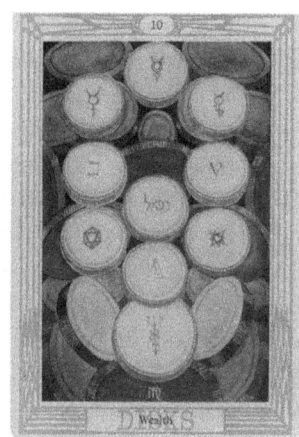

Decan: Mercury in Virgo.
Timing: 13 to 22 September.
Sefirah: Earth in Malkut.

This card is the final number, ten, of the final element, earth. As such it is a card of endings. In the Rider Waite Smith image, there is only one tower in the background as one's fate is now decided. The scales of morality are behind the aged figure on the pillar of the archway. The only thing to do is to look back in nostalgia. It is the end of a life stage or it is the final stage of life. The other figures show that life continues once our role is done.

It can also be a card of legacy if the other people are the old person's relatives. The pentacles in the image are arranged in the shape of the ten Sefirot, a completed Tree of Life. This card may come up when one retires, or one finishes a career. It also asks one to consider the old people in one's life. Their concept of time and mortality is quite different to that of younger people. The card asks 'What will you leave behind?' and dares one to leave the world a better place tan one found it.

Crowley calls the card 'Wealth'. The attitude of attention to detail (Virgo) and ability to understand commerce and flows of information (Mercury) has allowed the accumulation of wealth. At some point, one needs to shift the focus from the accumulation of wealth to putting the wealth to use, or no fulfilment will be reached. Negatively aspected or reversed, the goal is unobtainable, and one feels that one's time has been wasted.

The Court Cards in depth

Where the Major Arcana are the archetypes in a story, and the number cards are like plot points in the narrative, the court cards more directly address the cast of characters. Each court card represents a role played by a person in the reading. They can be people in the querent's life, the querent themselves, or occasionally, the Tarot reader in relation to the querent.

Gender

Each of the court cards represents a masculine or feminine role and an element. The Tarot was created at a time when gender roles were very different in society than they are now in the early twenty-first century. For that reason I find it is important to note that while, for instance, the Knight of Swords can be a daredevil, and men are more likely to engage in this type of behaviour than women, that there have at times been female daredevils. Likewise, while the Queen of Cups is usually a poetic woman with powerful ability to communicate her emotions, there have been men who take on this role; writers, artists, actors and nurturing fathers (especially solo dads).

This understanding that the human mind is, at its deepest core, androgynous, is not something new. Before there was psychology, we explained the human psyche to ourselves using magic, astrology, alchemy and other systems of learned thought. In all of these, and going right back to the roots, Shamanism, the androgyne was considered especially magical. Usually, it was thought that no human had truly understood themselves until they had engaged and incorporated their 'shadow' gender. Carl Jung termed the psychological feminine aspects in the male, the 'Anima', and the masculine aspects in the female the 'Animus'.

Those who had a tense relationship with their Anima/Animus were said to be inclined to project these tensions onto other people. In my experience, these things do play out in relationships and come into readings if one is aware of them.

In some decks, such as Crowley's Thoth Deck, pages are called 'princesses' which balances out the gendering of the Court Cards. Each of the Court Cards is assigned a letter of the Tetragrammaton and one of the four elements.

׳ Fire, Kings
ה Water, Queens
ו Air, Knights
ה Earth, Pages

This means that each Court Card has a pair of elements or a double-up of one element. For instance, Kings are Fire, and Cups are Water, so the King of Cups has the fiery properties of water. The King of Wands is therefore double fire, or fire amplified.

As much of the structure of Tarot is alchemical, these ideas apply to qualities in nature and in chemical experiments that were noticed by alchemists, as well as being applied to the Temperaments and psychology of people.

Each of the Court Cards from Kings to Knights also combines two of the signs of the zodiac, taking on a mixture of attributes of both. This idea was central to Crowley's interpretations of his Thoth Deck. As there are 16 cards rather than 12, the pages are the exception (who Crowley calls 'princesses'). These are instead assigned a quadrant of space around the north pole. Each of these quadrants can be thought of in terms of places on the map or as groups of three zodiac signs. These are shared by the Aces of the same suit as follows:

- Ace and Princess of Wands rule the quadrant of space occupied by Cancer, Leo and Virgo.
- Ace and Princess of Cups rules the quadrant of space occupied by Libra, Scorpio and Sagittarius.
- Ace and Princess of Swords rules the quadrant of space occupied by Capricorn, Aquarius and Pisces.
- Ace and Princess of Discs rules the quadrant of space occupied by Aries, Taurus and Gemini.

The court card categories are:

- **Kings (Called Knights in the Thoth deck)**
  Letter: Yod ׳
  Element: Fire (Wands)
- **Queens**
  Letter: Heh ה
  Element: Water (Cups)

- **Knights (Called Princes in the Thoth deck)**
  Letter: Vav ו
  Element: Air (Swords)
- **Pages (Called Princesses in the Thoth deck)**
  Letter: (final) Heh ה
  Element: Earth (Pentacles/Discs)

A quick alchemical summary of the court cards

King of Wands: Fire of Fire: Pure intent or one intent causes another. This card has an enormous amount of will, energy and like fire is quick to action. It can refer to both figurative and literal explosions and ignitions. This includes electricity such as lightning bolts, and arching electrical currents.

Signs: 21° Scorpio to 20° Sagittarius.

Timing (based on the movement of the sun): 12 November to 11 December.

King of Cups: Fire of Water: Intent affects emotion. Fire in this case is energy, so this implies fast-moving water. Physically this is floods, tidal waves and high water pressure. Figuratively this is powerful emotionality with intent.

Signs: 21° Aquarius to 20° Pisces.

Timing: 10 February to 10 March.

King of Swords: Fire of Air: This is a powerful drive in the intellect. For instance a powerful and commanding debater. Physically manifested it would be high winds, storms, hurricanes and cyclones.

Signs: 21° Taurus to 20° Gemini.

Timing: 11 May to 10 June.

King of Pentacles: Fire of Earth: This is intent in motion. It can be a purely intuitive action without justification or explanation. It is a drive for hard work focusing on acquiring or building tangible material things or the acquisition of money. Physically it would be things like earthquakes, landslides and rockfalls.

Signs: 21° Leo to 20° Virgo.

Timing: 13 August to 12 September.

Queen of Wands: Water of Fire: Emotionality affects intent. It is the ability to charm people into action. Physically it is combustible liquids such as gasoline.

Signs: 21° Pisces to 20° Aries.

Timing: 11 March to 9 April.

Queen of Cups: Water of Water: This is pure emotion, or the act of one emotion causing another. Physically it is phenomena such as waves.

Signs: 21° Gemini to 20° Cancer.

Timing: 11 June to 11 July.

Queen of Swords: Water of Air: Emotion-causing concept. One thinks of heartfelt spoken poetry or lyrics. Physically I think of mist and rain. Damp air. Emotional thoughts.

Signs: 21° Virgo to 20° Libra.

Timing: 13 September to 12 October.

Queen of Pentacles: Water of Earth: This is emotion acted out. Physically I think of rivers, swamps or mud, and especially of slow floods. It can also be, the once-solid Earth collapsing like a fluid, so landslides, and liquefaction. The formlessness of water washes away the once-solid Earth.

Signs: 21° Sagittarius to 20° Capricorn.

Timing: 12 December to 10 January.

Knight of Wands: Air of Fire: Intellect, or spirit causes intent. One thinks of volatile chemicals, volatile situations, and volatile people. Lightning storms and shock waves. It might also be explosive gases, such as hydrogen, not yet ignited.

Signs: 21° Cancer to the 20° Leo.

Timing: 12 July to 12 August.

Knight of Cups: Air of Water: Concepts act on emotion. This is the hero of romances and the pursuing partner who woos. Physically I think of water turned into gas, steam and vapour.

Signs: 21° Libra to the 20° Scorpio.

Timing: 13 October to 11 November.

Knight of Swords: Air of Air: Intellect acts on intellect. Words on words. This is the unseen, the purely conceptual, the spiritual, and unseen subtle forces like gravity, and physical fields like electromagnetism and entanglement.

Signs: 21° Capricorn to 20° Aquarius.

Timing: 11 January to 9 February.

Knight of Pentacles: Air of Earth: Concepts act on matter. Ideas are manifested. Blueprints are built into solid things. In action, it is plans made manifest. Physically one thinks of Earth becoming air such as dust storms, and their settling to produce sand bank islands and sand dunes.

Signs: 21° Leo to 20° Virgo.

Timing: 13 August to 12 September.

Page of Wands: Earth of Fire: The manifest causes new intent. It is the act of being fired up by one's environment. Physically it is combustible solid fuel waiting to be ignited: Fireplaces and contained and controlled fires or contained electricity.

Quadrant: The space occupied by Cancer, Leo and Virgo.

Timing: 21 June to 22 September.

Page of Cups: Earth of Water: The manifest causes emotion. For instance the effect of a painting or sculpture, on the heart. Physically it can be ice, snow and springs.

Quadrant: The space occupied by Libra, Scorpio and Sagittarius.

Timing: 23 September to 21 December.

Page of Swords: Earth of Air: That which is manifest inspires new concepts, or acts on the intellect. It is the action of reading a book and being affected by it. It is the ability of a tool or object such as a musical instrument to produce a conceptual effect; music. It can be writing, and recordings such as film and sound recordings. Physically it can be solids that turn into gas, such as dry ice (frozen carbon dioxide) or iodine.

Quadrant: The space occupied by Capricorn, Aquarius and Pisces.

Timing: 22 December to 20 March.

Page of Pentacles: Earth of Earth: Matter acts on matter, manifestation directly on manifestation. One thinks of the hardest objects such as stone and crystals. It is a force pushing on a force, one cancelling out the other. A hammer on a nail.

Quadrant: The space occupied by Aries, Taurus and Gemini.

Timing: 21 March to 20 June.

Pages

Also called Princesses, these are apprentices, youth or children. They are initiates, students and 'noobs'.[57] They are also usually people who are younger than the querent and represent someone at the beginner stage of a new field of study or career.

Pages can be literal children, youths, or the 'inner child' of the querent or of someone they know.

---

[57] 'Newbies' are those who are trying something new.

Page/Princess of Wands/Batons

Earthly properties of Fire.
The quadrant of space occupied by Cancer, Leo and Virgo.
21 June to 22 September.

This card shows someone full of enthusiasm for a new undertaking. It is naivete and exploration for a young person or beginner in a creative field. They have a manic energy and an excitable curiosity. It is the quality of being obsessed with a new undertaking. As people, they are attention-seeking to a charismatic leader. They can be playful and imaginative children. When the Page of Wands sees someone doing something impressive, they want to copy it and do it themselves. Sometimes they will leap in before they are ready. They are individualistic, brilliant, and daring, but usually not original in their thought. They are impulsive rather than calculating. They are theatrical and creative in a child-like way and very optimistic.

Negatively aspected or reversed, the card can mean a dabbler, someone who starts many pursuits and projects but never finishes anything. There can also be a gullibility that is easily taken advantage of alternatively, it can mean, wanting to start something new but not finding an opportunity to do it. Because the Page of Wands is not practised in their craft, they can be inclined to produce work that is derivative. They may also be inclined to present their work to the world before it is finished resulting in failure, embarrassment or a lacklustre response.

In the Rider Waite Smith image, the Page wears a jerkin covered in Salamanders, a reference to the elemental spirit of fire described by Paracelsus (1493–1541) and which was only later in English associated with the newt.[58] This card represents the earthy properties of fire; Crowley says this is associated with solid fuels which can be ignited: Wood, coal, and even plutonium. Crowley calls the card the Princess of Wands and ascribes her much more femininity. She is the idealised youthful beauty, Helen of Troy, and young female movie stars. One thinks of Marilyn Monroe in *Some Like It Hot*. Crowley says she may be shallow, but perhaps she is so because she becomes a projection of the 'Anima' in the 'male gaze', for whom she is a symbol to either be lusted at from afar or else conquered, affirming the male drive to prove himself in sexual conquest.[59] If legend and mythology is anything to go on, this will often be his undoing, and unfortunately often hers also. This is told in the tragedies of Romeo and Juliet, Lancelot and Guinevere or even Merlin and Morgan Le Fay. In real life, the result will often be less dramatic, he will at some point have to understand her as a human being, at which point she will either transform in his eyes to something more three-dimensional, or else she will disappoint and embitter him, for which he usually has only himself to blame for pursuing an illusion.

Similarly, this role can occasionally be played in reverse. One thinks of the boy band phenomenon marketed at teenage girls, especially those assertive enough to try and encounter these young men. Similar 'projections' can affect gay men such as the unobtainable 'twink', who simultaneously entices them sexually while reminding them of their own youth. This is a folly. One cannot date oneself.

Examples:

- Elmo from *Sesame Street*.
- Jim Hawkins the boy hero from *Treasure Island*.
- Alice from *Alice in Wonderland*.
- Morgan Le Fay, the enchantress and apprentice to Merlin in Arthurian legend.

---

[58] There was an idea that Salamanders were immune to fire and were in the habit of extinguishing fires. This mytheme appears to go back as far as Aristotle and Pliny, but the exact reason for the association of salamanders (newts), with fire seems to be lost to history.
[59] Some women have the same 'masculine' drive.

- Romeo from *Romeo and Juliet*. Juliet herself would be Page of Cups.
- 'Manic pixie dream-girls'.[60]
- Bart Simpson
- An idealised form can be found in the children's book character Pippi Longstocking created by Astrid Lindgren (1907–2002). Pippi, a tomboy, is 'the strongest girl in the world', and like Peter Pan she never wants to grow up.

---

[60] The film critic Nathan Rabin coined the term in 2007 in his series of columns 'My Year of Flops', on the website *the A.V. Club*. The original reference was to the actress Kirsten Dunst's character in Elizabethtown (2005), a film to which Rabin was deeply critical.

Page/Princess of Cups

Earthly properties of Water.
The quadrant of space occupied by Libra, Scorpio and Sagittarius.
23 September to 21 December.

This card represents a young romantic dreamer, someone who is waiting for their dreams to come true. In this way, they are not quite the same as the idealist, for whom the dream remains a concept, strived for, but never fully manifested.

The Page of Cups is a person with a child-like imagination, who is over the top with sweetness and kindness. They are, enthusiastic, a free emoter and often an empath. They tend to be very dependent on others, but also helpful. They are often a youth who is trying to 'find themselves', someone who is on a voyage of self-discovery.

Alchemically, earth of water represents chemical solutions that can produce crystallisation. Symbolically the Page of Cups is the manifestation of dreams and emotions. For this reason, some New Age readers interpret the card as someone who has burgeoning 'psychic' abilities, sixth sense, or an ability to sense or see spirits, such as fairies.

Other readers interpret the card as the quality of being receptive to new love and to relationships completely without cynicism.

Reversed or negatively aspected it can be a time of emotional confusion, emotional immaturity, and especially a crisis of self-identity. It can be someone who is very emotionally immature, or in a state of emotional arrested development. This person is not active, and may wonder why they are always attracting one 'type' of person when they would do better to take charge rather than waiting for a 'knight in shining armour'. It may also represent emotional wounds that were arrested during childhood and have formed an 'inner child' complex which has never grown up.

A reversed position, or a connection to another card such as Death, or the Devil, may bring out the 'gothic' aspects of this card. In this case, none of the romance is lost, but instead of optimism we have a romantic preoccupation with death and 'spookiness'. This type of person will strive to stand out and imagine they are very individualistic though it will be apparent to many people that they are following a subcultural trend: The gothic subculture, emos, punks, metallers, gangsta rap fans, etc.

Crowley interprets the card thusly:

> The character of the Princess is infinitely gracious. All sweetness, all voluptuousness, gentleness, kindness and tenderness are in her character. She lives in the world of Romance, in the perpetual dream of rapture. On a superficial examination she might be thought selfish and indolent, but this is a quite false impression; silently and effortlessly she goes about her work.[61]

Examples:

- Juliet from *Romeo and Juliet*. Romeo as the wooer, would be Page of Wands.
- Snow White.
- Rapunzel.
- Wednesday Addams.
- Characters suffering 'teenage angst'.

---

[61] Page 160 (Crowley 1944).

Page/Princess of Swords

Earthly properties of Air.
The quadrant of space occupied by Capricorn, Aquarius and Pisces.
22 December to 20 March.

This card presents us with a 'gatekeeper'. Someone who guards paltry amounts of information and who likes secrets and power. They tend to be immature, and petty, and enjoy being a contrarian. It can be a difficult 'problem child', who is prone to fibbing, a braggart or a bully. Given any responsibility, they will generally hold back instead of helping, or their idea of 'helping' is to affirm their own ego rather than to genuinely engage with the problems of the other.

On a more positive note, this card represents the early stages of learning to think and judge for oneself. In this sense, it can be a self-affirming youthful rebellion or 'going through a phase'. This is often annoying for one's elders, but perhaps it is necessary in the long run, as long as one eventually outgrows it.

Negatively aspected or reversed, this card represents being argumentative under the guise of being 'rational'. The page is motivated by a weak ego and prefers to try and score points rather than pursue any kind of truth or agreement.

Alchemically it is 'Earth of Air'. This can represent a rushed process or a lack of substance. Things built upon shaky foundations or strongly held ideas or concepts that have not been tested. It can be the skipping of the hypotheses stage directly to the thesis with none of the hard work done in between.

Crowley calls the card the Princess of Swords and suggests someone who is all theory and no praxis.

> He is full of ideas and designs which tumble over each other. He is a mass of fine ideals unrelated to practical effort. He has all the apparatus of Thought in the highest degree, intensely clever, admirably rational, but unstable of purpose, and in reality indifferent even to his own ideas, as knowing that any one of them is just as good as any other.[62]

The more positive incarnations of the Page of Swords are bookworm kids, intellectual children and those who experiment playfully with new ideas.

Examples:

- Ross from *Friends* (when he behaves like a know-it-all).
- Internet 'debates' that get out of hand, and in which opinions are presented as if they are facts.
- The negative side of the so-called 'Woke' subculture, especially kids who want to cancel things. Likewise, those on the other team who react in like, for instance, Incels, 'Red Pill' people, conspiracy theorists and similar internet subcultures.
- Mass movements like 'New Atheism' or those who have recently signed up to be religious fundamentalists.
- Followers of conspiracy theories, especially the more outrageous ones: Flat-Earthers, 'Space is Fake' or Qanon.
- The worst aspects of the 'self-help' movement.
- The websites 4Chan, 8Chan and other 'edge-lords'.
- The Alt-Right.
- Marilyn Manson fans, and other 'shock culture' celebrity followers.
- Poor quality cults.
- Multi-level Marketing and pyramid schemes.
- Fundamentalist evangelists.
- Young-earth creationists.

---

[62] Page 163 (Crowley 1944).

Page/Princess of Pentacles/Coins/Discs

Earthly properties of Earth.
The quadrant of space occupied by Aries, Taurus and Gemini.
21 March to 20 June.

A hardworking apprentice in a practical trade. A new job opportunity. A positive time of material growth, an opportunity for employment, and a child-like person who is hardworking. A playful worker who is externally focused. An earthy, natural beauty. A health-conscious person. Fertility. An outdoors person. A working-class kid.

Alchemically, it is earth of earth. Solid, stubborn, dependable, hard to manipulate, but also adverse to change. Someone who only considers real, that which is in front of them: 'Seeing is believing'.

Negatively aspected or reversed it is a materialistic person of little means. A worshipper of money, labels and the nouveau riche. They may reduce everything to monetary value. They may also sell their time for little gain.

Crowley takes a different interpretation. Calling the card Princess of discs, he considers it a full manifestation of the feminine principle.

> The Princess of Discs, the last of the Court cards, represents the earthy part of Earth. She is consequently on the brink of transfiguration. She is strong and beautiful, with an expression of intense brooding, as if about to become aware of secret wonder ... She contains all the characteristics of woman, and it would depend

entirely upon the influences to which she is subjected whether one or another becomes manifest.[63]

Aside from this, his interpretation is a little hard to understand. I would assume the implication is of full and final manifestation of one's ideas and fertility, in particular childbirth. The next stage after 'earth of earth' is the beginning of a new cycle. A fertile woman and the womb, marriage, family and motherhood.

Examples:

- A new factory worker.
- A farm worker.
- Bilbo Baggins.
- Rocky Bilboa from the *Rocky* franchise of films.
- Small town kids.
- Young supermodels.
- Mona Lisa.

---

[63] Page 169 (Crowley 1944).

Knights

Knights represent people at a professional or knowledgeable level in their field or career. Or people around the same age group as the querent. They are the 'doers' of the court cards. In Crowley's Thoth Deck, these are called princes and the cards he calls knights are really the kings in comparison to other decks.

Knight/Prince of Wands/Batons

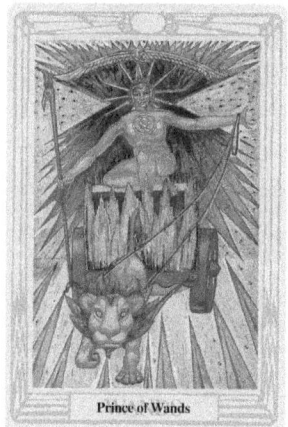

Airy properties of Fire.
Signs: 21° Cancer to 20° Leo.
12 July to 12 August.

A *Prima Donna*. A fast-moving person with charisma. They like to be the centre of attention and are ambitious, and larger than life. A bossy, headstrong person with dramatic gestures. At their worst, they can be narcissists of the vulnerable type.[64] They are people with rare gifts and talents. They are impulsive, but they sometimes struggle with indecision. Their insecurities can result in occasional meltdowns, and these will often be projected onto other people. They can have a martyr or victim complex if challenged. They have difficulty with, but also sometimes an attraction to people who are aloof. They have very strong opinions at the moment, but these opinions will often change from week to week or from moment to moment, creating a situation where everyone else is always trying to catch up. Often very quick-witted they are secretly able to see the different sides of an argument and therefore can find it hard to make up their mind. Their insecurity or obsession with dominance means that they often 'perform' a strong opinion that they may not actually strongly believe in. Despite their difficulties, they have

---

[64] Some psychologists classify two types of narcissists, the vulnerable type who are competitive and put others down in order to affirm a fragile ego, and the grandiose type who simply think they are superior to others all the time. The former pertains for us to the Knight of Wands and the latter to the Knight of Swords.

a strong sense of morality and fairness, when not feeling challenged, and can be extremely courageous. They are full of energy but are often very inefficient in how they use it. They present the airy properties of Fire. Volatile combustibility. When positively aspected, you may benefit from this person's high energy and inspiration. When negatively aspected or reversed, you will be involved in a drama or battle with this person.

Crowley calls the card Prince of Wands and his interpretation is similar. His image includes many more esoteric symbols:

> He is a warrior in complete armour of scale mail, but his arms are bare on account of his vigour and activity. He wears a rayed crown, surmounted by a lion's head winged, and from this crown depends a curtain of flame. On his breast is the sigil of To Mega Therion.[65] In his left hand he bears the Phoenix wand of the Second Adept[66] in the Ritual of 5060[67] of R.R. at A.C.,[68] the wand of Power and Energy, while with his other arm he reins the lion which draws his chariot, the chariot which is fortified by a wheel radiating flame. He rides upon a sea of flames, both waved and salient.[69]

One gets the feeling that Crowley identified with the card, and it certainly fits his reported and self-reported exploits as a young man. The 'Air of Fire' attribution to this card means that this person is impulsive, quick to act, and a performer of concepts. These qualities would suit a musician, especially one who improvises, an actor, or a public speaker. The card is attributed to 21° Cancer to 20° Leo, so this person would do well at emotional performances that cut to the core of the human experience, and get 'under the armour'.

---

[65] The Great Beast.
[66] A Golden Dawn ceremonial staff with gold painted bird-like head at top and striped shaft. Based on an ancient Egyptian staff topped with a stylised representation of the head of the god Set.
[67] Grade 5=6 from the Golden Dawn. Five is the Sefirah Gevurah and six is the Sefirah Tiferet.
[68] Rubidae Rosae and Aureae Crucis (Rose of Ruby and Cross of Gold). The name of the 'inner order' of the Golden Dawn who were dedicated to ritual magic.
[69] Page 153 (Crowley 1944).

Examples:

- Indiana Jones (in the first three movies).
- James Bond.
- Norma Desmond from *Sunset Boulevard*.
- Axl Rose, especially doing his 'snake dance'. (Both wands and snakes are phallic symbols).
- Miss Piggy, from *The Muppet Show*.
- Rambo from the movie *First Blood* (1982).
- 1980s action heroes.
- Hermione from Harry Potter.
- Paul McCartney of the Beatles, especially during the 'Get Back' era.
- Jimi Hendrix (1942–1970).
- Nina Simone (1933–2003).
- Mulder from *X-Files*.
- The young Aleister Crowley.

Knight/Prince of Cups

Airy properties of Water.
Signs: 21° Libra to 20° Scorpio.
13 October to 11 November.

A noble and unique talent who offers a generosity of mutual gain. They are often lost in their own thoughts, though they are self-aware. They are prone to escapism and isolated experimentation of their passions and sometimes drugs. They often put self-expression before well-being. In males, they can have intense issues with the Anima, which if not well understood, can be projected onto their lovers, mothers, and female authorities. At worst this becomes a Madonna/Whore complex where women are first idealised and then vilified when they don't meet their standards. One thinks of Lancelot and Guinevere from the tales of King Arthur. Alternatively, they will make every female partner their mother and emotional counsellor. They often engage in individualistically expressed rebellion. Though they can be very inspiring to others they are often themselves confused as to why.

The Knight of Cups rules from 21° Libra to 20° Scorpio. Scorpio has deep ambition and a desire to uncover mysteries along with a dramatic death or sex drive. Libra is an orientation towards fairness, diplomacy and engagement with people. (A negatively expressed Libra, however, will become the ultimate manipulator, playing people off against each other.) The result is someone who engages with people by revealing deeply personal aspects of themselves. 'Confessional' poets, musicians, or similar.

Negatively aspected or reversed they are bent on self-destruction through escapism, drugs and other vices. Or so over-committed to romance that it can only end badly. The airy properties of water produce steam, and a kind of formless power. While not well directed, this power has the ability, like steam, to penetrate into places that directive power can't go.

Crowley calls the card the Prince of Cups and discusses the more negative aspects of the card. Again one wonders if he didn't sometimes self-identify with this card.

> The moral characteristics of the person pictured in this card are subtlety, secret violence, and craft. He is intensely secret, an artist in all his ways. On the surface he appears calm and imperturbable, but this is a mask of the most intense passion. He is on the surface susceptible to external influences, but he accepts them only to transmute them to the advantage of his secret designs. He is thus completely without conscience in the ordinary sense of the word, and is therefore usually distrusted by his neighbours. They feel they do not, and can never, understand him. Thus he inspires unreasonable fear. He is in fact perfectly ruthless. He cares intensely for power, wisdom, and his own aims. He feels no responsibility to others, and although his abilities are so immense, he cannot be relied upon to work in harness.[70]

Examples:

- John Lennon (1940–1980).
- George Harrison (1943–2001).
- Kurt Cobain (1967–1994). (Towards the end of his career especially.).
- Charles Bukowski (1920–1994). American writer of confessional novels.
- Brian Molko (b. 1972) from the band Placebo.
- Brett Anderson (b. 1967) from the band Suede.
- Bowie as the Thin White Duke.
- Don Draper of *Madmen*.
- Edgar Allan Poe (1809–1849).

---

[70] Page 159 (Crowley 1944).

Knight/Prince of Swords

Airy properties of Air.
Signs: 21° Capricorn to 20° Aquarius.
11 January to 9 February.

This card presents us with overconfidence, brashness, arrogance, jumping the gun, and a personality full of 'fuck you' energy. They are youth too smart for their own good or those who enjoy arguing for the sake of arguing. Because they are full of quick ideas and opinions, they appear clever to most people until they argue with a pragmatist. In this sense they are good at spoken debate, but bad at written ones. In psychology, they fit the definition of the grandiose narcissist. With this card, I'm always reminded of the saying: 'fools rush in', and here there is an element of the daredevil.

Alchemically, this card is Air of Air. Ideas without practicality or grounding. As such the Knight of Swords will adopt whatever opinion they see fit for a sense of sport, without strongly held beliefs, and they will portray a lack of emotion until their pride is challenged, resulting in senseless rage. In a more stable person, they are pure intellect, having ideas that tumble over each other, and thinking fast on their feet. A rhetorical debater, or philosopher prone to 'smart person traps', they may reduce everything to ideas by removing the substance. As debaters, they are prone to using the 'Gish Gallop',[71] where one overwhelms

---

[71] The term was coined in 1994 by the anthropologist Eugenie Scott. It was named after the American creationist Duane Gish who was said to employ the technique when debating atheists.

one's opponent by rattling off such a flurry of ideas that they can't possibly respond in time. This is a sneaky tactic in any debate with an imposed time limit, where one presents more ideas than can possibly be argued against within the time constraints. The equivalent in martial arts or sports is to keep one's opponent on the defence with a flurry of attacks. They may excel as leaders in politics but can be difficult to control or predict once they have power.

Though the Knight of Swords seems brash and careless from the outside, their approach, when well-timed can achieve things that can seem nearly miraculous. When the system has become so full of rules, checks and balances that all work has seized to a snail's crawl, the Knight of Swords can find the chink in the armour that bursts the bubble. This will spur a shock reaction and render them the hero of those left out of the system, and the enemy of those who the system served. In the most dramatic examples, they may be able to bring faith in the whole system down by showing the weaknesses in its defences.

For this reason, a Knight of Swords may excel as a lawyer. They have the right timing to win over the jury while keeping their opponents on the back foot. The Knight of Swords also presents us with a primary tactic in martial arts and war. A gap in the defence is noticed and only a small window of opportunity will allow an attack to get through. Only a quick, intuitive, risky attack will allow a winning blow. In sports, this approach is necessary to understand, deploy and train against. In politics or war the Knight of Swords, having won the battle may stand confused about what to do next.

The successful opponent, who has spotted the Knight of Swords tactic, will lure the Knight to a predicted attack, move out of the way and then take advantage of the fact that the Knight, in all his bravado, has not prepared a proper defence himself. As he is a rebel at heart, the Knight of Swords is mostly a reactionary. He defines himself as the opposite of the person he is attacking. As the enemy keeps trying to define him, he will keep changing his persona in reaction. To him, this is a game. To his enemy, he looks inauthentic or dishonourable. The wise tactician, a King of Swords, can set up a straw man for the Knight of Swords to attack and then while he is distracted show him to be a fool, thus stabbing him in the back. A perfect example of this is the boxer Nicolino Locche, who was so genius at dodging that despite looking 'wide open' to his opponents, they were almost never able to land a hit. The results were so extraordinary that it looked like Locche was able to see into the future and his opponent's actions looked futile and comical in response.

To become a King or Queen of Swords the Knight must become humble enough to master their field. The best Knights of Swords stumble upon genius and inspire others to follow. Seeming to get away with the impossible, they can empower people to action and help them escape the feeling of being 'trapped'. For this reason, many cultural heroes can be thought of as the Knight of Swords.

They can charm unintellectual people into thinking they are extremely intelligent but will piss off 'earthy', practical or ambitious people. They are better at toppling sandcastles than building them. They can be without remorse when accused and it is usually impossible to get them to admit defeat in argument. It is also hard to figure out what they truly believe in because to them any idea is as good as any other. They will often be an aficionado of a political or philosophical system that is impracticable, such as Trotskyism, extreme libertarianism, hardline communism, post-modernism, post-structuralism, fundamentalist, conspiracy theories, and young-Earth creationism. etc. As such they can be faddists, jumping on whichever topical viewpoint is controversial at the time. Of this card, Crowley says: 'It is as if an imbecile offered one the dialogues of Plato'.

Examples:

- Donald Trump (b. 1946). President of the US from 2017 to 2021.
- Evel Knievel (1938–2007).
- Muhammad Ali (1942–2016), heavyweight champion boxer and civil rights activist.
- Charlie Parker (1920–1955). Jazz saxophonist and originator of 'Bebop', one of the most challenging forms of improvised music.
- John Coltrane (1926–1967). Jazz saxophonist who took Charlie Parker's art to a higher level.
- Alex Jones, David Icke, and other famous conspiracy theorists.
- Martin Luther (1483–1546).
- Ancient Greek sophism.
- Post-structuralist philosophy.
- Trotskyists.
- Don Quixote.
- Accelerationists.
- Young-Earth creationist debaters.

Knight/ Prince of Pentacles/Coins/Discs

Airy properties of Earth.
Signs: 21° Aries to 20° Taurus.
13 August to 12 September.

This card presents us with someone who is slow, cautious, protective, reserved, dependable, and responsible. They have a deeply thought-out plan and an enduring energy. They like routine and do not change course easily. Fitting with the theme of pentacles, they are materialistic with a strong work ethic. Generally stoic, they may lack emotional expression. Because of this, they may also be insensitive or tactless socially. They make no effort to understand ideas which are beyond their scope. They tend to be slow to anger, and fixed in their opinions.

In careers, they fit well with engineering, mechanics, or any subjects where ideas lead to material outcomes. As earthy types, they are well-presented and dress conservatively. However, they also enjoy beautiful things and will often have collections of objects, especially things that, though valuable, other people tend to throw away.

They may be found on a committee for heritage buildings or on the board of an art gallery. They enjoy machines, gadgets or sciences like biology. They can also be farmers or craftspeople, but they will tend to make useful objects rather than expressive ones. Despite this, they have an eye for aesthetics and may be found browsing an antique store. They can be uncomfortable with emotions and would prefer the people around them to be rational, though exceptions will be made for their spouse and children. In times of need, they will turn up and help with practical concerns, like mowing the lawn or organising the shed. They are hard to convince and may insist that their point of view is rational even when disproven. They are only able to maintain this belief because they are dismissive of that which doesn't make sense to them. Rather than engage with new theories they'd, rather other people sort them out first and come back to them when they are tested or scientifically proven. They do however love gadgets and conceptual ideas presented in a material way. They can be low in empathy, but can also be sympathetic when they are made aware of other's emotions. They are undramatic and may act as an emotional 'rock' for their partner. Positively aspected, they are hardworking assets if you know how to talk to them on their own terms. Negatively aspected they are stubborn, dismissive and controlling over their sphere of influence. Crowley says of this card:

> He is the element of Earth become intelligible. Clothed in light armour, his helmet is crowned with the head of a bull [Taurus]; and his chariot is drawn by an ox, this animal being peculiarly sacred to the Element of Earth. In his left hand he holds his disc, which is an orb resembling a globe, marked with mathematical symbols as if to imply the planning involved in agriculture.[72]

Examples:

- Richard Dawkins (b. 1941). Famous geneticist and anti-theist.
- James Randi (1928–20 October 2020). Stage magician, escape artist and debunker of those claiming psychic abilities.
- Ringo Starr (b. 1940) from the Beatles.
- The Catholic Church.
- Fred Dagg, the New Zealand comic farmer character.
- Hank Hill from *King of the Hill*.
- Sigmund Freud (1856–1939). Pioneering psychoanalyst.
- Brienne of Tarth from *Game of Thrones*.

---

[72] Page 155 (Crowley 1944).

Queens

Queens represent matriarchs, some female bosses (who can also be kings), mothers of adult children, grandmothers, and counsellors. They are the element of Water.

Queen of Wands/Batons

Watery properties of Fire.
Signs: 21° Pisces to 20° Aries.
11 March to 9 April.

The Queen of Wands is a person who finds power in traditionally feminine roles. They can be matriarchal mothers and grandmothers who organise a group of women and children, fiery and powerful female movie stars who play the seductress, provocative female artists, or people gender-bending or 'playing' at the feminine, such as drag queens.

In the mother or grandmother role, they have answers to all the challenges that children can bring. This role is very important in multigenerational communities, such as schools, churches, community groups and maraes (or other indigenous meeting houses). In Māori they are called Kuia: Female community elders, known affectionately as 'aunties'.

In the nurturing role, they are capable and proud and are beneficial to most. They can however become hoverers or smothering to their own children, even when they are beloved by the children of others.

Negatively aspected, or reversed they can be women who struggle to express their animus, as wands are the most active of masculine energies. In this way, they can be both, attracted to, and simultaneously resentful of masculine authority, especially in situations where they aren't in control of their own domain. When animus difficulties present she can suddenly turn on, or display dominance to her friends or children rather than standing up to the one who caused her resentment, perhaps a dominant lover, her father, her boss, etc. When her animus is positively expressed she is ambitious, a leader to her friends, a creator of fun, a counsellor and an emotional confidant.

As a seductress, she is in full power over her effect on straight men, and she celebrates this energy. This same energy can sometimes be harnessed by gay men, drag queens and others for whom the 'feminine' energy is accessible. Very occasionally, young straight men learn this also and in that case, they tend to target older women, who can have a 'masculine' drive to their sexuality.

Her children may find they are overshadowed by their well-known parent. Because of this, she can be inspiring if her children are like her, but difficult if her children are shy. Other children will often be asking about the parent and this can cause difficulties in the child's own sense of identity.

They are Water in Fire. Emotionality is directed by the will. They have an adaptable fluidity, and the ability to act in many different roles in order to get a job done. They have persistent energy but may brood when it comes to adult problems.

Examples:

- Madams of brothels.
- Carmen Miranda (1909–1955).
- Mae West (1893–1980), the Hollywood blonde with the sharp tongue. She had some of the best one-liners in the business.
- Marlena Dietrich (1901–1992). German actress who was successful in both German and American cinema.
- Billie Holiday (1915–1959). Jazz singer.
- Ella Fitzgerald (1917–1996). Jazz singer.
- Ziggy Stardust David Bowie's alien alter ego.
- Little Richard (1932–2020). The king and 'queen' of rock'n'roll.
- Drag Queens.
- Marina Abramović (b. 1946). World famous performance artist.
- Frida Kahlo (1907–1954). Famous painter.
- Mata Hari (1876–1917). A Dutch dancer, courtesan and spy for Germany during World War I.

- Josephine Baker (1906–1975). A black American dancer, singer and actress. She was a civil rights activist and aided the French resistance during World War II.
- Yoko Ono (1933). Performance artist, outsider musician and late wife of John Lennon.
- Male gigolos, especially those who have female clients.
- Baba Yaga, the mythical Russian witch. Her symbol is the pestle and mortar, a very Queen of Wands image.
- Glinda the Good Witch, from *The Wizard of Oz*.
- The Witch archetype in general, especially those who fly on broomsticks, a phallic symbol.
- Lady Gaga (b. 1986). Singer and pop star. Her best work is her music videos and onstage costumes. She is highly influenced by Marina Abramović.
- Elizabeth I of England (1533–1603). The 'Virgin Queen' who turned Britain from a group of backwater isles to a world-spanning Empire. Her femininity, which should have been a disadvantage, became the pride of England.

Queen of Cups

Watery properties of Water.
Signs: 21° Gemini to 20° Cancer.
11 June to 11 July.

A mystical woman with great intuition, who has solutions to problems of love and family. She is an emotional supporter. Though brilliant, she can also be manipulative, moody, and depressive. She is a laissez faire mother.

This card presents us with the watery properties of water. This is formlessness and the emotional world expressed in its full power. Highly empathetic, she has a 'sixth sense', almost to a fault. She is exceptional at observing situations and understanding them at an experiential, human level. For this reason, she can be an incredible poet, writer or lyricist, able to express what was thought to be inexpressible. Her arts are capable of great subtlety and sensuality.

When negatively expressed or reversed she may pick up all the subtle emotions from the people around her, but because she has little air (concept and rationality), she may come up with strange narratives on why the person is feeling that way. It can be nearly impossible to hide one's true emotions from this kind of person. She is very impressionable, but also highly individualistic. She loves to feel attractive to those she is attracted to, and may seek attention in this way through flirtatious behaviour or dress, or otherwise presenting herself as available; without expressly saying so.

This card is rarely attributable to men, as when they have these inner qualities, they are often covered over, or disguised by male social training. What was in the female a rich and overt emotional expression can instead come across as flat and deadpan, though their work will be extremely expressive.

Negatively aspected, she can become self-absorbed in her art, writing or work, which ironically is about connection to others, but at the cost of her actual relationships. Alternatively, she can become emotionally manipulative, something which she is, unfortunately, a master at, and which would otherwise be a positive force and drive behind her art. (20° Libra to 20° Virgo.)

Examples:

- Silvia Plath (1932–1963), 1960s American poet and writer.
- Virginia Woolf (1882–1941). An early twentieth-century modernist writer, and one of the pioneers of the 'stream of consciousness' technique.
- Mary Shelley (1797–1851). A Genius early nineteenth-century writer. She was a pioneer of both the horror and science fiction genres and is most famous for Frankenstein (1818), which she started writing when she was 18 and was fully published when she was 20.
- Kate Bush (b. 1958). Singer, dancer, composer and music producer. Most famous in the 1980s.
- Björk (b. 1965). Singer, composer and music producer. Most famous in the 1990s and early twenty-first centuries.
- Queen Victoria (1819–1901). Monarch Queen of the United Kingdom of Great Britain and Ireland from 1837 until her death in 1901.
- Margery Tyrell of *Game of Thrones*.
- Jacinda Ardern (b. 1980). Former Prime Minister of New Zealand between 2017 and 2023.
- Eckhart Tolle (b. 1948). A German self-help author.
- Jack Kerouac (1922–1969). The central voice and writer of the 'beat generation' authors. He tried to write the way that jazz musicians of the 1940s and 1950s were improvising music.
- Anne Rice (1941–2021). Writer of an entire franchise of vampire and supernatural novels with homoerotic themes.

Queen of Swords

Watery properties of Air.
Signs: 21° Virgo to 20° Libra.
13 September to 12 October.

A female intellectual, military leader, teacher, scientist, lecturer, academic, advocate, politician sports-person or communicator in a position of power. She is an expert in her field with a dominion over public life. She is often someone with pain in the past. A communicator of ideas, she understands the core issues when all around her may be confused. She is an intelligent person who is intellectually stimulating and a translator of ideas. She is not motherly in the traditional sense, so if she is raising children, they will benefit from also having a gentle father. She is a woman with ideas and someone who has been through it all.

This card can be a male if they are an especially sympathetic counsellor or psychologist, a gentle father, (often a single parent), or a male Tarot reader or fortune-teller.

If negatively aspected or reversed, they are cold, aloof and distant, or overly critical. The usually enthusiastic communication becomes a 'cold shoulder'.

As swords are traditionally ascribed to the military, this card can also be a female soldier, or a woman who has a competitive career, such as a sportswoman.

Examples:

- Ripley from *Alien/s*.
- Hillary Clinton (b. 1947).
- Scully from *X-Files*.
- Serena and Venus Williams (b. 1981 and 1980).
- Helena Blavatsky (1831–1891), founder of Theosophy.
- Dion Fortune (1890–1946), occult writer.
- Anna Kingsford (1846–1888), mystic and founder of the Hermetic Society, a precursor to the Hermetic Order of the Golden Dawn.
- Marie Curie (1867–1934), pioneering scientist in the field of radioactivity. She was the first woman to win the Nobel Prize, the first person to win it twice and the only person to ever win it in two separate scientific fields. She discovered the elements polonium and radium along with her husband Pierre Curie.

Queen of Pentacles/Coins/Discs

Watery properties of Earth.
Signs: 21° Sagittarius to 20° Capricorn.
12 December to 10 January.

A woman of means, at peace with material possessions. She thrives in modest comfort, is very private and practical, and finds joy in what she has. Industrious and hardworking, she has found her success in life. She can be a perfectionist. She is interested in nature and believes in community.

She likes ornaments and may collect antiques or paintings. She is not particularly artistic but will often be a patron to those who are. Despite this, she may discourage her own children from pursuing the arts in favour of more financially secure careers. She is materialistic but appreciates history and family lineage. She is usually the matriarch of her family. Externally focused. She may have a career in real estate, geology, farming or mining.

She works for the higher good whether that be by joining community groups or giving to charity. Though introverted, she is a socialite, and a person of grace and etiquette, keeping track of a large number of acquaintances and family. She may also be a proud gardener. She is practical, not philosophical.

Although conservative, she is not necessarily close-minded and is interested in the way other people live their lives as long as she doesn't have to participate herself. In this way, she may live vicariously through her children while sticking to the straight and narrow herself. If male, he is a graceful and dandy man with an assertive and ambitious partner.

Negatively aspected or reversed, she may put appearances and reputation before truth, and avoid confronting family dramas to the detriment of those affected. She toes the line and puts her community first, which will cause tension to a close family member or friend who is trying to express themselves as an individual.

Her close family may be frustrated when their own cousins or family friends are tolerated or even admired for their differences, quirks and self-expression when they themselves are told or taught by her to toe the line.

Examples:

- Elizabeth II (1926–2022). Queen of England from 1952 until her death.
- Margaret Thatcher (1925–2013).
- Gina Rinehart (b. 1954), mining magnate.
- Pannonica de Koenigswarter (1913–1988), the 'Jazz Baroness'. Patron to jazz musicians Charlie Parker and Thelonius Monk.
- Carl Jung's wife, Emma Jung (1882–1955).
- Carmela Soprano, from the TV series *The Sopranos*.
- Marge Simpson.
- Sybil Fawlty, from the TV series *Fawlty Towers*.
- Catelyn Stark, from the TV series *Game of Thrones*.
- Nanny Ogg, from Terry Pratchett's Discworld series.
- Olenna Tyrell, from *Game of Thrones*.

Kings

Somewhat confusingly these are called 'Knights' in Crowley's Thoth Deck, and the knights are replaced by 'Princes'. Kings represent patriarchs, fathers of adult children, grandfathers, authority figures (usually male) and leaders in their field. They are 'ideas people' who motivate and organise others. They operate with responsibility on behalf of their family or a group of people.

King of Wands/Batons

Fiery properties of Fire.
Signs: 21° Scorpio to 20° Sagittarius.
12 November to 11 December.

In Crowley's Thoth deck, Knights are equivalent to Kings. A Charismatic and inspiring leader. Full of ambition, they take command. An innovator, who creates something new and communicates it to an audience or his followers. A respected teacher of many. A lecturer or motivational speaker. They are enormously inspiring, forthright and engaging. They have worshippers, not friends. He does not stop for others and can be brutal to those who don't follow him. He can inspire bitterness. In his most negative manifestation, he is a cult leader.

His opinions are based more on his aesthetics more than his rational faculties. For this reason, he makes an engaging art critic, but only if one buys into his sense of taste. As a parent, he is forthright, overbearing, and unconventional, but can produce successful children if they can only get out from under his thumb. He may withhold his attention and love as a disciplinary tool rather than other kinds of punishment, which can cause complexes in his children.

Crowley calls the card Knight of Wands. He says the card embodies activity, fierceness, carelessness, pride, impulsiveness, swiftness, and unpredictability. As Fire of Fire, they are not only full of energy but being in their presence is itself energising.

If wrongly energised he is cruel, brutal and bigoted. He has no ability to modify his actions for different circumstances. If he fails in his first effort he has no plan B. As a combination of Scorpio and Sagittarius, the idealistic goal shooting of the latter is turned inward, as is the nature of Scorpio. Here is a combination of self-improvement and trying to change the world to their ideal.

Examples:

- Captain Kirk from Star Trek.
- Ayn Rand (1905–1982), and the male heroes of her books.
- L. Ron Hubbard (1911–1986).
- Tony Robbins (b. 1960), motivational speaker.
- Father Yod (James Edward Baker) (1922–1975) leader of the Source Family cult.
- Bhagwan Shree Rajneesh (Osho, 1931–1990). Cult leader and founder of the Rajneesh movement.
- Arnold Schwarzenegger (b. 1947).
- Mick Jagger (b. 1943).
- Tony Soprano, from the TV series, *The Sopranos*.
- J.Z. Knight (b. 1946) from the Ramtha cult.
- James Brown (1933–2006). The godfather of funk.
- Fela Kuti (1938–1997). Nigerian bandleader, singer, saxophonist, songwriter and civil rights activist. He is often compared to James Brown and also Malcolm X.

King of Cups

Fiery properties of Water.
Signs: 21° Aquarius to 20° Pisces.
10 February to 10 March.

In Crowley's Thoth Deck, Knights are equivalent to Kings.

A patriarch struggling in a tenuous position with dignity. An inspiring, nurturing caring father. He will fight for those dear to him. A Godfather, for whom the family is everything. He is an empathetic master of emotions. He promotes civility and is a defender of others. His family comes before all other morality.

When positively aspected, they are on your side and a powerful ally, when negatively aspected or reversed they can be an intense and irrational enemy or roadblock. They might also exhibit emotional instability which can, in the worst situations be manipulative or dangerous. As a parent, they are protective and brave. The child will grow up feeling safe from outside dangers but will have to learn to deal with their parent's ever-shifting moods.

As a man, he may struggle with his Anima. If this is not brought into balance within himself, then his ideals about femininity may be projected onto the women in his life. He is a romantic, who makes the people he loves feel special, but his ideals may not always be realistic. He is a sentimental man who has high empathy but often struggles emotionally. If out of balance, he is attracted to overly feminine, motherly, or submissive women, but can become resentful to them if they don't live up to his expectations.

The fiery properties of water are heavy rains, floods, high-pressure systems and water's power to dissolve. Crowley says the card presents a 'weak Jupiter', quick to respond to attraction, but not enduring in his attention. As his elements are Fire and Water, Crowley feels that this type of person has trouble being effective. The watery properties fizzle out or dilute the fiery properties. He may have minor addictions to minor drugs; smoking, caffeine, or a few drinks. Combining Aquarius with Pisces he is the humanitarian ideal focused on the family.

Examples:

- Elvis Presley (1935–1977).
- *The Godfather* as portrayed by Marlin Brando in the 1972 film.
- Martin Luther King Junior (1929–1968).
- A Catholic priest.
- Leonard H. McCoy (Bones) from *Star Trek*.
- Jordan Peterson (b. 1962). Psychologist, self-help guru and conservative internet personality.

King of Swords

In Crowley's Thoth Deck, Knights are equivalent to Kings.
Fiery properties of Air.
Signs: 21° Taurus to 20° Gemini.
11 May to 10 June.

A judge, or a leading thinker in their field, who commands authority and respect. They are fair, impartial, distant. They see both sides of an argument. An idealist with fixed rational beliefs, they are however capable of nuance. They may work in academia, government, as a consultant to business, science, in law or the military. They are a master of deep balanced decision making and a good advisor for the hardest decisions. They have the courage and intellect to accomplish things that other people can't. They excel at intellectual strategies, large-scale planning, and logistics. They are excellent at creating theories from observing patterns. These could be in the realm of scientific, technology, the internet, artificial intelligence, logistics or military planning. As generals, they are cunning and ingenious.

Reversed or negatively aspected, the person doesn't command the respect that they expect; they are questioned by their underlings, or they lose face. It could also mean that they don't have the full understanding that one needs in order to see a goal through. They might be putting to work a theory, based on incomplete data.

As a parent, they are distracted by their own interests, but can be very close to their children if they find something in common. They often engage with their children through hobbies, education and reading. The child may grow up with a teacher for a parent.

He is steady in his beliefs but despondent if he loses faith.

In the Rider Waite Smith Image, the butterflies on the throne signify transformation. There is also an angel on the throne near his left ear. In the past Angels were thought to inhabit the world of concepts. As the fiery Properties of Air he has energy for ideas. Alchemically this could also denote storms and high winds. As a mixture of Taurus and Gemini, he encompasses ideas and communication put to practical work. He seems to always have a solution to every problem.

Examples:

- Dr Spock from *Star Trek*.
- Charles Darwin (1809–1882).
- Isaac Newton (1642–1727).
- Albert Einstein (1879–1955).
- Stephen Hawking (1942–2018).
- Sherlock Holmes.
- Dr Strange from the Marvel Universe. (He later becomes the Magician card.)

King of Pentacles/Discs

Fiery properties of Earth.
Signs: 21° Leo to 20° Virgo.
13 August to 12 September.

In Crowley's Thoth Deck, Knights are equivalent to Kings.

A hardworking boss. Calm, cautious, proud and self reliant. A 'salt of the earth' personality. He intends to stay in charge. He plays it safe, and doesn't move until he knows how to get the job done properly. He has a depth of life experience and is an expert problem-solver. He doesn't not like being beholden to anyone, and repays his debts. Those that work for him value his approval. He is usually a master craftsman and can also be a farmer, a tradesman, or merchant of goods. He is externally focused, and may neglect his own emotional well-being.

He can be immovable in his opinions unless they are proven wrong in practice. He may have trouble relating to airy/intellectual people. He is highly respectful unless disrespected. A materialist, atheist or someone for whom religion is purely practical. He puts great stock in community.

Alchemically, this card is the fiery properties of Earth: Mountains, earthquakes, and volcanoes.

Crowley associated this card with the production of food, hence the field of grain and the flail that he wields in the Thoth deck image. Virgo, though a detail focused air sign, is also fertility and Leo is leadership, but also implies the sun. So here we have the combined image of the sun, the earth and the fertility of the field.

Negatively aspected or reversed, he puts time, money and riches before all else.

Examples:

- Karl Marx (1818–1883).
- John D. Rockefeller (1839–1937), American founder of the Standard Oil Company, his family name became associated with riches and philanthropy.
- Andrew Carnegie (1835–11 August 1919). Tycoon of the American steel industry who became a philanthropist. He gave away 90 per cent of his fortune to charities and institutions in his own lifetime.
- Cecil Rhodes (1853–1902). An English mining magnate and politician in South Africa, he set up the De Beers diamond company and worked to expand the British Empire in the region.
- Mining corporations.
- Scotty from *Star Trek*.
- Ned Stark from *Game of Thrones*.
- Ebenezer Scrooge from Charles Dickens' 1843 novella *A Christmas Carol*.
- Antonio Stradivari (1644–1737), luthier who crafted some of the most famous violin family instruments in history under the name Stradivarius.
- Gorō Nyūdō Masamune (1264–1343). Considered Japan's greatest swordsmith.

Reversals revisited

The reason that I have waited this long to discuss reversals is that I feel that it is easier to start by reading without them. Reversals are an oft debated option amongst Tarot readers, professional or otherwise, with many loud opinions both for and against.

The spirit of this book is to explore the options, and I personally always offer to the querent the option to read with reversals before I shuffle for a reading. I do this in part to show my confidence that the reading will work either way. This may ruffle the feathers if those who believe that the truth in Tarot is in the cards rather than the reading, as a reversed card ought to produce and opposite reading than one which is the right way up. I have however tried every option, and though reading with reversals is harder for the reader at first it still works.

Crowley discusses that magical symbols, including Tarot card meanings, always have within them a contradiction. That is to say, each contains its own opposite, and an ability for a positive expression or a negative expression. For this reason, it made more sense to him to use the context of each symbol as the determiner for whether the card it is positively or negatively expressed, rather than leaving this factor to a randomised reversal. I think this is the reason he never discusses reversals.

The Golden Dawn, and their Tarot manual, *Book T* also don't mention reversals.

Etteilla, however, the writer of the first ever Tarot manual, printed reversals right on the cards themselves. This suggests that there was a tradition of using reversals that predates him, which is to my knowledge, lost to time. Therefore reversals, though optional, have been a part of the Tarot tradition for a long time.

The difference between reading with reversals vs without reversals is this: Reversals leave to chance the positive or negative attributions of each card, whereas non-reversals leave more of the positive or negative attributions to the jurisdiction of the reader.

Depending on one's working explanation as to how the Tarot works, one might think that reading one way would give superior readings than the other, especially given the fact that reversals can reverse the meaning of a card.

Strangely, I have found that one style of reading gives much the same effectiveness as the other. Which suggests that the art of Tarot lies more in the reader than in the fate of the cards and that the magic lies more in 'making it work', than in the universe sending you messages or synchronicities. In any case my results surprised me, yet I must honour them whether they are explainable or not.

How to shuffle reversals

Reading with reversals necessitates adding a step to how you shuffle the cards. Normally one would have all the cards facing the same way and one would shuffle in a way that maintains that orientation.

Because I let the reader decide whether I use reversals, my decks usually contain reversed cards, and if they ask for 'no reversals', I simply turn them up the right way when I draw them (which will probably cause steam to come out of ears of Tarot readers who believe in fate!). Again, in my experience this works just fine, and the alternative would be to spend a lot of time reorganising the deck before starting.

To shuffle for reversals, split the deck in two. Rotate half of the cards 180° and then add them back together. Shuffle again. Split the deck in two again. Rotate half of the cards 180° and then add them back together. Do this several times. Now your deck will be randomised for reversals.

Pro:	Con:
• Reversals force the reader to think about positive and negative expressions of each card. Over time this can make one a better reader.	• Reversals can be daunting for beginners. Now there are dual meanings for each of the 78 cards. Many see this as more work.

- Reversals randomise a factor, the positive and negative expressions of the cards, which would be at the jurisdiction of the reader if they weren't reading reversals. Some would prefer to make the choice themselves.

Many of the readers who don't use reversals feel that the positive and negative aspects are 'inside the card', and become readable according to whether they are well aspected or poorly aspected: The position in a spread, or their relations to other cards. For instance a Devil card next to a King of Cups, might bring out all the worst properties in that card. Likewise if you have a card out of balance, i.e. there are too many sword cards in a spread, then some of the negative properties of 'too much air' will come to bear.

A.E. Waite, in his own book *The Pictorial Key to the Tarot*[73] describes reversals for court cards, but doesn't mention them for the Major arcana. His reversals are not, for the most part, however the cards in negative aspects, and his reasoning for his interpretations are therefore hard to understand.

---

[73] (Waite 1910).

Example spreads (advanced interpretation)

Using the Rider Waite Smith Deck

The three-card spread

Question: A woman in her 30s wants to get married but her partner is resistant. She knows he loves her, so what is going on with him?

Left card, the past: 0—The Fool

As the Fool denotes someone without any experience, this is the first long-term relationship of the male partner, and possibly even his first sexual relationship. It felt adventurous to him to have a girlfriend and he was deeply attracted by the sense of mystery to the relationship. For her, he was a highly spontaneous and imaginative person, with a child-like charm, often very funny, sometimes without realising exactly why. He lived life in the moment and she loved experiencing the world through his eyes. Like a curious child he was seemingly interested in everything. Coming from this place, marriage may seem quite an alien concept to him. He doesn't make a lot of plans for the future. In his mind, he may be too young for marriage, or not understand why it might be important to her.

Middle card, the present: VI—The Lovers

Their romantic life is strong. The Lovers card is associated with the sign Gemini, and their relationship is very idealised, imaginative, spontaneous, entertaining and everchanging. The best approach to bringing her partner around to the idea of marriage would be to first reassure him that he won't lose his freedom, and that the wedding itself could be a creative exercise celebrating the union of their personalities. He will likely be put off by the idea of a conventional wedding, with a bride in white, a bland suit, in a church. He may become more excited if the wedding is a creative event, perhaps with more interesting costumes, humorous surprises or a bit of adventure.

Right card, the future: XIV—Temperance

The woman will get her wedding, but it will end up quite different to the one she has had in her head. Only by a lot of compromise, and allowing her lover to express himself, even when some of his ideas are spontaneous and seemingly haphazard will he comply. He likes to throw paint at the proverbial canvas and figure out what the picture represents afterwards. In this way she will probably need to have easy expectations of him in regards to the logistics of planning the wedding. On the other hand, he is a man with a lot of energy, and if she can manage planning the wedding with him, she too will find herself excited by the results. He will probably take some time to be fully on board with the wedding, perhaps seesawing on it for a while. They would be wise to find an experienced and appropriate wedding planner who can handle the practical matters to assure the success of the wedding. The Temperance card is an excellent one for marriage, showing two cups sharing waters, and pointing to balance.

The six-card spread

Question: A man in his late 30s is trying to take over the family business; his father says he wants to hand it to him but he won't get out of the way.

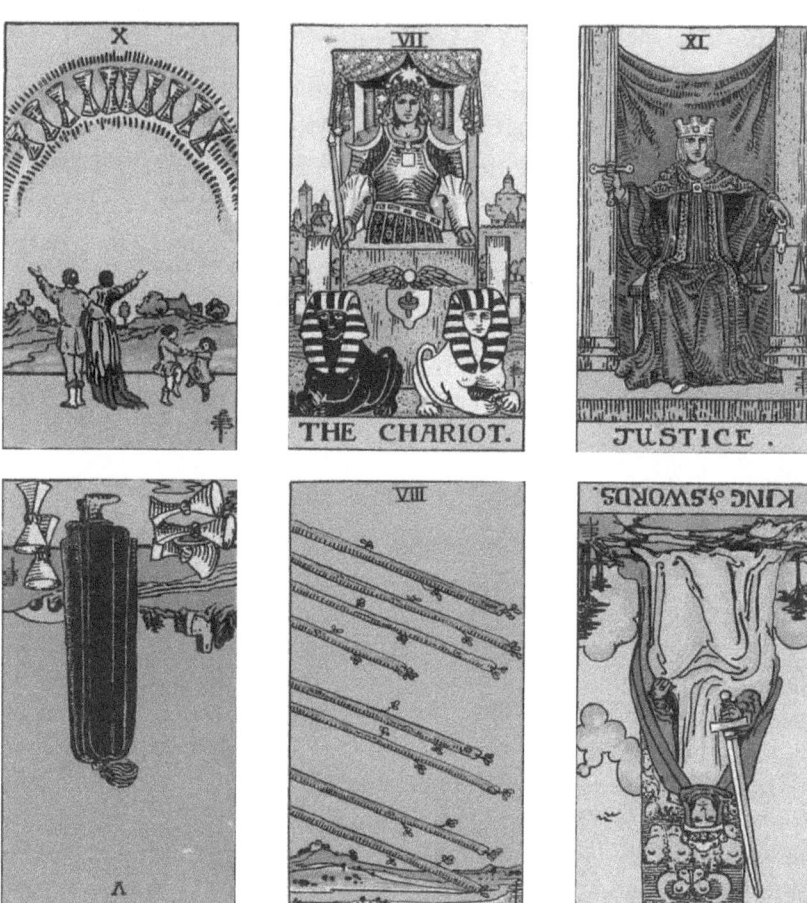

Left top Card, the past, what is known: Ten of Cups. The young man has fond memories of family life and his childhood. As the main financial provider and loving family man, his father provided a strong base and secure home life for him. Tens signify completion. The son saw the finished product of the father's work life, a kept home and childhood provided for him where he didn't have to worry about finances.

At home his father left work behind and focused on the family relationships, signified by Cups. In Kabbalah Ten is the number of the Sefirah, Malkut. This is the realm of the sensory world or the physical plane. Home life for the father was about provision and care, and served as his primary motivation to work. Implicit is that the son never went away with a clear idea of who his father was at work, or how difficult his father may have found his work. This bias, and the chance to live up to his father's role model is a driving and motivating factor for the son wanting to take over the business.

Left bottom card, an underlying reality: Five of Cups reversed. This card would normally be emotions getting in the way of progress. In this case the father, though he is an emotional man, had to put away his resentments, stresses and attachment to losses in order to live up to his ideals as both a boss and a father. This didn't mean that he didn't suffer internally. The father has worries both about revealing his emotional world to his son and also about whether his son is resilient enough to handle the stress. The son may find the father's emotional repression old fashioned.

Middle top, the present, what is known: The Chariot. The need to unify opposing forces towards a common goal is playing out in several ways. The business requires a constant management of workers, clients, expenses, profits and cashflow. The boss must be trusted by the staff for the business to work. This means a steady, diplomatic discipline. There is a risk if weakness or ineptitude is shown. The father has always been careful to hide his stress from his workers. The Chariot is associated with sign of Cancer, the crab, who separates its inner world from the outer world by the armour of its shell. The father has some anxiety now about showing his emotions about his work to his son. This must happen however in order that his son can understand the responsibility of the position. He must also show the son his work persona which the son never got to experience fully during a regular work day. As the boss, the father had to defend himself against opposition, and took it on himself to sign off on all major business decisions. Sometimes this meant acting out of intuition rather than in a calculated manner. The father, like the figure in the Chariot card, is a believer in acting on instinct and has some fear that this may be hard to teach and also that is may not be a trait which the son has inherited. He believes in a kind of 'magic touch'. The son might feel that this is not a particularly 'modern' or 'democratic' way to run a business. The father did not want to be slowed down by stopping to calculate every decision, even if that resulted in some trivial inefficiencies.

Middle bottom, an underlying reality: Eight of Wands. Swiftness, action and communication. Despite his stress, the father has prepared the business to be handed over. Fast action, hard work and initiative are required by the son. He must communicate clearly to all the staff and the clients, and this is best done by direct communication. The logistics need to be fully organised, and orders for parts fulfilled in order to avoid future shortages. The best way is to meet with all the site managers in person. If the son is ahead of schedule then the father will feel relieved.

Right top card, what is known: The future. Justice. The son will do okay if he leaves the past in the past, and listens to his father's 'case' diplomatically. He will need to accept a higher level of responsibility that he may realise. Being the boss is about balance (Justice, ruled by Libra), not about power. Being humble and setting his father's heart at ease is an important step in running the business. He will go a long way if he takes the initiative to settle all accounts, and make good on previous business relationships, even those that were based on 'spoken contracts' i.e. 'I'll scratch your back if you scratch mine' and 'gentleman's agreements'. A couple of the clients are still the friends of his father. Ultimately the son must settle for a pragmatic resolution rather than an idealistic one.

Right bottom card, an underlying reality: King of Swords reversed. The son is a much more rational actor than his father. His natural tendency is to try and understand everything and then act logically in response. In a business that is as complex as this one, and which relies so much on relationships with the workers and clients, this approach is not going to be possible. Similarly if the son is too distant, not seen enough in person, as is his tendency as an introvert.

Some tension is inevitable, and this personality difference with his father, not the workings of the business itself, will be the most difficult part of the change over. This will become most difficult when the father has fully retired.

There will be some tension from the workers for a period that 'things have changed around here'. This suggests that though the father may be an annoyance to the son, his concerns are real and the son has a big task ahead of him to keep the business running smoothly.

The Celtic Cross

Question: A young man has just finished high school, and is trying to decide to train in a trade, or if it's even worth trying. He asks what's the point of it all?

The cross

The middle top card, what you think is going on: Nine of Wands. The querent had a very hard time at school. He felt like he was often battling other students and may have been subject to bullying. Though he completed his school work and passed, he was left with resentments about education. Astrologically, the Nine of Wands is the Moon in Sagittarius. The young man has high idealised hopes for his future, and while school didn't live up to his expectations, his idealism also provided motivation to pull through the difficulties and uncertainties.

The middle underneath card (which is crossing it) is an underlying reality: Three of Wands. The querent is having trouble making a decision and stepping out into the unknown. Now the teenaged struggles of high school are over and if he goes to trade school, or university, he will find it very different. The initial difficulty is in making a decision, and this decision ought not to be coloured by his 'battles' in high school. He can leave that behind him, as depicted in the card. Every decision involves a sacrifice of what could have been, and there is no way to have it all. If he accepts this, his decision will be easier for him.

Astrologically, the Three of Wands is the Sun in Aries. Aries is a sign of individuality and the Sun is often representative of the self. For those of you who know a little more about astrology you may know that the Sun is exalted in that sign, which is to say, strengthened. The young man should accept that his choice is his own to make and that in this case, he doesn't need to factor in the concerns of others. He will feel better if he makes a decision fully under his own power, a first step towards reclaiming his own freedom and escaping his feelings about high school where her felt 'trapped'.

The left card is the past: Page of Pentacles. Despite his troubles with bullies, the young man's attitude to school work was commendable. When push came to shove he worked diligently on projects and exams, even when he felt out of his depth. Alchemically this card is 'earth of earth'. He works well in practical situations. A hands on trade may be very well suited to him. Part of his problems with school was a desire for a practical outcome to his studies. That oft-asked question of students; 'but what is this for?'

The top card is what is helping the situation: The World. An opportunity to get out and see the world would be great for him. The adult world is very different to school and choosing a path that broadens his horizons will help him. One thing that may work very well for him is spending some time working, especially in a practical trade, where he gets to move around. Perhaps deliveries or onsite work. He might consider working hard, saving some money and then travelling as an alternative to tertiary education.

The World is associated to Saturn. The young man will gain some self assurance if his hardworking efforts are accepted by an institution and older men. In Kabbalah the World card maps to the path from Yesod, the Sefirot of creation, communication and the moon, to Malkut, the Sefirot of the 'physical' (or sensory) realm. A job or trade making real things happen would suit him.

The bottom card is what is not helping the situation: Six of Wands. His school friends are in a state of celebration of their leaving school. Many of them feel nostalgic and excited. Our young man however is more keen to move on, leaving his school days far behind him and therefore feels at odds with the other school leavers, who revel in memories. It is a time of parties for them. This card is also Jupiter in Leo. A general feeling of good fortune that our querent feels apart from.

The right card is the future: The Devil. In the near future, the next few weeks, there is going to be a great letting loose, amongst his friends. I predict a lot of partying, with a lot of alcohol, tomfoolery, and perhaps drugs. While the other kids are partying in celebration our querent will find himself drinking to dampen his negative emotions. This will amount to difficulties with self-control and disenchantment with the group and his past education. To prevent this getting worse he might want to delay further education, and take a direct path into work, saving money and travelling to see the world. His time of debauchery and 'experimentation' might in the long run be important both to let off steam and also to gain some necessary emotional experience.

The Devil is also Capricorn. 'Necessary evils' in the light of a practical result. The young man should accept a less that perfect job for a time, in order to earn a little money.

The column

The bottom card of the column is what is motivating the querent: Knight of Swords. The young man has amongst his heroes, adventurous daredevils. Men who rush into adventure. Perhaps he grew up watching action films and reading adventure novels;—Knights of Swords, heroes that bravely rush in. Some travel and adventure on his own terms would serve him well. He needs to be able to express himself in terms of his own ego. A time of rebellion is ahead. He desires action.

The next card up represents the behaviour of people around the querent: Five of Wands. There is competition amongst his friends and comrades from high school. Most of them are going to university in order to compete for very similar goals. Our querent may want to avoid this in order not to return to the competitive and catty Nine of Wands environment of the first card. Five of Wands is Saturn in Leo. Saturn is in detriment in this sign, which causes tensions and perhaps depression around how one would like to be seen in the world. Leo is the 'performer', and Saturn tends to slow down all that it touches.

The second card from the top represents the hopes and/or fears of the querent: The Star. The querent wants a clear path towards perfection or an ideal that he is going to struggle to find from further education. Again the idea of travel to other countries and far off goals is clear. Once he has the money, a back-packing adventure governed by a 'star' and under his own terms, (the Knight of Swords), is in order.

The top card in the column is a conclusion card. Six of Cups. Nostalgia. Despite the down-trodden emotion expressed from his question, the querent is about to build some fond memories and enter a time of his life that he will be proud of in retrospect.

There is an intensity of experience to come (Sun in Scorpio) that will be formative for him.

One card pull

Though one card is usually not enough by itself for a full reading, sometimes the querent will have an additional quick question, especially after a primary reading. If you have already formed a rapport with them and feel 'in the zone', a one card pull can be useful.

Question: A woman who has just retired has always loved reading murder mysteries and wants to know whether is worth writing one herself.

Card: Knight of Wands. As wands is ambition, fire and desire, and the knight is a card of action, the Tarot says yes to expressing herself as a writer. If nothing else, she will enjoy the experience and scratch an itch to express herself that she had been putting off for some time. As the Knight of Wands is full of personality, she should go all out in expressing herself with her writing.

Using Crowley's Thoth Deck

The three-card spread

Question: A female high school student has gotten into trouble in school. She has fallen behind on school work. What can she do to save the semester?

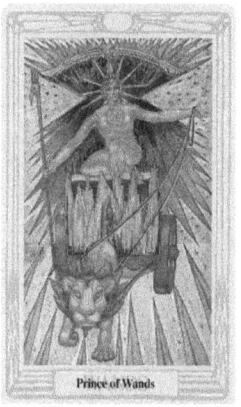  

Left card, the past: Prince of Wands (equivalent to Knight of Wands). The girl has fallen in with a very difficult friend. At first this friend appeared charming, confident, talented and exciting. The attention felt good. Over time this friend has become manipulative, bossy and unpredictable. It is very likely that this friend is a boy and that there is some romantic attraction from the querent. At times this 'friend' has had temper tantrums, first at people around them, but eventually he turned on the querent, and this has caused much mental upset. The card is attributed to 21° Cancer to 20° Leo, so this is a person who wears their dramatic personality(Leo) as a type of 'armour', like a crab, to defend their own insecurities.

The querent needs to know that the fiery source of this behaviour, though projected outwards comes from insecurities in this person, and that she would do well to learn to separate their tantrums from her own feelings of anxiety and guilt. If she is unable to do this then perhaps the friendship needs to end.

Middle card, the present: The Star. The querent has not found the support she needs at school, so she has looked elsewhere for guidance.

This has actually been a positive thing, despite the withdrawal from school work.

The loss of confidence in her circle of friends has led to a reassessment of what she cares about. She has realised that she is currently very different to her friends, and is especially interested in spirituality, which has lead her to having this Tarot reading. The Star represents a renewal of faith, especially in the face of difficulty. The cynicism and cattiness of some of the other teenagers is not serving her. I suspect she has been reading a lot of spiritual websites, books and perhaps podcasts or internet videos.

Her emotional well-being is as important as her school work. As she is young, and not a senior, she has a little time and can cut herself some slack. She ought to make sure she gets good enough grades to pass, but not to overwhelm herself. The interests she is building now will become lifelong pursuits while her grades will not haunt her forever. Crowley says that the path from Yesod to Netzach, to which this card is assigned, can be the act of getting ready to take a leap of faith. The querent is developing a belief system and values that are quite different from those held by her friends or taught to her at school.

Right card, the future: The Tower. The Tower represents a faith-breaking calamity or event that affects us as a group. In this case, because it is preceded by the Star, the shake-up that the querent has had, her self care, and her new found interests are actually preparations. While the querent currently feels like an outsider, there will be an event that shocks the school and shakes the faith of her fellow students. In the aftermath of this, the querent will be better prepared to cope than her friends, and may actually be able to support them. By dealing with her anxiety early on, she is ahead of the curve, ready to catch the wave. In the wake of this event academic troubles will seem somewhat diminished. I recommend that as long as she can pass there will be time to fix her academic record next year, her final year of high school.

When this happens she will find that the confidence that was attracting her to the Prince of Wands is now a quality that she can find in herself. Though the calamitous event will be a result of something negative, there is an opportunity in it for the querent to grow as a person.

The six-card spread

Question: A young man at university is playing competitive football. He likes playing on his team. However he says the coach is a 'prick' and is ruining his enjoyment of the game. Should he stay on this team or find another team?

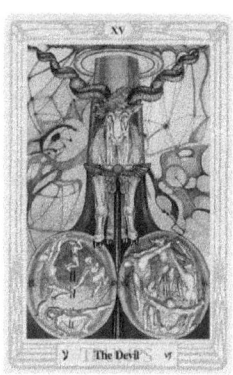

Left top card, the past, what is known: Queen of Swords. Due to the youth of the querent, who is about 19 years old, the Queen of Swords is most likely to be his mother. She is an intelligent and intellectual career woman with an intellectual job possibly as a teacher. She can be quite critical and the young man does not always get the support from her that he requires. In the past when he has complained about difficulties with his team, the coach or his studies, his mother has suggested that the important thing is to focus on playing 'the game' in order to 'get ahead'. She is not very concerned with his emotions and would like him to achieve his ambitions and to become motivated like her. As a result he often feels she is overly critical, though he admires her. He has stayed in the team longer than he might of otherwise at her insistence. This card is a combination of the signs Virgo and Libra, a combination of the peace-keeper and a critical, focused intellect.

Left bottom card, an underlying reality: The Devil. This is the card of corruption and toxic relationships. The coach is a deeply problematic person. He is obsessed with competition and often turns a blind eye to unfair play. He also harbours a secret, perhaps a drinking problem or something illegal. The young man's sense is correct, and his distrust of the coach will at some point become validated. If the young man was to quit the team now, perhaps causing his mother concern, there will come a time when the corruption of the coach is uncovered that the young man will become validated in this decision.

Middle top, the present what is known: The Hermit. This card represents a withdrawal in order to learn, especially the type of learning that involves direct personal experience in solitude. The young man is, at the moment, more suited to solitary activities. If he wants to remain in sports, a solitary sport such as running, marathon, shotput, etc., would suit him well. This is a compromise that ought to keep his sporting interest, nurture his talents and appease his mother's desire for his success.

The Hermit is also assigned to the sign of Virgo, an intellectual sign interested in details and technique. This makes a good connection with the Queen of Swords who rules 20° Virgo to 20° Libra. The querent and his mother may form a rapport over an interest in the details of technique in a new sport.

Middle bottom, an underlying reality: Queen of Wands. The querent's relationship to his mother is changing. She may be more ready to accept his change in sport that he realises, and she may already have heard some things about his bullying coach. He ought to discuss this with her. She may switch from being distant and critical to being more involved and he may start to see more of her own life's passion more directly.

Though she may never be a particularly emotionally supportive mother, she will defend him if she knows about the coach's behaviour. As her role changes to Queen of Wands she will become, more fiery, expressive and less distant to our querent.

The Queen of Wands rules 20° Pisces to 20° Aires. Though she may often live in a world of her own, she will put the full force of her ambition (Aries) behind defending her family (Pisces). In a sense she sees the son as an extension of herself. Though this can sometimes be trying for the youth who wants to express himself, she will take it personally if the coach is abusive to her son and defend him, as if the coach had offended her.

Right top card, the future, what is known: Five of Wands, Saturn in Leo. Crowley calls the card 'strife' and says that it can signify a proverbial volcanic eruption. Initially the coach will be angry and throw his weight around about the querent leaving the team. He will probably become verbally abusive. This may rub off on some of the young men in the team. However, the coach is exerting more authority than he possesses. He doesn't have power over the querent's decision, and it is likely that he is about to get in trouble with the university over concerns about his behaviour. The querent's mother, who is a persuasive woman, is ready to back him up in this regard if he properly explains the situation to her. If it is required, threatening to complain to the coach's boss will reign him in (Saturn's restricting effect). He is close to losing his job.

Right bottom card, the future, an underlying reality: Six of Wands, 'Victory'. The querent will be successful in his dealing with the coach with the support of his mother. The other team mates are more concerned than he realises and a successful confrontation with the coach, even if it involves his quitting the team will win their admiration. The Six of Wands is connected to Tiferet, the heart centre, which denotes connection to others. Although the immediate future will be unpleasant, the long-term outcome will be successful, the continued friendship of his team mates, a pursuit of a new sport talent, a closer relationship with his mother, and a development in in confidence in dealing with authority figures.

The Celtic Cross (with reversals)

Question: A woman in her late 30s is getting the sense that she and her partner are drifting apart, she asks if her fear is based on something happening with him, or if it is unfounded.

The cross

The middle top card, what you think is going on: The Fool. Sometimes when people ask a question like 'what is going on with my partner?' they already have a fair idea, or some suspicions, in this case however, the querent really does have no idea. As the predecessor to action, sometimes the Fool represents a total blank slate. This suggests that we can rule out the common suspicions. The husband is unlikely to be angry, to be having an affair, to have fallen out of love, etc. The probable reason for this, is that the querent is very intuitive, and has predicted somehow that something is about to happen that perhaps hasn't happened yet.

The Fool is assigned to the Sefirah of Keter, which is pre-manifestation. Though some attribute the Keter to Uranus, a planet of change and disruption, I prefer to consider it the 'Primum Mobile', or 'first action'. That is, it is the state of potential just before concept or form. Something is about to happen, but it hasn't taken any form yet. Because of this, asking the husband what is going on with him is probably going to produce a shrug or a response such as: 'nothing'. However, this won't be the case soon. Something is about to change.

The Fool is often an inversion of values. The husband is likely to do something that is very out of character. The Fool can be intoxication or foolish behaviour. Though the husband is normally controlled, predictable and sober, he might become for a short period, unpredictable, or drunk and/or do something strange and normally out of character for him. The outcome of this will be ambiguous. Neither ill-intended nor positive. He might not even understand or be able to explain it.

The middle underneath card (which is crossing it) is an underlying reality: Prince of Swords (equivalent to a Knight of Swords) reversed. While the husband is not able to currently explain what is going on, there is a discomfort growing inside of him. He has become bored of doing 'the right thing'. He is about to act out, thought this is out of character for him.

A rebellion will occur, not particularly triggered by any one thing. A kind of 'fuck it' energy. When he does act out, it will be in a sudden dramatic way. A fight with another man, a gamble, a sudden unpredictable act. Because this card is reversed this action will immediately be blocked, thus making the husband appear a 'fool' to his wife. Perhaps he will lose the fight, lose the bet, crash the car while speeding. In one way or another the lightning bolt of energy will take its path to ground.

The card is attributed from 20° Capricorn to 20° Aquarius. Capricorn is conservative values and pragmatism, making a shift towards the change and unpredictability of Aquarius. Because this is reversed. The energy will be blocked. The action will probably be regretted.

The left card is the past: Seven of Discs (pentacles) 'Failure', reversed. The husband has been living steadily, without change for a long time. No great successes, no great failures. For some reason, perhaps ennui (existential boredom), he sees this as a negative thing.

The top card is what is helping the situation: Nine of Discs (pentacles) 'Gain'. The husband is going to come into some money. I predict a bonus or a raise at work. Because of boredom at always towing the line, this will lead him towards talking a gamble that will not go in his favour. Leading to him becoming, temporarily, a 'Fool' in the eyes of his wife, the querent. In this case the 'helping' the situation is not what is necessarily 'good' about the situation, but what is allowing it to take place.

The bottom card is what is not helping the situation: Eight of Discs. 'Prudence'. The sudden windfall is going to push him out of his boredom towards 'blowing off some steam'. This will lead him into the trouble. He has, for a long time been hardworking, always saving for a rainy day. Perhaps a workaholic. He has been ignoring some mental distress that has been building up and is about to 'flash'.

The card is assigned to Sun in Virgo. This is a focus on details and methodical thinking and problem-solving. This pertains to the type of work he does. Someone who has to do things by the book. Things have become too routine. This card is also Earth in Hod. Hod is the Sefirah of getting stuff done. Earth in this case is a blockage, or such a focus on the material, that the soul feels neglected.

The right card is the future: Six of Discs reversed. 'Success'. This card is an inversion of the 'failure card' This time we have 'success', only it is reversed. This suggests that whatever was gained will be taken away again. What should have worked will stop working. The husband is heading for a change. This card is assigned to the Moon in Taurus. Taurus the homely bull is appeased by fine things. In this case the fine things will be taken away and the good mood will go with it.

The card is also Earth in Tiferet. The manifestation of the heart's desire. Again, because it is reversed, the husband will lose that which he desired. Normally a card of good fortune, he will likely receive some money then immediately lose it.

The column

The bottom card of the column is what is motivating the querent: Five of Discs. 'Worry'. The worry is the wife's. She is very perceptive and has somehow picked up on a misfortune before it has happened. It is also 'worry' in the sense of gnawing away at something. This applies more to the husband. Crowley says of this card 'The economic system has broken down'. It would be wise for the wife to allow her husband his embarrassed foolery, understanding it as an out-of-character moment. The windfall should have been positive but has by the fifth Sefirah, Gevurah became restricted or blocked.

The card is Mercury in Taurus. A stalemate. Mercury wants to move, but the stubborn bull has blocked the flow.

The next card up represents the behaviour of people around the querent in regards to the situation: Four of Discs. 'Power'. The home life and family of the husband and wife have been very stable. This is the source of the problem. Boredom for the husband. The 'imp of the perverse' within him wants to take a risk to make things interesting. Stability has been achieved but all flow has stopped. The husband thinks 'why don't I use my money for once'. The type event where one buys a beautiful sports car, and then crashes is on the ride home. This card is Earth in Chesed. A blocked flow.

The second card from the top represents the hopes and/or fears of the querent: The Magus (magician) reversed. The magician knows what he is doing and is a master of his actions. Reversed he is out of control, perhaps even maniacal. This card is 'talking' to the Fool card from the beginning of the reading. The magician is normally the first spark of action towards form. In this case the husband will act out and the result will, instead of order, which is typical of the magician, be a mess. This will become the fear of the wife.

The top card in the column is a finality, or conclusion card: Three of Discs 'Works'. Mars becomes exhalted in Capricorn, energy moves towards pragmatism. After his foolish outburst, the husband will return to form. This will lead to better success at work, perhaps a raise. Perhaps the raise is what caused the outburst in the first place. In any case the foolish act will not be lasting nor will it have a lasting effect.

As a couple the husband and wife, might try and spice up their marriage by living in the moment now and then. Maybe go on holidays or dates. This could really improve their home life and prevent future 'foolish' moments.

One card pull

Question: A young woman asks: 'Do you mind pulling a card for me about money. My budget is tight, is it worth it looking for a part time job or should I just save money'.

Card: Ten of Wands, 'Oppression'. As ten is a finality card, a desire or dream is dashed. Any effort will be blocked resulting in exhaustion if force is continued. Therefore the querent will not receive a job and it would be better to wait. She ought to reduce spending, and put efforts that cost money on hold, until the situation clears and opportunities present themselves. Saturn in Sagittarius means this is a bad time for big dreams.

The history of Tarot

Paper-making and printing

The history of Tarot and card games starts with the invention of paper. While paper has predecessors in papyrus and parchment it replaced both by being easier and cheaper to manufacture in bulk, and capable of producing a more versatile range of products.

Official Chinese history puts the invention of paper at 105 CE, though there was further development over time, and some argue for an earlier date, with other earlier types of paper existing since as far back as 300 BCE. The inventor is said to have been Cai Lun (蔡伦), a eunuch of the Han court. His invention replaced bamboo slips as the primary media for record keeping in the Han Dynasty Court, and was soon adopted widely.

Woodblock printing soon followed, with still-existing artefacts dating as far back as 220 CE. This provided the necessary technology for playing cards.

The Kuei T'ien Lu, a book of anecdotes written in the eleventh century by the historian Ou-yang Hsiu (歐陽脩), places the invention of playing cards in the middle of the T'ang dynasty (618–906), a similar time as the first printed books in

Figure 1. Bamboo Slips from Shanghai Museum dated 300 BCE.

the ninth century. The Chinese word for playing cards is pái (牌), which is also used for gaming tiles including domino tiles and domino cards. These are the predecessor to playing cards as we recognise them today.

The earliest forms of playing cards and dominoes were based on pairs of dice, where the numbers were drawn from a deck of domino tiles rather than being rolled. It appears that these games were used for gambling and divination via numerology. Over time the paper cards became more elaborate while the tiles, often made of expensive materials such as ivory remained simpler.

The game Mahjong, is an evolution of these original simpler domino type tiles. For the first 600 years, paper-making was a Chinese monopoly. It is said that later when Samarkland (in present day Uzbekistan), was conquered by Arabs in the battle of Talas in 751 CE, two Chinese prisoners taught the Arabs the secret and this product spread along the silk road to the Mediterranean. Even if this tale is inaccurate, we know that paper was being manufactured in Samarkland from around this time.

By the ninth century, we have the first extant complete printed book containing a date, This is the Diamond Sutra, a Mahāyāna Buddhist text, translated into Chinese from Sanskrit. By the tenth century, printing had taken off, with up to 400,000 copies printed of some pictures and texts including sutras and the Confucian classics. A skilled printer of this time was able to print up to 2,000 double-page sheets per day. A huge advance on hand-copied documents.

Because they had adopted the Chinese logograms, printing quickly spread to Korea and Japan. From here it spread to Turpan and Vietnam, where it was adapted for their own scripts. Now proven internationally, the technology was picked up in Persia and Russia.

The guarded secret of paper-making eluded the West until the Muslim occupation of Spain from around 711 CE—known as the caliphate Al-Andalus. From here the secret of paper was eventually leaked to the rest of Europe starting around 1238 CE when Christians conquered some of the Muslim territories. Italy had its earliest paper factory at Fabriano about 1276 CE and became a centre for trade.

Block printing, was first used in Europe to print cloth by 1300 CE, but as paper became more widely available in the early 1400s CE the technique was transferred to the paper industry. By this time printed cards became available in Europe and were popular from the 1425 CE onwards. The Gutenberg Bible of 1455 CE was the first mass-produced book in Europe using moveable type the next breakthrough in printing technology.

Paper money

As the originators of paper, the Chinese were also the first with a paper currency. These began as 'Promissory notes' issued by merchants; receipts of deposits created in order to reduce the amount of haulage required to deposit or bank heavy coins. These were also an early form of bank account. The Chinese used coins that were round with a rectangular hole in the middle. These are still common today, and they allow the coins to be strung together for convenience.

By the eleventh century in the Song Dynasty, these promissory notes had evolved into true paper money, called 'jiaozi'. The story goes that in 960 CE a copper shortage forced the government to issue the first paper currency, with the idea being that the recipient would be able to redeem these notes for the more familiar copper coins once they became available. Over time people became used to paper currency being used alongside coins and soon the convenience of paper money caused these notes to be preferred by merchants and buyers. They were lighter, took up less space and were easier to defend and hide. The central government soon created a monopoly for the printing of these notes using woodblocks.

Around 1150 CE, the Knights Templar would issue notes to pilgrims travelling to and from the Holy Land. Pilgrims would deposit valuables with a local Templar preceptory before embarking on the journey and receive a document indicating the value of their deposit. They would then use that document upon arrival in the Holy Land to receive funds from the treasury of equal value. This helped prevent expensive robberies by organised bandits along the roads.

Play money and suits

With the popularity of gambling games, 'play money' soon appeared so that people could practice without having to lose their real currency. It is likely, as put forth by the British Sinologist William Henry Wilkinson (1858–1930), that this play money holds the origin of the first playing card suits.

One of the first of these types of games we know of is Madiao, a trick-taking game (like the later Tarot games) from the Ming Dynasty (1368–1644). The fifteenth-century scholar Lu Rong 陆容 described it as being played with 38 'money cards' divided into four suits:

- One to nine of 'coins'.
- One to nine of 'strings of coins' (counting as 1,000 coins each).
- One to nine in myriads (groups of 10,000 coins).
- One to eleven in tens of myriads (groups of 100,000 coins).

Over time, the depictions of strings of coins became simplified and started to be considered 'Sticks', and later, 'Wands'.

Mamluk Cards

By the eleventh century, playing cards came into Egypt. In the Benaki Museum and the Keir Collection, they still have fragments of the oldest surviving cards in the world, dated to the twelfth and thirteenth centuries.

The term 'Mamluk' originally revered to slaves, especially foreigners from Central and Eastern Europe, Persia, the Caucacus and Turkey. Over time the term became associated with indentured soldiers, including a class of knights in Egypt. These came to be a powerful class in their own right, though controlled by Arab rulers.

Card games were popular in Egypt and were associated with the Mamluks. These decks are often beautifully ornate and, derived as they were from Chinese decks, the four suits had evolved from the coins and strings of coins, to the, for us, more familiar Sticks, cups, swords and coins.

European playing cards

By the late 1300s playing cards, including gambling games, had spread to Europe, first to Spain via the Muslims. By 1380 they were widespread from Switzerland, to Italy, to France. Playing cards are mentioned in documents from around this time including calls to ban them due to the perceived immorality of the gambling habit.

The term 'Ace' itself comes from a dice player's term in the Anglo-Norman language, which is itself derived from the Latin 'as' (the smallest unit of coinage).

Educational decks and 'luxury cards'

While the minor arcana in the Tarot are simply an evolution from one type of playing card deck, the Major arcana have a separate origin from educational decks and 'luxury cards'.

Originally called *trionfi*, the Italian word for 'triumph', this evolved into the English word 'trump'. There seems to be a common origin with the Italian 'Trionfo', a traditional fancy dress processional parade given for victorious generals, or later simply for festivals similar to modern Christmas parades.

Like Christmas parades these processions included floats: Dressed up carts depicting scenes from cultural stories, pop culture, mythology and religion, as well as military chariots and other vehicles. Over time this parade trope was extended into other types of art, painting, and eventually cards.

Some commonly depicted 'triumphs' were:

- Personified virtues (and sometimes vices). For example, the seven heavenly virtues and the seven deadly sins.
- Personifications of the four classical elements: Air, Water, Fire, Earth.
- Allegorical categories such as Love, Chastity, Death, Temperance, Justice, Strength and Fame.
- Societal figures such as 'the Pope' and the 'Popess' and the Emperor and the Empress.
- Astrological figures such as the seven classical planets, and the signs of the zodiac.

Educational decks could have a large variety of themes, but as well as religious tropes, cards with figures from history or types of birds have been found.

Luxury cards were often highly ornate commissions from nobles, depicting family members in hunting scenes or other interests of the patron. Like a lot of art works, these were to be displayed as prestige items to impress upon visitors to the noble household. Sometimes entire playing card decks, including Tarot were created such as the Visconti-Sforza and Sola Busca decks from the fifteenth century. These luxury decks were hand painted rather than the cheaper printed cards made for public use.

Over time these decks which usually amounted to between 16 and 40 cards were included in some card games with special rules, becoming 'Trumps', cards that were allowed to usurp the rules of the minors. The Joker cards in the standard modern 'French' playing card decks are an example of the trump concept. The Tarot family of games expanded this with the 22 Trumps that diviners call the Major arcana.

Tarot card games

These are a family of games that are still played in some countries today, especially France, Germany, Italy, Austria, Slovenia Switzerland and Canada. They are 'trick-taking' games, which centre around a series of playing rounds, called tricks. Each trick ends with a winning play and the winner of the game is either the player who wins the most tricks or who scores the highest, with often intricate scoring rules determined by the value of the cards taken or left in the hand.

Games in the 'Tarot' family are known as Tarot, Tarock, Tarocchi and similar names. Rules are highly varied by region but the decks are generally of the 78 card type with 21 Trumps, and an additional Fool card of which we are familiar. In the French the Fool is often called 'the Excuse', and it variously is played in lieu of using up a trump, or else acts as the strongest trump. Tarot games are amongst the oldest European card games that are still played.

While many fortune-telling decks are not suitable for card games, the Marseilles deck from which most fortune-telling decks derive, is an example of a deck that is still suitable for both gaming and divination.

Despite the symbolism of the 'Trumps' (Major arcana), the numbers on these cards are the only thing that matters in modern Tarot card games. The particular pictures on the cards do not affect gameplay and are instead a remnant of the aforementioned educational 'triumph' decks. While in the English-speaking world, we are most familiar with the non-Tarot 56-card French deck, with the four suits: Diamonds, Clubs, Hearts, and Spades, there are actually many European decks with different suits, though there are normally four.[74] The Tarot suits: Wands (or Sticks), Cups, Swords and Coins (or Pentacles/Discs) are actually the oldest European playing card suits, dating back to the Egyptian Mamluk cards discussed earlier. These are still used in some French, Italian and Spanish playing decks today.

Our names for the standard English playing card suits are actually a little muddled and show that while we adopted the French suit system we used to have a different one. Diamonds make sense but are referred to as 'Tiles' in French. Hearts are Hearts, but Clubs are called 'clovers'

---

[74] There are actually rare decks, including Tarot decks, with up to six suits.

in French and this is clearly what they depict. 'Clubs' must be a hangover from the older suit which in Tarot we call 'Wands', but has in the past been called 'Clubs' or 'Sticks' and dates back to the aforementioned Chinese strings of coins. 'Spades' makes some sense for the shape, but in French they are called 'Pikes' and this makes it more clear that they were once weapons, equivalent to 'Swords'.

Modern Tarot gaming decks sometimes adopt the French suits rather than older ones, and the images on the Trumps vary enormously.

Legendary origins of Tarot from the Egyptians

Before the deciphering of the Rosetta stone in 1822 by the Frenchman, Jean-François Champollion, nobody had had access to the meanings of the Egyptian hieroglyphs since the fifth century CE. In this gulf of comprehension, many popular ideas arose about what the Egyptians, who clearly had impressive architecture and artefacts, might have known. Especially in light of the fact that the original ancient Greek philosophers Thales and Pythagoras claimed to have been trained in Egypt (and also Persia). The hieroglyphs[75] became legendary and were considered by many to be magical pictures that granted powers, and the secrets of the universe.

Renaissance thinkers like Athanasius Kircher (1602–1680) took the mystery of the Hieroglyphs and used it as a platform to syncretise spiritual teachings from a large variety of cultures, with a mission to describe the 'Prisca-Theologia', the idea that a single original theology, given by God to human beings, exists in all cultures for those who are learnt enough to decipher it. This later morphed into the similar concept of 'the perennial philosophy' which is at the core of the Western occult tradition. Claiming to be able to decipher the hieroglyphs, Kircher projected onto them nearly the entirety of Eurasian philosophy, theology, magic, philology and philosophy as he understood them.

The most legendary figure representing the perennial philosophy was Hermes Trismegistus, who was believed by many occultists to have originally been an Egyptian priest (or a god) and the key to the wisdom that produced the Greek philosophers.

---

[75] The term 'hieroglyph' itself comes from the Greek for 'sacred carving'.

Gébelin and Mellet

Taking the perennial philosophy as inspiration, the French-Swiss Protestant clergyman and occultist Antoine Court was the first to put forward the idea that the Tarot was a lost 'book' of Egyptian origin in his 1781 work *Le Monde primitif* (The Primitive World) written under the pseudonym 'Court de Gébelin'. The Tarot section of this book took the form of an essay which was credited to one Comte de Mellet. Also included was the idea that 'Gypsies' were a lost Egyptian tribe holding secrets of ancient Egyptian wisdom.

Neither de Gébelin nor Comte de Mellet wrote a complete manual on the reading of the cards. They were however the first to assign the Major Arcana to the letters of the Hebrew alphabet, paving the way for later correspondences with Kabbalah.

Etteilla

In 1785, Jean-Baptiste Alliette, who wrote under the pen name 'Etteilla' (his surname spelled backwards), wrote an answer to Court de Gébelin: *Manière de se récréer avec le jeu de cartes nommées Tarots* (How to Entertain Yourself With the Deck of Cards Called Tarot). This was the world's first Tarot manual and is therefore as far as we know the source for much of modern Tarot reading. In the book, Etteilla claimed that he had been introduced to the art of cartomancy in 1751, long before Court de Gobelin's work, though we have no way to verify this. Etteilla later started a correspondence course for Tarot reading.

Etteilla proposed correspondences between the Tarot, astrology, the four classical elements and the four humours. He was also the first to issue a revised Tarot deck specifically designed for occult purposes. As far as we know he is the first to describe the divinatory meaning of the pip cards, the first to use reversed cards in readings and the first to use the term 'cartomancy'.

Regardless of who came up with the idea first, these writers said that Tarot constituted a lost 'Book of Thoth', named for the Egyptian god of writing, scribes, magic and communication who had been a focal point of Western mysticism since the Hermetic Corpus, a group of writings, beginning in the third century BCE, that syncretised the Greek god Hermes and the Egyptian Thoth into the legendary figure of 'Hermes Trismegistus'.

Later, Aleister Crowley, the most famous and infamous of the Victorian occultists ran with the idea of 'the Thoth Tarot'; and created his own deck of the same name with the artist Lady Frida Harris (who had also commissioned the work) and his accompanying *Book of Thoth (Egyptian Tarot)*, a Tarot manual for his deck and this time an actual book. Although he was inspired by his idea, Crowley had nothing good to say about Etteilla who he referred to as a 'grotesque barber'.[76] Despite the charm of the idea, there is no historical evidence that the Tarot has any link to Ancient Egypt.

Legendary origins from the Romani

In his 1889 book, *Le Tarot des Bohémiens* (The Tarot of the Bohemians), the French occult writer, Gérard Encausse, writing as 'Papus' put forth the idea that the Tarot was brought to Europe by the Romani. At the time it was still thought by many that this ethnic group were a lost tribe of wandering Egyptians, the origin of the word 'Gypsy'. To Papus they were custodians of an ancient Egyptian lore which he said, like Athanasius Kircher before him, was the source of all Western wisdom.

We now know that the Romani are an Indo-Aryan people from India, and that their language is a descendant, like many other Indian languages, from Sanskrit. However, to this day the stereotype of the fortune-teller, especially that of a Gypsy woman reading cards, palms or scrying from a crystal ball remains, and there exists an entire subculture of people, who identify as 'Gypsies' without having any actual Romani lineage. In pop culture, Stevie Nick's song 'Gypsy' and Jimi Hendrix's album *Band of Gypsys* are prominent examples, as are a preponderance of 'Gypsy' Tarot decks, and 'New Age' or magic shops called 'Gypsys' or similar. Despite the fact that the Romani people are not Egyptian, nor were they the originators of Tarot reading, fortune-telling and magic are a real part of Romani tradition.

Legendary origins from Kabbalah

There is one version of the Prisca-Theologia, centring around Kabbalah, which comes from a Jewish legend in which Adam was the first Kabbalist, having been taught the 'language of creation' directly

---

[76] Page 210 (Crowley 1944).

from God. Renaissance writers such as Pico della Mirandola and Reuchlin took this idea and added to it that Jewish patriarchs such as Moses may have taught Kabbalah to the Greeks, especially Pythagoras.

This idea that Kabbalah was a focal point for the origin of Western Theology, was picked up by Éliphas Lévi, who identified the Tarot as a lost book of Kabbalah, especially focusing on the numerology of the 22 Major Arcana, which he laid out in correspondence with the 22 paths on the Sefirot, or Kabbalistic 'Tree of Life'. He also attributed the ten Sefirot themselves to the minor cards numbered one to ten.

While again unhistorical, the Tarot has been associated with the Kabbalah ever since, with the Golden Dawn using both the Sefirot and the Tarot as a central part of their teachings and for the hierarchy of their grade system,[77] which was also influenced by freemasonry. As Moses had an Egyptian name, and was said, in the Bible, to have been raised by an Egyptian princess, there are many legends that depict him as a spiritual teacher who understood both the Egyptian and the Hebrew mysteries.

Many if not most magical systems start with a legend like this. As I regard Tarot as a creative exercise rather than an objective one I have included the Kabbalitic associations, with the value that, if it gives results, it has magical value. Despite this, just like the other legends, there is no evidence that Tarot had any link with the Kabbalah before Lévi's publication of *Dogme et Rituel de la Haute Magie* around 1856.

---

[77] The Golden Dawn grade system was taken from the German masonic 'Orden des Gold- und Rosenkreutz' (Order of the Gold and Rosy Cross). This order was founded in the 1750s by the Freemason and alchemist Hermann Fictuld.

The evolution of Tarot decks, and Tarot Reading

Visconti Sforza Tarot

These are a collection of approximately 15 incomplete decks from the late fifteenth century that constitute the oldest existing Tarot decks. They are held in various museums and private collections around the world.

By this period we have the 78 card format we are now familiar with, Four suits numbered from one to ten with four court cards each, as well as the 22 Trumps. These Tarot decks were commissioned by the Duke of Milan, Filippo Maria Visconti or by his successor Francesco Sforza. The most complete deck was painted by the renowned Renaissance painter Bonifacio Bembo (born 1420 CE) and is now known as the Pierpont Morgan Bergamo deck. This is missing only the Devil, the Tower, the Three of Swords, and the Knight of Coins. There are several recreated Visconti decks in print which fill these missing cards with modern images, in a similar style, usually inspired by Tarot de Marseilles. In the original deck, six of the cards seem to have been painted by someone else perhaps as replacements for lost cards, but do not divert from the original style.

The three most famous Visconti-Sforza decks are as follows:

Pierpont Morgan Bergamo

This is the deck described above.

Cary-Yale Visconti

This is thought to originally be an 86-card deck of which only 67 cards still exist. Most interesting are the 24 Court Cards which include both male and female knights and pages. This deck is also believed to have been painted by Bonifacio Bembo and is held at Yale University.

Brera-Brambilla

Named after the man who purchased them in 1900 in Venice this is a set of ornate gilded cards of which only 48 still exist. They were commissioned by Francesco Sforza in 1463 and were most likely painted by Bembo.

Sola Busca

This is not only the oldest complete Tarot deck still in existence, created in the 1470s or 1480s, but also the oldest deck with scenes depicted on every card, including the minors, a feature only usually found in Rider Waite Smith and derived decks, which were inspired by the Sola Busca.

While the number and court cards follow the format we are familiar with, the 22 Trumps feature historical Roman rulers, military generals (including Alexander the Great) and figures from the Bible, not found in any other deck. It is clear from the luxury and condition of these cards that they were intended as an art piece and not used for playing games. Following the military theme, the 'coins' are depicted as shields, the 'batons' as ballista missiles (a type of enormous artillery crossbow), and the 'cups' as urns, perhaps those used for holy water.

Tarot de Marseilles

Tarot of Marseilles is a collection of decks of a consistent style which were initially created between the seventeenth and eighteenth centuries. The term is retroactive, first being applied, as far as we know, in 1856 by the French card historian Romain Merlin. These decks remain one of the most popular types for Tarot readers today and are the template from which most other fortune-telling Tarot decks evolved. Despite this, they still function as a set of playing cards, and for this reason, mark the point at the crossroads where card games separated from fortune-telling.

By the early 1500s, standard playing cards had gone through a stylistic change. The original four French suits, Diamonds (or Tiles), Hearts, Spades (or Pikes), and Clubs (or Clovers) had become standard as well as the 52 card format.

Tarot card gaming decks bucked this trend by sticking with the 78 card format and the original 'Mamluk' suits of Sticks, Cups, Swords and Coins. The name of the games using the Tarot deck changed to Tarocchi, Tarock or Tarot, to distinguish it from a popular game of 'Triumphs' played with a regular playing card deck. While various regional Tarot decks emerged, such as a smaller 62-card Bolognese deck and the expanded 97-card Minchiate deck, the Tarot de Marseilles, a French version of an older Milanese deck became the most popular deck for Tarot gaming.

Over time, with improved printing technologies and public fervour for card games, card-making became an industry with Tarot becoming mass-produced in France, Italy and Spain. The Tarot de Marseilles imagery, in one form or another, has been around since at least 1500. The first Marseilles deck that we have evidence for was printed in 1650 by the Parisian card printer Jean Noblet. This had only very minor differences to the Marseilles Decks still printed today.

The first 'modern' Marseilles deck that we know of was printed by Pierre Madenie of Dijon in 1709. Today Marseilles decks come from the 1760 Conver de Marseilles deck, which was copied from a 1736 Chosson de Marseilles deck which in turn was based upon the type of which Pierre Madenie is a specimen.

Eventually Tarot/Tarocchi gamers largely dropped the Marseilles deck in favour of new, more decorative, designs, with clearer numbering and often French suits, while an emerging group of cartomancers, deep in a French occult revival stuck with the Marseilles Deck. These esoteric groups centring around occult and Rosicrucian societies based on freemasonry developed the lore that the Tarot de Marseilles contained a secret occult symbolism described variously as Egyptian or Kabbalistic.

It is in these groups that the correspondences with astrology, and Kabbalah were created.

Casanova

Giacomo Girolamo Casanova (1725–1798), was a writer, adventurer, libertine, musician, gambler and magician, whose immense memoirs offer us one of the most authentic sources of information about European life and culture in the eighteenth century. Of interest to us, is the first historical mention of fortune-telling with cards.

He talks of a 14-year-old female Russian serf slave he owned and called Zaira, who would read cards.

> If it had not been for her furious jealousy and her blind confidence in fortune-telling by cards, which she consulted every day, Zaira would have been a paragon among women, and I should never have left her.
>
> I got home, and, fortunately for myself, escaped the bottle which Zaira flung at my head, and which would infallibly have killed

me if it had hit me. She threw herself on to the ground and began to strike it with her forehead. I thought she had gone mad, and wondered whether I had better call for assistance; but she became quiet enough to call me assassin and traitor, with all the other abusive epithets that she could remember. To convict me of my crime *she shewed me 25 cards, placed in order, and on them she displayed the various enormities of which I had been guilty.*[78]

Casanova also is credited with inventing the Lottery.

Tarocco Bolognese

The Tarocco Bolognese, a 62-card deck, is the earliest Tarot deck known to be used for cartomancy. It was developed to play the game Tarocchini. Bolognese cartomancers have always used the same deck as card gamers and do not make the same occult associations to the deck as later Tarot readers do.

Etteilla's Decks

Etteilla's original methods used a shortened 'Piquet deck' of 32 playing cards, which was popular in France. This deck includes only Aces, sevens, eights, nines, tens, Jack, Queen and King in each suit.

In 1788 Etteilla formed the *'Société des Interprètes du Livre de Thot'*, a society for Tarot readers. Later, in 1789, he published his own 78 card Tarot deck, called *Livre de Thoth, ou le grand jeu des 78 tarots egyptiens* (Book of Thoth, or the Great Game of the 78 Egyptian Tarot Cards). This was the first ever deck which was specially designed for divination, with reversed meanings clearly printed on each card. This deck is clearly a Tarot deck, though it has not proved influential in its design compared to Marseilles decks, and is quite a departure for those used to Marseilles, Rider Waite Smith or Crowley decks.

While only a few of these original cards remain, one of his students, Melchior Montmignon D'Odoucet, published a completely revised 'Grand Etteilla' deck in 1804. Later a third version of the Etteilla deck was published in 1840 by Julia Orsini, along with her own manual for the cards, *Le Grand Etteilla, ou l'Art de tirer les cartes*.

---

[78] Chapter XX (Casanova 1798; Machen 1894).

Éliphas Lévi

Alphonse Louis Constant (1810–1875), was a French occult author who wrote more than 20 books on magic, Kabbalah, and esotericism under the pseudonym Éliphas Lévi Zahed. More than anyone else, because of his influence, he is responsible for making the Tarot a central part of occultism. After a career as a Catholic Deacon, and shortly before being ordained as a priest, he left, perhaps in a crisis of faith and worked as a tutor in Paris. It was around this time that he met and became a follower of Simon Ganneau, a mystic, sculptor, socialist, feminist and occultist who preached androgyny both of the individual and of God and who presented himself as an androgynous prophet, wearing long hair and a beard and a mixture of men's and women's clothing. At the age of around 40 in 1850, Lévi had a spiritual awakening and dedicated himself to studying occultism, especially the Kabbalah. Over the next few years, he published his most famous three books, *Dogme et Rituel de la Haute Magie* (*The Doctrine and Ritual of High Magic*) in 1854–1856, *Histoire de la magie* (*The History of Magic*) in 1860 and *La clef des grands mystères* (*The Key to the Great Mysteries*) in 1861. These works made him perhaps the most renowned occultist in Europe in his era.

Lévi took Etteilla's theory and methods of Tarot reading and reorganised them to confirm his understanding of Kabbalah. More than any other figure, Lévi is responsible for Tarot's inclusion into high magic, and it is his correspondences to the Hebrew alphabet, and the paths on the Kabbalistic Tree of Life diagram, that were taken up by the Golden Dawn and then by Aleister Crowley, who decided that he was the reincarnation of Lévi (being born in the same year that Lévi died), undoubtedly in order to add gravitas to his own reputation. Lévi accepted Court de Gébelin and Etteilla's claims that the Tarot was a hidden 'book' of ancient Egyptian wisdom. He rejected Etteilla's own Tarot deck designs, however, instead using and reinterpreting the Tarot de Marseilles. He called it 'The Book of Hermes' and claimed that it had existed in some form since before the time of Moses, as a universal key of wisdom, combining Egyptian spirituality, Hermeticism, Kabbalah, Christianity and high magic.

Lévi also inspired the formation of the Hermetic Order of the Golden Dawn. Lévi was himself a Rosicrucian freemason initiated on 14 March 1861 in the Grand Orient de France lodge La Rose du Parfait Silence at the Orient of Paris. In 1854 Lévi made a trip to London where he caused a stir amongst the English occult revivalists. With his reputation preceding him, he was asked to perform tricks and miracles. Eventually, he found himself obliging in a ritual where he reported summoning the phantom of Apollonius of Tyana in the magical parlour of a lady occultist. Apparently, the results of the experiment spooked Lévi enough that he swore off ever performing necromancy again.[79]

In 1861, Kenneth R.H. Mackenzie, a Rosicrucian and future founder of the Golden Dawn travelled to Paris to meet Lévi allowing him to claim a connection to the French occult tradition which had continued uninterrupted. In English, occult writings appear to have paused for one or two generations.

In Tarot reading, Lévi was the first to suggest that the Magus (Magician) was to be depicted with the symbols of the four suits. His associations of the Hebrew alphabet with the Major Arcana were the direct inspiration for the Golden Dawn's attributions and inspired the Rider Waite Smith Deck as well as all derivative decks from the Rider Waite Smith and the Golden Dawn.

He claimed the court cards represented stages of human life and associated the four suits with the letters of the Tetragrammaton and its interpretation in Kabbalah.

> An imprisoned person with no other book than the Tarot, if he knew how to use it, could in a few years acquire universal knowledge, and would be able to speak on all subjects with unequaled learning and inexhaustible eloquence.[80]

Paul Christian

A student of Éliphas Lévi, Jean-Baptiste Pitois, variously known as Jean-Baptiste or Paul Christian (1811–1877), was a French author of *Historie de la Magie, du monde Surnaturel et de la fatalité à travers les Temps et les Peuples* 1870 (*History of Magic, the Supernatural World and Fate, through Times and Peoples*), an occult history that towed the line between esotericism and Catholicism. This work included astrological attributions of the Tarot, including the 36 Decans (which have Egyptian origin) and was cited in Helena Blavatsky's famous work, *The Secret Doctrine*.

---

[79] Page 81 (Leví 1896).
[80] Page 103 of the same.

His 'Egyptian Tarot' deck features depictions of Egyptian gods and is a precursor to Crowley's 'Thoth' Deck which itself incorporated many Egyptian themes. Taking seriously the dubious, and problematic idea that Kabbalah, rather than being a Jewish development, instead comes from an Egyptian root, Christian invented an original Egyptian alphabet of 22 letters, the supposed precursor to the Hebrew alphabet as well as an Egyptian Sefirot. Christian would probably be best confined to that part of history that has not well stood the test of time, were it not for the fact that he inspired Papus' *Tarot des Bohemiens* (1889) which borrowed ideas from him about the Major arcana, especially their astrological attributions.

He is of passing interest to us for this reason as a stepping stone in the development of Tarot reading and his Egyptian Tarot deck is very attractive.

Oswald Wirth

A well-known Swiss occultist and Kabbalist (1860–1943), Wirth designed a special Majors only Tarot deck in 1887 to fit with Éliphas Lévi's ideas. Based on Tarot de Marseilles, it features Hebrew letters on the cards and additional Kabbalistic and magical symbolism in the images, for instance Egyptian figures such as sphinxes drawing the Chariot (rather than horses). Some of these developments were included into the later Rider Waite Smith Deck. A later revised version of his deck was released in 1926, featuring much more detail in the images, and borders containing hidden symbols, especially Phoenician letters (the ancestor of the Hebrew, and all other alphabets).[81]

This later deck has been re-released with pip and Court Cards added, albeit designed by someone else. This deck, in either its full, or Majors only version, serves as a great middle ground between the Rider Waite Smith and the Tarot de Marseilles, for readers who want some of the flavour of both. Along with it Wirth published a second Tarot manual in 1927 *Le Tarot des imagiers du moyen-age*.

---

[81] Archaeology and linguistics show us that the Hebrews are descendants of the Canaanites, and the Hebrew language began as a Canaanite dialect. The term Phoenicians is simply the Greek term for those seafaring Canaanites who traded and fought in the Mediterranean Sea.

As well as the two Tarot manuals, His writings in French include books on astrology and Hermeticism. Wirth became one of the stars of the Parisian occult scene, and went on to have a following in the English-speaking world after the communication was opened by Lévi's visit to England. Wirth's *introduction à l'étude du Tarot* (1931) was translated into English and published in the United States in the 1980s as *Introduction to the Study of the Tarot*. His second manual was published in 1985 as *The Tarot of the Magicians*. While Earlier decks number Strength as VIII, and Justice as XI, Wirth's decks swapped these. The Golden Dawn and Rider Waite Smith used Wirth's system. Later Crowley changed it back, to the traditional numbering.

Hermetic Order of the Golden Dawn

Before Éliphas Lévi's visit to London in 1954, Tarot was nearly unknown to the English-speaking world. Perhaps in part because the English were introduced to the Tarot first as a repository of occult knowledge, especially ancient Egyptian, Hermetic and Kabbalistic mysticism, and not as deck for playing card games, the Tarot deck became elevated to a tool for communication to the godhead itself. In this way became seen as a divination system for 'serious' magicians, rather than crank 'fortune-tellers' or 'Gypsies'.

The seeds for the Golden Dawn come from numerous influences. The Theosophical movement founded by Helena Petrovna Blavatsky (1831–1891) in 1875, created a culture of interest in the occult, psychic abilities, spirits, Kabbalah and Eastern mysticism, especially Tibetan Buddhism. Many of the original members of the Golden Dawn were Theosophists first. The magical source material for the order was translated compiled, edited and organised by Samuel Liddell MacGregor Mathers (1854–1918) from grimoires in the British Museum, especially Agrippa's 'Three Books of Occult Philosophy', as well as Lévi's writings. MacGregor Mathers had been a freemason since 1877.

The idea of a Rosicrucian secret society based on freemasonry found it's precursor in Societas Rosicruciana in Anglia, founded by Robert Wentworth Little in 1865, and of which MacGregor Mathers became a member in 1882. In 1884, Anna Kingsford, then president of the London lodge of the Theosophical Society, founded the Hermetic Society, which existed until 1887, when her health declined, the same year that the Hermetic Order of the Golden Dawn was formed by the

Freemasons, William Wynn Westcott, MacGregor Mathers and William Robert Woodman. Kingsford had introduced MacGregor Mathers to H.P Blavatsky in 1886.

Mathers had also spent some time living in Paris with his wife, Moina Mathers, where he would have had access to French occult literature especially the works of Éliphas Lévi. Occultist Kenneth MacKenzie's visit to Paris in 1861 where he met Éliphas Lévi, inspired him to write up a proposal for an occult lodge whose teachings and rituals would be based on revisions of Lévi's system. A new Tarot deck was to be a core part of the lodge's syllabus. After Mackenzie's death in 1886, his writings, a collection of 60 folios later named the 'Cipher Manuscripts', found their way into the hands of the three founders of the Hermetic Order of the Golden Dawn. A legend was created that these were the papers of a secret German magical lodge, which was in contact with 'the Secret Chiefs', variously described to be a secret order of human magical wisemen, or a collection of incorporeal spirit teachers. This concept comes from the Theosophical idea of 'the Ascended Masters', which is itself inspired by the Buddhist ideas of the 'Matreiya' and the 'Bodhisattva'. These secret beings, or people who only spoke to a select few were thought to grant spiritual authority to teachers such as Blavatsky, and contact with these masters was claimed by various Theosophists, then by MacGregor Mathers, and then by Aleister Crowley. Arguments over who was and wasn't in touch with the Secret Chiefs lead to many power grabs and schisms in these organisations.

It seems that every magical organisation has a legendary origin linking them to a secret line of authority. Similar to how modern day conspiracy theories claim to know what is really going on with governments or cabals, and how religious founders have a secret line to God through revelations, the Cipher Manuscripts are the legendary origin story of the Golden Dawn. These folios were written in English using a simple substitution code, and contained outlines for a graded course in Kabbalah and ritual magic drawing from Alchemy, Christianity and Hermeticism. The secret of who composed the papers is not known, but they contained a mysterious German address for one 'Fräulein Anna Sprengel', claimed by Westcott to be a representative of a secret German 'Gold- und Rosenkreuzer' Order. William Wynn Westcott and Samuel Liddell MacGregor Mathers claim to have written to Sprengel, and to have received a reply from her granting permission to start a lodge for the order in England, the first Hermetic Order of the Golden Dawn lodge named the Isis-Urania Temple. Historians analysing these documents generally agree that Sprengel was an invention of Westcott in order to promote interest in the organisation, and it is known that Mather's created most of the later material for the Golden Dawn by studying and translating magical books such as Agrippa's *Three Books of Occult Philosophy*, Maimonidies, John Dee's works, *The Lesser Key of Solomon* and Éliphas Lévi's works. It is quite likely that he alone, or with Westcott also created the Cipher Manuscripts.

Starting in 1887, The Hermetic Order of the Golden Dawn grew, building itself in the model of a masonic lodge, as a mixture of a genuine magical society and an outer order which was more of a social club for theatrical upper-class eccentrics. Some of the more noted members were:

- Charles Henry Allan Bennett (1872–1923), also one of the first English Buddhists.
- Aleister Crowley (1875–1947), the most infamous of the Victorian occultists.
- Sir Arthur Conan Doyle (1859–1930), author of Sherlock Holmes.
- Florence Farr (1860–1917), Well-known stage actress and musician.
- Robert Felkin (1853–1925), medical missionary, explorer and anthropologist in Central Africa, author, and founder of the later New Zealand branch of the Golden Dawn.
- Arthur Machen (1863–1947), Welsh author of occult fiction, such as *The Great God Pan*, *The White People* and *The Hill of Dreams*.
- Moina Mathers (1865–1928), wife of MacGregor Mathers and sister of philosopher Henri Bergson.
- Pamela Colman Smith (1878–1951), British artist and co-creator of the Rider Waite Smith Tarot Deck.
- Arthur Edward Waite (1857–1942), British writer and translator of occult works and co-creator of the Rider Waite Smith Tarot Deck.
- William Butler Yeats (1865–1939), Irish poet, dramatist and writer.
- William Wynn Westcott (1848–1925), Coroner and founding member of the society. Supreme Magus (chief) of the Societas Rosicruciana in Anglia.
- William Robert Woodman (1828–1891). Medical doctor and founding member. Supreme Magus (chief) of the Societas Rosicruciana in Anglia.

Golden Dawn Decks

As part of their training material, MacGregor Mathers and his wife Moina created a special Tarot deck, outlined in *Book T*, the Golden Dawn Tarot training manual. Golden Dawn members of the appropriate grade were required to create their own copy of this deck by hand. The original deck was never shown to the public.

While no direct reprint has ever been published, there exist two decks inspired by this original deck, one by Robert Wang, published in 1978, who designed the cards to the specifications of Israel Regardie, the compiler and editor of the original published Golden Dawn book, and another published in 1991 by Chic Cicero and Sandra Tabatha Cicero, a husband and wife team dedicated to teaching the Golden Dawn material.

Some features of the Golden Dawn Tarot deck and instructions are:

- The Fool being allocated the initial position amongst the Trumps, the letter Aleph, rather than the Magician (as written by Éliphas Lévi). All the other Trumps are shuffled along by one position.
- The cards being laid out on the paths of the Sefirot, or Tree of Life, taken from Éliphas Lévi.
- The Justice and Strength being swapped in comparison to their traditional positions, taken from Oswald Wirth.
- The suits renamed from Batons and Coins to Wands and Pentacles. Both wands and pentacles being magical tools used in Golden Dawn rituals.
- The King and Knight being swapped in their order in the court cards and the King is renamed the Prince. This elevates both the Queen and the Knight while demoting the King.
- Pages are changed to Princesses, in order to equalise the male and female genders.
- The Court Cards are assigned to letters of the Tetragrammaton YHVH, and the four alchemical elements, fire, water, air and earth, respectively. This was taken from Éliphas Lévi.
- The 36 cards from twos to tens in each suit were assigned to the astrological Decans, as per Paul Christian.
- The ten numbers of the pip cards were assigned to the ten Sefirot, taken from Éliphas Lévi.

The end of the original Golden dawn

By 1896, up to 400 members had joined the Golden Dawn, with most of these being in the more social, outer order, rather than the more practical inner order of adepts who were engaging in ritual magic.

Over time MacGregor Mathers became the sole head of the organisation, and the only remaining founding member. Westcott had cut ties with the organisation, and it is thought that this was a result of an incident where he had accidentally left a folio of secret papers in a horse-drawn taxi cab. The papers were discovered by a third party, and brought to the attention of his employers. He may have been given an ultimatum to resign from his job as a coroner, or otherwise quit the order.

Personality clashes, and challenges to Mathers' leadership were causing rifts. In 1898 the brilliant and larger than life, Aleister Crowley had joined, who had an obsessive friendship with MacGregor Mathers. Crowley, who took Mathers as his magical role model, shot up the ranks of the order while simultaneously ruffling the feathers of other members, especially the celebrity poet Yeats, who thoroughly disliked Crowley, and A.E. Waite, who similarly to Crowley had a dominating and abrasive ego, if his writings are anything to judge by.

Crowley also had an intimate, if not homosexual relationship with Alan Bennett, who moved in with him, and taught him ritual magic, meditation and Buddhism. Both engaged in hedonistic drug use, and experimented with summoning spirits, especially through the Goetia of the Lesser Key of Solomon, a renaissance grimoire. Bennett was also Crowley's meditation teacher. When the London lodge members refused to initiate Crowley into the second order, Mathers initiated him in private. Crowley then tried to seize the 'Vault of the Adepts' temple space at 36 Blythe Road. He failed at this, and his arse was kicked down the stairs by an enraged Yeats. A court case ensued over the rights to use the space which was won by the lodge members, creating a schism between them MacGregor Mathers, Crowley and Crowley's few friends.

In 1899 there was a revolt, complicated by Florences Farr's secret society within the Isis-Urania, and the ousting of Crowley and Mathers. Remaining lodge members tried to claim access to the Secret Chiefs, which had previously been the sole privilege of Mathers. After several prominent resignations, the lodge split into three groups, one lead by

A.E. Waite and M.W. Blackden, claiming the rights to the original Isis-Urania temple, one more successful group lead by Dr Robert Felkin and other lodge members renamed Stella Matutina, and Crowley himself, who went on to use and expand upon the Golden Dawn system of magic for the rest of his life, and who started several magical orders over his time.

Although acrimonious, these splinterings are responsible for the continued legacy of the Golden Dawn, and eventually new chapters were opened, the Osiris temple in Weston-Super-Mare, the Horus temple in Bradford (both in 1888), the Amen-Ra temple in Edinburgh (1893), the Ahathoor temple in Paris (1893) and the Thoth-Hermes temple in Chicago (founded some time before 1900). The longest running temple however was Whare Ra, in Havelock North New Zealand, started by Reginald Gardiner and officiated by Dr Robert Felkin, running from approximately 1907 until 1978.

There are now numerous Golden Dawn societies around the world teaching from the original syllabus, none of whom have a direct lineage to the original London Temple.

The Equinox

In March 1909, Crowley began production of a biannual magical magazine titled The Equinox. Over time he published a large amount of the secret Golden Dawn syllabus, and founded his own order, the A∴A∴, teaching and expanding upon the Golden Dawn teaching. This served to end the era of the Golden Dawn as a secret society, and also to create public interest in the magical system, which ultimately preserved it, causing it to become the most famous occult system in the English-speaking world.

The Golden Dawn book

After serving as Crowley's student and secretary, (Francis) Israel Regardie (1907–1985) edited and published all the Stella Matutina rituals, first in a series of books and then later in a single volume. This book has became the most influential modern work of occult magic ever since. Amongst the material is *Book T* the Golden Dawn Tarot manual, which is the direct influence on the Rider Waite Smith Deck. In 1978, artist and Tarot historian, Robert Wang collaborated with Regardie to create 'the Golden Dawn Deck', which is based upon the secret Golden Dawn Deck created by MacGregor and Moina Mathers.

Papus aka Gérard Encausse

Gérard Anaclet Vincent Encausse (1865–1916), who wrote under the pseudonym 'Papus' was a French physician, hypnotist, and occultist. He founded the modern 'Martinist Order' in France. Directly influenced by Éliphas Lévi, Papus wrote his Tarot manual *Le Tarot des Bohémiens* in 1889 using Oswald Wirth's original Majors deck for the images. This book was translated by A.E. Waite who published it in English in 1958 as *The Tarot of the Bohemians: Absolute Key to Occult Science*.

Papus' numerological 'neo-Pythagorean' method for reading Marseilles style 'pip' decks is very useful for learning to divine with Tarot, and I have included and paraphrased his method it in this book in the earlier chapter: Understanding Tarot numerology. In March 1895, Encausse joined the Ahathoor Temple of the Hermetic Order of the Golden Dawn in Paris.

The name 'Papus' comes from Lévi's *Dogme et Rituel de la Haute Magie (1855)* where it is name of a Genius of the First Hour in the Nuctemeron,[82] and is translated in the text as 'physician'.

Rider Waite Smith

Arthur Edward Waite (1857–1942) joined the Outer Order of the Hermetic Order of the Golden Dawn in January 1891 after being introduced by E.W. Berridge. He withdrew for a time in 1893, only to rejoin in 1896. In 1899 he entered the Second (magical) Order of the Golden Dawn and entered the Societas Rosicruciana in Anglia in 1902.

In 1903 Waite founded an independent Golden Dawn order, R. R. et A. C. which existed until 1914. Although he published numerous titles on magic, alchemy, Rosicrucianism, Kabbalah and poetry, Waite's most important legacy is the Rider Waite Smith Tarot Deck, which he commissioned from his collaborator and fellow Golden Dawn member, the artist Pamela Colman Smith.

First released in 1909 by the Rider Company, the Rider Waite Smith Deck was the first complete Tarot deck designed exclusively

---

[82] The Greek writings attributed to Apollonius of Tyana.

for divination since Etteilla's original 'Thoth' Tarot. It has gone on to be the most popular and recognisable Tarot deck in the English-speaking world.

Its major feature was the inclusion of pictures on all the cards, including the Minor Arcana, a feature borrowed from the fifteenth-century Sola Busca deck, from which several of it's images are influenced. Many Tarot readers find this feature particularly helpful for learning, especially those who practise 'intuitive reading'.

Though the deck is often said to have been designed by Arthur Edward Waite, a reading of his accompanying manual, *The Pictorial Key to the Tarot* (1910), shows that Waite was primarily focused on the Major Arcana, which he describes in detail, and that he probably left the designs of the minors up to Pamela Colman Smith (1878–1951). Pamela Colman Smith, was not only a studied occultist in her own right, but also highly intuitive, claiming to have painted in a stream of consciousness trance and to have 'channelled' some of the images. Whatever the case, most of the minor arcana images, outside of the few influenced directly from the Sola Busca deck, appear to be Colman Smith's own highly original work. The two images inspired by the Sola Busca deck are the Three of Swords and the Ten of Wands (adapted from the Sola Busca's Ten of Swords).

There is evidence that some figures in the deck are portraits of Smith's friends, notably actresses Ellen Terry (the Queen of Wands) and Florence Farr (the World). Colman Smith also reported having synesthesia and would often paint to music, depicting what the sounds suggested to her.[83] As Smith wrote in a 1908 article she wrote for *Strand* magazine called 'Pictures in Music': 'When I take a brush in hand and the music begins it is like unlocking the door to a beautiful country … with plains, mountains and the billowing sea'.

The Rider Waite Smith Deck is based on the writings of Etteilla, Éliphas Lévi, Papus, the Golden Dawn Deck from MacGregor and Moina Mathers and MacGregor Mathers' *Book T*. Either out of respect for secret society oaths, or else as an act of self censorship the Rider Waite Smith Deck excludes some the more overt occult references such as the Hebrew alphabet and overt references to Kabbalah such as the Sefirot (though its there in more subtle form for instance in the Ten of Pentacles). Its astrological symbols are obvious enough for those in the

---

[83] (Ray 2019).

know but are not overt. This may have been a measure to get around anti-occult laws in England. The 'Witchcraft act' of 1735, made it a crime for a person to claim magical powers for themselves or others and was only revoked in England in 1951. It was then replaced by the Fraudulent Mediums act, prohibiting a person from claiming to be a psychic medium, for the purpose of making money, itself only repealed in 2008. Waite borrowed heavily from the Etteilla School's word lists in his interpretations of the cards as given in his manual *The Pictorial Key to the Tarot* (1910).

Crowley and Harris' 'Thoth Deck'

Aleister Crowley's (1875–1947) biography is extensive as the most famous, infamous and the most written about occultist in history. One biographer, Tobias Churton has written six volumes about him to date. For this reason I will not go into great detail about his very full life here. Crowley's 'Thoth Deck' was actually commissioned by his collaborator Lady Frieda Harris (1877–1962). She was the wife of Percy Harris, a politician of the Liberal Party. In 1932 Percy Harris was made a Baronet by the British Crown for his service, and Frieda Harris took the title 'Lady' as his wife. Crowley had expressed interest to his associates in creating a special Tarot deck for divination. A friend of his, the playwright Clifford Bax (1886–1962) introduced him in 1937, to Lady Frieda Harris, then aged 60, after several other artists had fallen through.

Crowley's original intention had been to refine the traditional Tarot deck, almost certainly informed by the Golden Dawn Deck. Harris, herself a well read occultist, including of Crowley's own books and the works of Rudolf Steiner, encouraged Crowley towards a much more ambitious and complex deck including Crowley's ideas. To spur on the project she paid Crowley a stipend for his work on the deck and his accompanying book *The Book of Thoth (Egyptian Tarot)* (1944).

Despite Crowley's deeply critical nature, abrasive personality and unrelenting drive towards perfectionism, the two appear to have maintained a deeply respectful professional relationship and friendship, which was unusual for Crowley. She was perhaps his longest lasting platonic friend.

> She devoted her genius to the Work. With incredible rapidity she picked up the rhythm, and with inexhaustible patience submitted

to the correction of the fanatical slave-driver that she had invoked, often painting the same card as many as eight times until it measured up to his Vanadium Steel yardstick![84]

Aside from Harris, Crowley's motivation and inspiration came from a desire to improve upon the shortcomings he saw in previous divination decks, especially those of the Golden Dawn, the Rider Waite Smith, and the decks of Etteilla and Oswald Wirth.

> The grotesque barber Alliete [Etteilla], the obscurely perverse Wirth, the poseur-fumiste Péladan, down to the verbose ignorance of such Autolycus-quacks as Raffalovitch and Ouspensky; none of these or their kin have done more than 'play the sedulous ape' to the conventional Medieval designs. (Their luck was out: The Tarot is a razor!). Eliphas Levi was a master scholar, and knew the true attributions; but his grade was only 6°=5° (Adeptus Major); and he had no instructed foresight of the new Aeon.
>
> Dr Gérard Encausse, 'Papus', who followed Eliphas Levi, felt himself even more closely bound by his Oath of Secrecy, so that his dealings with Tarot are worthless; and that although he was a Grand master of the OTO in France, and grand Hierophant 97° of the rite of Memphis on the death of John Yarker.[85]

Typically for Crowley this scathing diatribe fails to acknowledge just how influenced he was by all of these writers and deck designers. There is however much originality in the Thoth deck, which is dense with information from Crowley's take on Kabbalah, his deep understanding of astrology, probably the most refined of all Tarot writers, his take on Egyptian mythology, which while based on that of the Golden Dawn, had largely replaced their own dominant Christian and Rosicrucian themes, and elements from his own prophetic 'channelled' work *Liber Al Legis, The Book of the Law*, itself informed by the Book of Revelation.

Crowley added a key word for each of the minors, which is an enormous help in reading such a complex deck. Frieda Harris brought a studied almost proto-psychedelic and visionary style to the artworks. To prepare herself she had studied projective synthetic geometry, and

---

[84] Page 3 (Crowley 1944).
[85] Page 209 (Crowley 1944).

artificial perspective, styles inspired by the design theories of Rudolph Steiner and perfected by the artists Olive Whicher and George Adams. Harris had the perspective lines extend over multiple cards and used these techniques to envision the revelatory inner experiences that Crowley described.

In all they worked on the deck from 1938 until 1943. Crowley's accompanying book was released in 1944, and Harris' paintings were displayed at an exhibition at least four times during this period June 1941 at the Randolph Hotel in Oxford, March 1942 in Chipping Campden, July 1942 at the Berkeley Galleries on Davis Street in London, and August 1942 at the Royal Society of Painters in Water Colours (now known as the Royal Watercolour Society) in London. As well as to display her work these exhibitions were an attempt to raise money to print the deck by attracting subscribers and were given consent by Crowley. Though initially the cards were displayed anonymously, word soon got out about Harris' involvement. She asked Crowley to remain silent on his involvement due to his status as a feared 'black magician'.

> My business is to get money to publish these cards if possible & this is nearly impossible in the present war condition. I have been successful through using what influence I possess in getting at people with money to come & see the exhibition. This is using my social position fully. If they suspected that the cards were inspired by the Arch Magician of Black Magic they would withdraw their patronage. I have had this conveyed to me politely & impolitely. Therefore if you come to the Private View or show up in any prominence this attempt to launch the cards is doomed & all the work & money lost. Can you be so large-minded & detached as to keep away until the thing is launched. I am trying to keep out too because I am bored by occult people, loathe commercialism, do not want fame or notoriety, do not want money, but yearn, long, desire for solitude. Any financial success will be yours. I have had my reward in the work.[86]

As expected this ruffled Crowley who had worked hard on the deck and had his own plans for their publishing. This rift was eventually healed

---

[86] (Di Monda 2023).

and the two remained friends. Despite this the deck was not published in either of their lifetimes, eventually being released in 1969, and again in higher quality in 1977 by US Games. Since then it has become legendary, as one of the three most important divinatory decks along with the Marseilles and Rider Waite Smith.

The Thoth Deck uses Golden Dawn's Hebrew letter and astrological correspondences on the cards, which in turn were influenced by Éliphas Lévi. It also used the Golden Dawn's Court Cards, Knights, Queens, Princes and Princesses. This was done to balance the genders of the deck. Crowley also liked the idea of elevating the feminine to the most authoritative card, by removing the Kings. Crowley renamed Justice, Strength, Temperance and Judgment as Adjustment, Lust, Art and Aeon respectively, in line with his prophetic vision of a coming age of Horus, and he switched Justice and Strength back to their original Tarot de Marseilles order, though they retain their swapped associations in regards to the Hebrew alphabet. He also renamed the Golden Dawn's 'Pentacles' to 'Discs'. His reasoning for this is not clear.

Hermann Haindl

(1927–2013) A German artist and author of books on Tarot and the runes. Although not as well known or perhaps as historically important, I have included him here for his extraordinary attempts to progress the evolution of Tarot decks by including syncretic elements from Shamanism, native American mythology, Celtic mythology, Elder Futhark Runes, Hinduism as well as the more common Egyptian and Kabbalistic symbols.

Influenced by both the Rider Waite Smith's and Crowley's Thoth decks, Haindl incorporated many unique ideas. Each suit is themed for a particular culture:

- Wands are Hindu, with Kali, Brahma, Radha, and Krishna as the Court Cards.
- Cups are Celtic and Germanic, with Venus von Willendorf, Odin, Brigit von Ireland and Parzival as the court cards.
- Swords are Egyptian with the gods Nut, Re, Isis and Osiris as the court cards.
- Stones are Native American, with Spider Woman, Old Man, White Buffalo Woman and Chief Seattle as the Court Cards.

Each of the Major arcana features both a rune as well as a Hebrew letter. Haindl as a German wanted to reconcile Germanic symbolism with that of the Jews. Finally the Hexagrams of the I-Ching are also incorporated. Perhaps the Haindl deck offers us a vision of where Tarot might evolve in the future, or perhaps at least an example of how one might design one's own magical deck, a subject which we will explore in a following book.

Oracle cards

'Oracle cards' is a blanket term for divination card decks other than Tarot. These can range from divination decks that have their own tradition, to one off original works released by magicians and/or artists following their own magical ideas. As such, they run the full range from highly effective to utter nonsense, and being offered an 'oracle card' reading can leave you with no idea what you are signing up for.

For those new to Tarot there can be a lot of confusion, with some readers, even professionals referring to all divination decks as 'Tarot' even if they bear no relation to true Tarot cards. On the other hand, it is wrong to assume that all 'oracle decks' are necessarily inferior or ineffective in comparison to Tarot. The wide variety of oracle cards is too numerous to go into here, with each being a system unto itself, and with new decks being designed all the time.

Lenormand cards

The oldest oracle decks are the Lenormand cards, named after the famous cartomancer Marie Anne Adelaide Lenormand (1772–1843). The original Lenormand cards are a deck of 36 cards first printed in 1799 as a card game called 'Das Spiel der Hoffnung' (The Game of Hope) and invented by the game designer Johann Kaspar Hechtel (1771–1799). The symbols on these cards were similar to those used in coffee ground reading, so Hectel's game itself may have its roots in fortune-telling. These were soon repurposed and marketed as 'Lenormand cards' ignoring Hectel's original game rules. This goes back as early as 1846, but after Madame Lenormand's death.

Marie Anne Adelaide Lenormand herself was, along with Etteilla, the most famous cartomancer of her time, as well as being an author of many books, mostly to do with prophecy, especially involving French public figures. It is claimed that she read the fortunes of many celebrities at the time including Empress Joséfine Bonaparte (Napoleon's wife), Tzar Alexander I (Emperor of Russia), and the famous French revolutionaries, Jean-Paul Marat, Maximilien Robespierre, and Louis Antoine de Saint-Just.

It is thought that she used both playing cards and cards that were similar to Hectel's Game of Hope in her readings. In her own writings, Lenormand claimed to have been reading since she was 14, taught by gypsies who also gave her first deck. Shortly after Lenormand's death a different deck of cards called 'Le Grand Jeu de Mlle. Lenormand' was first published by the playing card brand, Grimaud. This 54 card deck was created by a Madame Breteau, who claimed to be a student of Madame Lenormand. It consisted of the 52 standard playing cards, elaborated by extra symbols, and with two extra cards to represent either a male or female querent.

It was sold with a set of five books describing various types of divination, including cartomancy, palmistry, astrology, numerology, and talismans. Though emerging perhaps earlier than the 36-card 'Petit Lenormand' decks the 54-card deck has not proved as popular. Neither deck was used by Lenormand herself.

The Lenormand cards and method of reading have since become a tradition in their own right. Each card has one symbol, and one associated playing card, which is also pictured. The symbols on the Petite Le Normand (Game of Hope) decks have precursors in 'Sibilla cards' from the 1700s which have been found in Italy, France, Germany, Austria and Hungary. These earlier decks do not the have numbers or suits printed on them.

An early deck has also been described by the Tarot historian Mary Greer, while doing research at the British Museum called *Les Amusements des Allemands*. This is accompanied by a 31 page booklet describing how the card's symbols are derived from coffee ground divination. Many of the cards match the symbols used in the Lenormand decks, and it can therefore be concluded that Lenormand decks have evolved from coffee-ground fortune-telling, which has historically been popular in Eastern Europe and performed with the left over coffee grounds from the preparation of Turkish coffee.

To read coffee grounds, water is poured into a white cup on top of ground coffee beans, as is common when brewing Turkish coffee. The client may sip the coffee until sludge is left in the bottom of the cup.

Then the reader places a saucer on top of the cup and turns it over so that the excess liquid pours out, leaving the grounds clustered on the bottom and sides of the cup. The remaining dark grounds form patterns and shapes against the white cup. The reader looks for images in the shapes, and notes their darkness, lightness, and position on the cup. When reading the grounds, each image and position adds meaning. Darker shapes are considered negative and light ones positive. The same shape positioned on the side or bottom will have a different meaning. There are hundreds of possible images the reader might envision in the blobs of coffee. Over time, lists of standard images emerged.[87]

Madame Lenormand was herself said to have performed divination using coffee grounds.

Below is a list of the 36 standard Lenormand cards:

- The Messenger (or Rider), 9 of Hearts
- The Clover, 6 of Diamonds
- The Ship, 10 of Spades
- The House, King of Hearts
- The Tree, 7 of Hearts
- The Cloud, King of Clubs
- The Snake, Queen of Clubs
- The Coffin, 9 of Diamonds
- The Bouquet, Queen of Spades
- The Scythe, Jack of Diamonds
- The Rod (Or Whip or Broom), Jack of Clubs
- The Birds, 7 of Diamonds
- The Child, Jack of Spades
- The Fox, 9 of Clubs
- The Bear, 10 of Clubs
- The Star, 6 of Hearts
- The Stork, Queen of Hearts
- The Dog, 10 of Hearts
- The Tower, 6 of Spades
- The Garden, 8 of Spades
- The Mountain, 8 of Clubs
- The Path (Or Crossroads), Queen of Diamonds
- The Mouse (or mice), 7 of Clubs

---

[87] (Place 2015).

- The Heart, Jack of Hearts
- The Ring, Ace of Clubs
- The Book, 10 of Diamonds
- The Letter, 7 of Spades
- The Gentleman (or Animus), Ace of Hearts
- The Lady (or Anima). Ace of Spades
- The Lily, King of Spades
- The Sun, Ace of Diamonds
- The Moon, 8 of Hearts
- The Key, 8 of Diamonds
- The Fishes, King of Diamonds
- The Anchor, 9 of Spades
- The Cross, 6 of Clubs

LEVEL 3

Understanding Tarot

Congratulations, you are psychic!

To understand what a psychic is, it is better not to ask whether or not psychics or psychic phenomena are 'real'. Instead, a better initial question is: 'What information is the person valuing as evidence that they are psychic, and is it possible for me to have the same type of experiences?'. Put another way, 'What thought-game is the psychic playing?' and 'Can I play the same game?' To focus on whether something is real or not real before first trying it on its own terms, risks missing the point and reverting back to one's prejudices about what is true or untrue. This may be affirming, but really there is nothing to be truly gained from this approach. Instead it can be interesting to try on the belief system of another person like one would try on a hat. Just don't forget to take the hat off again once you are done!

Different people define 'real' and 'not real' in different ways and talking across these belief systems often requires a translation of terms. It can, however, be enormously rewarding, and at best, reality redefining. Once one has repeatably achieved results (or repeatably failed to), then one can make a useful sceptical judgement, but not before.

Right-brain thinking

In his acclaimed book *The Master and His Emissary*, and it's follow up *The Matter with Things*, Iain McGilchrist,[88] a psychiatrist and neuroscientist, made several stunning conclusions from more than 20 years of research on brains and human subjects. In studying the hemispheres of the brain and their differing abilities, he came to the conclusion that it is the right side that is dominant in both perception and the processing of information. This is contrary to what many people in the modern world had been led to believe.

According to McGilchrist the left hemisphere of the brain has evolved to focus on detail. It breaks subjects apart (analysis) and tends to deal with abstractions, especially by focusing on the differences between concepts rather than the relationships. It tends towards dichotomies: 'True/false', 'either/or', 'included/excluded', 'relevant/irrelevant', 'good/bad'.

In contrast to this, the right hemisphere operates with a broad and flexible attention that is open to new information. It looks at things in their wider context, appreciates the implicit, and favours 'both/and' type connections. This is 'holism' and 'synthesis'.

It is the right hemisphere that has a better appreciation of both itself and the left, whereas the left, especially because it is the language centre, feels somewhat 'isolated' from the right. While both types of processing are vital and complementary, it is McGilchrist's view that the left hemisphere's operation ought not to dominate the right. He writes that the left brain makes 'a good servant, but a very poor master'.[89]

The right brain operates through association, through pattern recognition, and through making links to that which it can recognise. It takes in a vast amount of information in comparison to the more limited amount processed by the left brain, which organises that information. One of McGilchrist's conclusions is that we take in information first and then rationalise it afterwards.[90]

---

[88] (McGilchrist 2012).
[89] (McGilchrist 2021).
[90] (McGilchrist 2023).

Intuitive problem-solving

Though most of us are taught in an education system that emphasises left brain hemisphere dominant activities such as language, mathematics, logic, analysis and categorisation, it is wrong to think that these are the only ways that humans are able to solve problems.

Artists, musicians, poets and writers and other creative people, know well that answers to problems and inspirations can pop or drift into the mind, and that when they do, they frequently take the form, not of language or maths, but of symbols, images, sensations, feelings, smells, textures, music or thoughts, that occasionally appear as if they were generated not from one's own mind, but from outside. For those of us who value these inspirations, the rewards can be manifold. Just because these experiences are hard to put into words, does not mean that they are rare, unimportant, or 'unreal'. Given the ease at which these inspirations flow into the mind-space, and the comparative effort required for rational thinking, this 'intuitive' type of thinking or problem-solving is much more common that logical thinking. It is quicker and more efficient, but also much less certain, being clouded by subjectivity.

Considering that many cultures downplay the role imagination has as an interface to reality, and instead favour logic or rationality as the closest to what is 'real', it is no wonder that people who particularly inclined towards intuition consider themselves outliers, and in some cases as 'psychics'. Perhaps they feel they are born with special talents that most other people don't understand.

Flow states

This is a psychological term for the states of consciousness that are more colloquially known as 'being in the zone'. These are the states where we are completely absorbed in a task, and they correspond to hypnotic trances.

While the majority of these experiences, for many people, are had alone, it is interesting and important to note that these states of mind can also be shared, and when they are shared they often bring about a feeling of a merging of 'selfhood' with the other people tuned into the same state. This can happen with musicians playing, or improvising in a group, lovers having sex, sports teams deeply concentrating in a game, and other teams, such as soldiers completing a physical task without speaking. What's more, many of these group tasks can *only* be completed at full efficiency in these 'flow states'.

What is less often discussed is how group flow states often allow an individual to 'know' the thoughts of others in the group. The core ingredient seems to be a mutual focus on the task. Whether or not this a type of telepathy, is secondary for my purposes. It is enough that the information is useful, and that it feels like it is coming from outside one's own imagination. These are amongst the phenomena that psychics and spirit believers experience personally, and count as evidence for their belief.

I have had this apparent 'telepathy' many times as a musician while improvising in a group. While studying jazz double bass at polytechnic (our term for a technical college), I made a close friendship with a pianist, Mike, which centred around our uncanny ability to get into a mutual flow state while improvising. This flow state somehow allowed us to predict each other's 'moves'. One day a saxophonist friend joined in our jam. Mike, and I entered into a simultaneous soli improvisation, which finished with us seamlessly playing a phrase together that went from the lowest notes on our instrument to the highest. The saxophonist was shocked and exclaimed: 'How did you do that?' Mike and I shrugged. We didn't know how we had done it, but it was something that happened for us often.

Tarot has all the necessary ingredients for the same types of quasi-telepathic experiences. The factors needed seem to be:

- A reader who is relatively fluent with the Tarot symbols.
- A deep state of mutual attention between the reader and querent.
- A suspension of 'disbelief' for the duration of the 'game'.
- A willingness to notice intuitive 'flashes' or unusual thoughts as important information to be reported on during the 'game'.

When one has had enough of these experiences, one might well start to seriously entertain the idea that perhaps our minds are not in our heads, and that, like a Venn diagram there seem to be ways in which one person's mind can overlap with another's. It's as if, from time to time, one person's thought can spill out of their own private mind-space, into the 'shared area' and be noticed by the other.

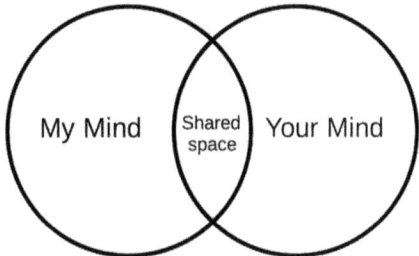

With practice, these experiences are easy enough to have. There are however differences between this type of 'telepathy' and that depicted in fantasy and science fiction. For the most part, it is hard to control which thoughts 'spill over'. This renders the idea of a telepath fully invading the mind of another and rifling through their thoughts and memories like a spy raiding a filing cabinet, as unlikely, or at least very rare (I have never met a person who can do this, though I've had it happen with spirit experiences). Also, most of the time, peoples thoughts are shut off from us. The creation of the shared space seems to require a flow state of shared attention. The types of thoughts that 'pop through' tend to be emotional states, such as anxiety or excitement, or memories and images with emotional content.

What's more, these shared thoughts, in my own experience seem to correlate to strong reactions. One time I was observing as my friend Ciaran gave another friend of mine a palm reading over an internet video chat. Ciaran, who up to then had given a perfect reading, which had deeply impressed the woman, had a 'miss' when he said to the querent 'You probably enjoy getting out in the garden'.

I, who was up until then a silent observer had a sudden flash of a woman's hands covered in dirt, and a strong feeling of anxiety and fear about needing to get her hands clean as soon as possible. In particular the owner of the hands detested the feeling of dirt under her fingernails. I interjected: 'No she hates the feeling of dirt on her hands'.

The woman was stunned: 'Can Ari read palms too?'

I said: 'No it just popped through as an image, I don't know why'.

By the end of the reading she was stunned not only at Ciaran's abilities as a palm reader, but also at that uncanny thought we had shared. At the time it felt like her strong aversion to dirt had caused the thought to pop out of her head and into mine, like a projectile launched by the feeling of unpleasantness. It is worth noting that I didn't know this woman very well and that I had never met her outside of cyberspace.

It is possible that the pre-lingual, right side of my brain picked up part of her body language, a micro movement or twitch of the face. However, the way the thought presented itself to me was as if it was a flash of telepathy with an image and an emotion. It also wasn't picked up by Ciaran in the same way (though he got the rest of the reading right). In any case I believe this experience and many others Ciaran and I have had in our experiments, is in line with the types of experiences considered 'evidence' by people who identify as psychics.

To engage with 'psychic' results like this, start paying attention during Tarot readings, or other tasks of shared attention, to ideas that 'flash though'. Report them to the querent and see if they identify with these thoughts. Sometimes the thoughts that flash through seem to be conscious thoughts of the querent, while other times they are unconscious. This must be kept in mind as unconscious thoughts may take the querent longer to recognise as their own.

Thinking without language

Another useful aspect of Tarot, is that it gives us a symbol set that can be used without language. This allows us to engage in a type of thinking that has more to do with the right side of the brain. The language centres of the brain in most individuals are held in large part (but not entirely) in two left brain regions called Broca's area and Wernicke's area. Damage to these areas can produce a reduction in, or a total loss of language.

Tarot offers us a way to, in part, subvert the language regions of the brain and engage with the more associative right lobe. This of course correlates with McGilchrist's idea that the right seeks connection to others and our environment, and the left is more concerned with our individuality. Whatever else is going on, this might be a factor in the 'shared thought' feeling, associated with psychic phenomena. Perhaps the attraction that some people feel to Tarot reading, especially those of us who tend towards being intuitive, is that it gives us a mode of communication with others that is difficult using conversation alone. The skill of a good Tarot reader relies on one's ability to pay attention to one's intuition, and then to be able to translate that into a narrative for the querent through language.

Dreaming as a right brain activity

If you are still having difficulty relating to the difference between left and right brain activities and their associated 'rational' and 'intuitive' thought processes, it might be interesting to try and understand what human experience is like when the left brain hemisphere is turned down and the right brain is turned up. It turns out that life without a left side of the brain might be a lot like the state of dreaming.

Dreaming as a neurological state, specifically during the REM (rapid eye movement) stage of sleep, correlates to increased blood flow in the right side of the brain, particularly in the temporal and parietal regions, and a decrease in activity on the left side. In brain scans of dreaming patients there is an enhanced activity in this right temporal and temporal-occipital region.

It is thought by neurologists that the right side of the brain creates and displays dreams, and that this correlates to the increase blood flow on the right side during the dreaming phases of sleep. These types of experiences are visual, spatial and emotional, and create a narrative by association with the dreamer's own emotional memories.

This association may be the brain's own 'natural divination', with the dream state being, at least in part, a random shuffling of thought, and the connection to existing memories creating the meaningful story. In a sense, the right brain is presenting the dream material, and the left brain (or both sides working together) is trying to organise the dream into some sense that can be understood and remembered. It appears that much of this processing actually takes place, after the dreamer is awake.

While it is possible to dream outside of the usual REM, right brain dominant state of sleep, in phases where the left brain is more excited than the right, these types of dreams are reported as being quite different. In particular, they are devoid of imagery and are instead often more like a running spoken monologue. It is this type of dreaming that is theorised to produce 'sleep talking'.[91] To improve one's intuition for Tarot reading, it may help to try thinking like a dreamer.

---

[91] Roberge, Pierre R. *Sleeping Brain.* https://www.corrosion-doctors.org/Dreaming%20is%20Personal/Brain.htm#:~:text=The%20right%20hemisphere%20of%20the,in%20that%20hemisphere%20during%20REM. Last accessed 3 April 2024.

Scientific evidence for psychic phenomena

An unfortunately common interjection by critics to claims of psychic phenomena, is the idea that there is no scientific evidence for their existence. While this is commonly taken for granted, it simply isn't true. The United Kingdom's Society for Psychical Research has been going since 1882, and the parallel study of parapsychology has been practised since the term was coined in 1889 by Max Dessoir.

Over more than 140 years there have been, and continue to be numerous scientific tests that have delivered valid results in favour of psychic phenomena from telepathy to telekinesis to manifestation (producing real-world physical results through intentional thought).

For a fair minded, scientific and clear understanding of the scientific testing of psychic phenomena I recommend the book *Real Magic: Ancient Wisdom, Modern Science, and a Guide to the Secret Power of the Universe*.[92] by Dean Radin PhD (b. 1952). Radin is a former president of the Parapsychological Association, founded in 1952 in the North Carolina US.

In the following Radin describes a psychic test designed by another important scientist in the field, Rupert Sheldrake (b. 1942):

> British biologist Rupert Sheldrake's book on this topic, The Sense of Being Stared At, describes many experiments he and others conducted to test if these anecdotal reports are due to sensory cues, peripheral vision, or a genuine psi sense. In a simple form of this experiment, one person of a pair is assigned to be the starer (let's call him Mulder); the other is the staree (let's call her Scully). They sit within few yards of each other, with Scully's back to Mulder. To begin the experiment, Mulder flips a coin to decide if he should stare or not stare at the back of Scully's neck. If the assignment is to stare, Mulder intensely gazes at Scully for ten seconds. Then he alerts her with a 'cricket clicker' (a handheld device that makes a cricket sound) to respond yes if she thinks Mulder is staring at her or no if she thinks he isn't.[93]

Radin analysed a total of 33,357 trials of this experiment by Sheldrake and others. The overall success rate was a 54.5 per cent average in

---

[92] (Radin 2018).
[93] Page 146 (Radin 2018).

favour of psi, where pure chance would have been a 50 per cent average. While this effect may appear small, Radin calculates the overall chances of this figure remaining consistent over so many trials at 202 octodecillion to one.[94] This test is indicative of most scientific tests of psi. The rate of success in favour of psi phenomena being real often hovers between roughly 54 per cent and 56 per cent.

This puts us in a frustrating place; 56 per cent is not dramatic enough to build a new model of reality that incorporates a theory of psychic forces. On the other hand the results are too good, over too many well designed tests, to be dismissed as chance or error. To put it in perspective, a success rate of 54 per cent would be considered strong evidence for effectiveness in many drug and vaccine trials.

My conclusion of the data is that our model of reality is a little bit wrong, but also that psychic results are not particularly dependable. We have come to a stalemate. A grey area. The phenomena are real, but they are not explainable. In any case, it is my lived experience teaching Tarot that psychic type experiences are within the grasp of everyone who makes a practice of them, and that these are a part of divination.

Tarot as a narrative game, provides a compartmentalised way to safely practice being 'psychic' without the need for this belief to spill over or cause problems in the rest of your life. Put simply. I propose you entertain the belief that you are psychic while reading Tarot, but not necessarily outside of the game. For a more detailed exploration of magic and the nature of belief check out my first book *Pragmatic Magical Thinking: Real Magic Explained*, especially Chapter 7: Believing different things on different days.

---

[94] Octodecillion: A number equal to 1 followed by 57 zeros.

Finally understanding what is going on with Tarot

A sceptical understanding

The human mind is a wonderful prediction machine. Given a set of prompts it is quite possible to quickly imagine how they might link together to tell a story or provide meaning. Often despite not having all the ____ we can still quite often ____ the meaning. Add to this our susceptibility to persuasion, and the sometimes dramatic effect on our perception when things are pointed out to us, (such as how you can see the end of your nose right now, but you have been ignoring it this whole time) and you have almost everything you need for a narrative game like Tarot to work, even if there were no 'psychic' component.

The issue then is less 'is Tarot reading real', and more 'is Tarot reading interesting?' I predict with my copious psychic powers that Tarot reading is in fact very interesting to you. At this point arguing that Tarot isn't real, is akin to playing *Dungeons & Dragons* for a month and then in a middle of a session standing up from the gaming table, announcing 'sorry I just don't believe in *Dungeons & Dragons* anymore' and walking out, leaving the other players bewildered as to why that should matter.

Put another way, Tarot reading only needs to be believed in for the duration of the game. Afterwards you can take off that belief and put on a different one. Though some of you may protest, this is actually something that functional human beings do all the time.

What Tarot can't do

Too often aficionados and true believers make grandiose claims about what their favourite thing is able to do. To me, it is just as interesting to ask what something can't do, and this question is vital if one intends to become a master at anything.

As Tarot was designed for creating narratives, it is not good at simple yes or no answers. Its 'vagueness' is precisely what allows it to be applied in many useful ways, and most attempts to make it more precise will also result in narrowing what it can be used for. This is also why the effectiveness of Tarot mostly lies outside of the realms of what can easily be tested scientifically. There are simply too many parameters to test. If this wasn't the case, which is to say, if it could easily be proven to work in scientific tests, Tarot and divination would rightfully become part of scientific models of reality. There is a sense in which functional magic ought to be defined, as the things which work, but which have eluded our ability to test them. This is in part, because every Tarot reading is different. There's too much variation, and scientific certainty requires a high degree of repeatability.

Instead Tarot has much more in common with art. Almost nobody has ever been bothered to try and test scientifically whether fine art paintings 'work'. We know that paintings work because they affect us. So we generally accept art on its own terms. To me, divination is in a similar category as art.

I have found that Tarot won't predict, or allow you to win, the lottery. If we accept that 'intention' is a magical force, then every lottery ticket is already a spell with intent, and your intention would have to cancel out everyone else's intention to work! To test if intention can reorder the universe in order to manifest what you want, you are better off choosing something with better odds of occurring, and which is not being cancelled out by someone else's wish.

It is very hard to figure out if Tarot and other forms of divination really know anything that you aren't already capable of knowing, or if they are tapping in to a latent ability that is always in us, to divine, and make working predictions. As you may have guessed I tend towards the latter opinion. Divination certainly brings out knowledge that we 'don't know how we could know'.

Perhaps our minds do reach out beyond the confines of our heads, a topic which I have explored in my first book *Pragmatic Magical Thinking* in a chapter entitled *'Why you aren't just your brain'*. Perhaps there is a section of our minds that can be accessed by other minds. A kind of 'public domain' zone where snatches of emotion, symbol and thought can be accessed in the way that is usually termed 'psychic phenomena'. This is an interesting question, but it is beyond the scope of this book to try and answer it.

Though through systems like the astrological decans, people have tried to use Tarot to time predictions, it is not good at doing this in a very specific way. Part of this is simply statistics. It is certain that my city will experience an earthquake within the next five years, but it is nearly impossible to tell on which exact hour that earthquake will happen.

Tarot, or any form of divination is simply not great at specifics. It won't accurately predict which team will win a football game, or by exactly how many points. I've tried it. If you want to master Tarot, it is important that you test some of these things out for yourself. If you haven't worked something until you've found it's failure points, then you also haven't fully discovered what that thing is capable of.

I urge you not to take my word for any of these limitations, but rather that you ask these questions yourself, test them, and come to your own conclusions.

Dealing with misses and failed readings

Many of us are raised in a risk-adverse culture that frames success as a lack of failure and failure as a lack of success. This is something that I've had to unteach myself in order to become a professional musician and a guitar and singing teacher.

I now see failure as a necessary component in all successful performances. Small failures show you and the audience, that you are performing at your human limit. My audience doesn't come to see me play without flaws, they come to see me play with drama; tension and release and to see me perform with bravery. For this reason, if everything I am doing is working all the time, I know that I am not playing at my human limit and also that I am not learning anything new. If I never make a mistake, then I'm simply not playing the best, most entertaining way I can play. I really can't emphasise this enough. The audience doesn't count your mistakes, and a performance where no risks are taken is usually a disappointing performance.

I treat Tarot reading the same way. I've never regretted getting something wrong in Tarot, but I have regretted not leaning into an intuition strongly enough. When you find out you are right about something that you chickened out of saying it, that can hurt.

I feel this is a good approach to magic, divination and Tarot reading. Don't be perfect. Be interesting. When the querent tells you that you have 'missed', accept it immediately and move on. Take note of repeated misses over many readings, and if you can find a pattern to them, adjust to a new approach. Even a completely failed reading shows you something. Have a break, pick up the cards and try again.

While making mistakes is an important part of performing to one's human limit, and necessary for learning, it is also just as important to never be too proud to accept one's mistakes. This is where being too emotionally invested in the idea that Tarot reading is 'real' can actually prevent one from getting good at it. Tarot is a thing you do, not something you are.

As a performer, it is equally important to me that I never blame my audience. If Tarot reading is best framed as a performance for a querent, then how can the querent be 'wrong'? For this reason, I try to refrain from defensive habits such as explaining away a failed reading as 'blocked energy' from the querent, or dismissing a disagreement from them because of the idea that doubt somehow prevents magic from working, or worst of all, refusing to read for a sceptic out of fear of failure, or of being 'found out'.

As long as you have not over-promised a result before a reading, a sceptic will generally not write off a whole reading because of a couple of small 'misses', as long as the rest of the reading was interesting to them and contained some 'hits'. While true believers may be easier to read for, I have always most enjoyed reading for sceptics. They may be a tougher audience, but for me they are also a more rewarding one. For one thing, when a sceptic is wowed, the affect can be world changing for them. Some of the sceptics I have read for have later become Tarot readers themselves.

A 'sceptic' whose entire goal is to debunk a reading will generally not agree to being read. Such extreme positions are not truly 'sceptical' at all, as scepticism comes from the Greek word for 'enquiry' (σκέψις, *skepsis*). These people are instead merely doubters who are only looking for reasons to be proven right. Even so, there can be something to be gained by reading for these people. They toughen us up. When someone has tried to tear you down and you remain standing, that is something to be proud of.

You might not actually be psychic
Confirmation biases, deception and self-deception

Here I will take seriously some of the explanations critics use to dismiss divination and discuss several 'cold reading' techniques which can be used both knowingly and unknowingly by readers. We will also explore some of the biases that can affect a reading, and which can make it seem, perhaps, more effective than it actually is.

The Forer effect, or 'blanket statements'

Between statements that are so general, that they obviously apply to everyone, such as 'You sometimes feel run down', and statements that are so specific that they can only apply to one person such as 'You are the third child in your family, and you are named after your grandmother who was also a third child, and who married a clergyman', lies an interesting territory. These are the pieces of information that sound convincingly specific, but which actually apply to most people.

Called the 'Forer effect', or the 'Barnam effect', this is a psychological bias, which is often invoked by sceptics in order to explain away the effects of fortune-tellers and stage psychics. It is also often employed both knowingly and unknowingly by fortune tellers, and is worth knowing about if we are to be effective readers.

The terms Barnum effect, and 'Barnum statements' are named after Phineas Taylor Barnum (1810–1891 CE) a circus showman, philanthropist and 'shuckster' who became the archetype of the show biz charlatan. He is often said to have coined the phrase 'there's a sucker born every minute' (though by an almost cosmic irony, there is no record of him actually saying that).

The 'Forer effect' which is the other name for this same phenomenon is named after Bertram Forer (1914–2000) the American Psychologist who first made a study of it. Forer studied the effect of Barnum statements while working at the Veterans Administration Mental Hygiene Clinic. In 1948, he gave a psychology test to 39 of his psychology students, who were asked to fill out a questionnaire and told that they would each receive a brief personality profile from an expert, based on their test results. One week later, Forer gave each student an 'individualised' response and asked each of them to rate it for accuracy. In reality, each student had received the same piece of writing, inspired by statements from magazine horoscopes and graphology (divination by handwriting).

A description of his test and the following 'Barnum statements' which he presented to his class can be found in his 1949 paper, 'The Fallacy of Person Validation: A Classroom Demonstration of Gullibility':[95]

Here are the original statements with which he tested his classroom in 1948.

- You have a great need for other people to like and admire you.
- You have a tendency to be critical of yourself.
- You have a great deal of unused capacity which you have not turned to your advantage.
- While you have some personality weaknesses, you are generally able to compensate for them.
- Your sexual adjustment has presented problems for you.
- Disciplined and self-controlled outside, you tend to be worrisome and insecure inside.
- At times you have serious doubts as to whether you have made the right decision or done the right thing.
- You prefer a certain amount of change and variety and become dissatisfied when hemmed in by restrictions and limitations.
- You pride yourself as an independent thinker and do not accept others' statements without satisfactory proof.
- You have found it unwise to be too frank in revealing yourself to others.
- At times you are extroverted, affable, sociable, while at other times you are introverted, wary, reserved.
- Some of your aspirations tend to be pretty unrealistic.
- Security is one of your major goals in life.

This list was presented to his class as if it was a personalised profile of each individual student who then were asked to rate its accuracy. On average, the students rated it at 4.30 on a scale of 0 (very poor) to 5 (excellent). The Forer effect works because we tend to underestimate our similarity to other people, and overestimate our differences.

If our purpose is to win over sceptics or to prove the 'hidden powers' of the Tarot, then we ought to push beyond Barnum statements.

---

[95] (Forer 1949).

Therefore the goal must be to include some information that is more specific. Otherwise a Tarot reading is no better than a generalisation.

If, however, your goal is merely to 'perform as if' one is a psychic, then these and similar statements are useful, though they also provide a potential for sceptics to see through the performance. Since Forer's experiment, many people have become aware of this effect.

Here are some more Barnum statements, to either avoid, or employ, in your own jurisdiction. (As a disclaimer, I a not encouraging you to mislead people, and as such I accept no responsibility for what happens if you do so. Having said that, if you were going to mislead people, these would work really well, and they may even give you money.)

- You tend to be too self-critical.
- You're an independent person.
- You do not accept what others tell you to believe.
- You don't suffer fools (or arseholes) lightly.
- Some of your goals seem to be a little unrealistic.
- You're a creative thinker.
- You have a unique personality and grew up feeling different to the people around you.
- You have many interests but find it hard to find time to commit to all of them.
- You would like to connect to other people more deeply.
- Your personal boundaries are very important to your mental health.
- Though you are usually a good judge of character, you have been hurt by people in the past.
- You have many ideas but have trouble getting most of them finished.
- You hold very high standards for the things you care about.

(I came up with a lot of these myself, so if you do make a lot of money by fleecing people, you ought to spend some of that money on my books. Thanks.)

Rainbow statements

Similar to Barnum statements, these are phrases that trick us into thinking they are specific, but actually present both a statement and its antithesis; having it 'both ways' and are thus always true.

A few examples:

- You are closer to one of your parents than the other.
- Sometimes you love a party, while other times you prefer solitary activities.
- Though usually cheerful, recently you have been upset.
- Though you generally get things done, recently you have found yourself to have run out of energy.
- You are often shy and quiet, but when the mood strikes you enjoy being the centre of attention.
- Though generally you are polite and considerate, you strongly resent when someone crosses your boundaries.
- You can be a spontaneous person, but in your private life you tend to stick to a routine that works.
- Though you are an open-minded person, you tend to dispense with bad arguments quickly.

Prejudice and projection

If you are finding yourself doing the same readings over and over for different people, then it's likely you are falling into one of these two traps, prejudice or projection.

Prejudices are your ideas about 'types' of people. These need not be especially negative, or strong in order to bias a reading. In many cases, your querent will not be aware of your prejudices while you are reading for them, but you may become aware of them yourself over time. If you are to get better as a reader, and you wish to get more dramatic positive responses from your querents, it can be helpful to move beyond your own personal set of stereotypes. For instance, if all your readings for women tend towards being about relationships, and all your readings about men tend towards being about careers and interests. Likewise, if you tend to frame one type of person as being oppressive, and another type as being the victim or recipient of that oppression. Real-life situations are rarely so black and white.

Projection happens when we take an aspect of our own psychology or something that is happening to us emotionally, and then try to make the other person 'wear it'. Put another way, projection is the overreliance of our own personal experiences in trying to understand what someone else is going through, instead of listening closely to how they explain it themselves.

If you find that in most of your readings, you have a strong feeling of 'I've been through the same thing', then you may be projecting too much of yourself onto the situation. Likewise, most of us carry prejudices and projections that can push us into self-fulfilling prophecies. Such as having high standards for how a partner or a friend ought to behave, that they never signed up for, and then blaming them for not living up to those standards.

People who are frequently resentful towards others are often suffering from this habit.

Here are some extreme examples of projection or prejudice that may come up for yourself or your querents:

- The Madonna–whore complex: Women are either epitomised or denigrated with no in-betweens. In reverse, this is sometimes referred to as the knight-beast complex. In this case, men are either rescuers or oppressors.
- Older women are always being framed as mothers or grandmothers.
- Funnelling a Tarot reading towards the topic of trauma with a querent because of one's own past hurt. Sometimes the querent will respond in like resulting in 'Trauma bonding'. While this is not necessarily a bad thing, it can become a problem or a bias if it is happening too often. One way out of this is to emphasise the querent's own power for change, over their status as a 'victim'.
- Inserting one's own romantic feelings onto someone else's relationship story.
- The idea that macho men are 'secretly gay'.
- The idea that boyish women are 'secretly gay'.
- The idea that the secret motivation for everything is sex (pseudo-Freudianism).
- Strong nostalgic feelings from your own life, when reading for younger people.
- Having a strong sense of 'right or wrong' over something the querent is doing, or which is being done to the querent, because it is something that you yourself have been doing or has been done to you.
- Trying to talk a querent out of taking a risk, because of your own fear of things going wrong, despite the situation not being something you have personal experience with.

- A tendency of people who have cheated or are considering cheating on their partner, to also be more jealous of that partner's potential to cheat.
- A tendency to want to fix all negative situations for a querent instead of remaining impartial.
- Giving a negative reading to a querent who has unknowingly annoyed you.
- A tendency to label all people who abuse another or who are sometimes manipulative as 'narcissists'.
- A tendency to define all power dynamics as an interaction between three clear cut roles of 'victim, rescuer, persecutor',[96] instead of recognising a complexity of roles and interactions.
- A tendency to label all people that someone has chosen to separate from, as being 'toxic'.
- A tendency to tell querents to break up with their partner at the first sign of difficulty.
- An inability to put oneself in the shoes of a querent who is going through something you haven't, such as a male reader not understanding a female querent's concerns around pregnancy, or a female reader not being sympathetic to a male querent whose wife has left him.

Self-fulfilling prophecies and their ability to empower and disempower

The Baader–Meinhof phenomenon is a type of observation bias whereby one notices many more instances of a thing after one has been primed to notice it. For instance, one buys a red Toyota Corolla (a very common type of car in a very noticeable colour), and one starts noticing many other red Toyota Corollas out and about on the roads that weren't noticed before. This phenomenon is so prevalent that it is almost unavoidable in all magic, and might actually be a large part of how magic and divination function. This can however lead to a belief

---

[96] This is a model of human interaction proposed by psychiatrist Dr Stephen B. Karpman, called the 'Karpman drama triangle', first proposed in 1968. Though he was trying to outline traps in thinking that people fall into rather than objective roles, many people missed the memo and try to group people into these three roles. In any case I find the whole concept overly reductive.

that the frequency of the occurrence of something has increased after one has been made aware of it, and is sometimes also referred to as 'the frequency illusion'.

Seeing as how all opportunities to act are preceded by noticing an opportunity to act, the priming of oneself to look for opportunities and to avoid pitfalls is actually a powerful tool towards achieving what you want. This is clearly part of what is going on with 'manifestation magic'. The Baader–Meinhof phenomenon is very powerful and can be used both to 'bless' or to 'curse' someone, by priming them towards positivity or negativity.

As such, it is a bias to beware of, but not necessarily to be avoided. The goal should instead be to push the bias towards a positive outcome. Because of this frequency illusion, it is possible that part of what makes Tarot readings work is a manipulation of what the querent pays attention to. In this way, one element of what makes a Tarot reading come true, is an amount of 'self-fulfilling prophecy'. This is not necessarily a bad thing, as sometimes a querent needs an extra push to do something that will benefit them, for instance, applying for a new job.

Where this can become a negative, is when it presents a problem that was not actually there beforehand, for instance a tension in a relationship which becomes 'noticed' as a problem only due to it being pointed out. In the worst case scenario, the Tarot reading might itself be the cause of the tension. This is to be considered and avoided if possible.

The power of talking about yourself

There is something built into the human being where undivided positive attention from another person usually feels good. Tarot, and all other counselling, works partly due to this effect. People simply love to talk about themselves. This is not at all a negative thing, but it is important to keep in mind as otherwise the positive outcome of any type of counselling (including Tarot reading) can be over attributed to the specific techniques used, when in fact the power of undivided attention, and allowing a person to talk about themselves is universal for all counselling.

This technique of providing undivided attention can be misused by cults or fringe therapies on targets who have been deprived of positive human attention, when the effectiveness of the therapy is credited to 'special' techniques rather than the general use of attention. To progress towards being a better Tarot reader, it is important not to attribute all your positive results to your own special techniques. One can get around this by either switching techniques frequently (like we have explored in this book), or else by observing readings given by others in order to notice these generalised effects, over those effects which are due to the particular skills of the reader.

Sunken cost fallacy

People tend to try to justify to themselves an increased investment in a decision based on their cumulative prior investment, despite evidence suggesting that the decision was wrong. For this reason, it is possible that longer Tarot readings may be rated as more effective than shorter ones, and more expensive 'professional' Tarot readings might be rated more effective than cheap or free readings.

This bias can be hard to grade for. If one is inclined to get to bottom of its effect, in order to become a better reader with more 'hits', then one ought to perform a variety of readings of different lengths, and if professional, at different price points, and take note of the effectiveness as reported by the querent.

The generation effect

People are better able to recall memories of statements that they have themselves generated, than similar statements made by others. For this reason, conversational readings where the querent participates in telling the reader what is going on, might actually be rated as more effective in terms of 'hits' than they should be.

I have noticed in observing Tarot readings that suggestible querents often give the game away, through nods, facial expressions or other body language, despite thinking they are being 'poker-faced'. This is not easily avoided, but I try and get around this partially by offering the querent the opportunity before the reading starts of remaining silent and or 'poker-faced' throughout the reading in order to test me. Though my own findings have been that my readings are roughly equally effective either way, I recommend that you test for this bias in some of your readings as it can only improve your skill.

The 'stepping stone' memory

In his work *A Mind So Rare*,[97] Merlin Donald, Emeritus Professor at the Department of Psychology at Queen's University, Kingston, Ontario, puts forth the astounding theory that all human memories of events cannot exceed moments of longer than approximately 15 seconds. This means that our memories of events are like stepping stones of remembered moments, and that our understanding of these memories is like a game of 'join the dots'. This opens up the power of new narratives to reform our ideas about the past. It seems that we are doomed to never have a fully objective understanding of what has happened to us. Instead we must make do with 'better' or 'worse' stories, and we ought to choose these stories based on how they affect our future and the future of those around us.

All of our ideas of the past depend on 'stories' and the generation of these stories are always, in part, a creative exercise. Tarot can then be seen as a 'story construction set', or at least as a set of prompts for the formation of, hopefully better stories. This is true of all narrative therapy relating to remembered events. If the goal is to help the querent, then stories ought to be chosen based on how they allow the querent to act positively, rather than simply how well the story 'sticks'. Stories about the past that paint us into a corner are therefore worse than stories that grant us new options to act.

Making it work might be the point of the exercise.

As the purpose of this book is not to dispel Tarot divination, but rather to teach it and understand it, all of these biases can equally be seen as real working parts of why Tarot reading works. In my experiments I, and my collaborators have found that readings work regardless of whether or not they are framed as being 'magical' or 'psychic'. Likewise the inherent morality or immorality of a reading lies entirely in what the querent is led to expect. My policy is one of general honesty. I have found that the game of Tarot reading is enjoyable and fascinating even when all pretences of magic are avoided.

This is precisely why I find Tarot interesting.

The really interesting question then is not, 'Is Tarot fake', but rather, 'What can Tarot tell us about ourselves and about our general

---

[97] (Donald 2001).

perception?' As all human perception through senses, as well as our opinions about time and fate are at best, imperfect representations of reality, Tarot, and all other forms of magic are a fascinating window into how we may become active manipulators of our own 'reality tunnel'.

Regardless of any 'spooky; goings on, Tarot reading is a way to shape the way one observes and behaves in the world, and a way to 'talk ourselves into' narratives that may serve us better. The power of associative thinking to pull patterns and order out of randomness is the fundamental aspect of human creativity. Tarot reading is, therefore, a powerful technique that can be applied to all creative acts, from writing a song or a novel, to sorting out one's life.

The hard-nosed 'sceptic' is as equally guilty of self-enchantment, as the 'true believer' if they make the claim that they go through life in an entirely 'rational' or 'objective' way. The options given to us are not a choice to be or not to be enchanted, but merely what kind of enchantment we choose to roll with.

Put another way, you will always have magical thinking in your life. The choice then is not between magical thinking all the time, and rational thinking all the time, but rather between bad magical thinking and better magical thinking. True rational thinking is much harder to achieve than many give it credit for, and is therefore simply not available to us in every moment.

The closest we can often truly get to 'objectivity' then is to try wearing many hats, with the understanding that no single hat will serve for all purposes. The approaches to Tarot I have explored in this book honour this approach.

Dealing with problematic querents

As an activity that has never been mainstream, and always relegated to 'the occult' or 'New Age', Tarot reading is bound to attract not only thoughtful people who want to explore their psyche, or people curious about the fringes of consensus reality, but also people who live in a fantasy, and, like trying to push square pegs into a round holes, these people will gravitate towards the things that they believe will maintain their fantasy.

These people may come to you, not for your input, but rather for validation on what they have already decided to be true, and they may not like appreciate being contradicted. A common signs that you are dealing with this kind of person is that they have had multiple readings from you where they've asked the same question, despite your giving them the same reasonable answer each time. They may have also been to several Tarot readers and won't give up until they get the answer they want. If you have broached this issue gently with the querent, the worse case scenario is that these people need to be cut off.

Picking up on hopes

I've found it's much harder to read for people you are close to, or for yourself, than it is to read for perfect strangers. The reason is as follows: When you know the querent well, you may have your own personal hopes for them and you may want nothing but the best for them in a way that may actually cloud your understanding of the cards. With perfect strangers of whom you know nothing, and whom you are unlikely to see again, it can be much easier to read impartially.

As a Tarot reader, I have only ever done one reading which I regret. This was for a female friend who asked to know about a new relationship she was getting into. She was considering moving herself and her children to another town to live with a new man. The reading came out very positive, centring around the Sun card. I read it as if a positive outcome was most likely.

Unfortunately in this case, eventually the relationship did not work out. The man was withholding from her that he was a drug addict, and that he was having financial difficulties and, from what I heard later, that he had some emotional difficulties caused by mental illness. The relationship failed and the querent had to move back home. I considered whether the reading had been a flat out failure. A 'miss'. Things had certainly gone the other way than I had interpreted. I realised that if I had have framed the reading in terms of her hope rather than what was actually going to happen, then I could have given her much sounder advice and also regulated her expectations.

During the reading she had given me such undivided belief, not only in the cards, but also in the relationship she was having. Rose-coloured spectacles. Her friends and I had our doubts, but the cards were overwhelmingly positive. I have since learnt to interpret the Sun card, not only as a positive omen, but also, when negatively aspected, as a sign that the querent might be avoiding looking at the negative sings in a situation.

Perhaps the cards 'read' her belief more than they read her fortune. With this refined approach I've not had a failed reading like this since.

Using Tarot to stalk your ex

While most people know how to regulate their intrusive thoughts and negative emotions, there are unfortunately those who not only lean into them, but who also try to recruit others to act them out. One common type of question that comes up, especially from female querents are questions about ex-partners that have clearly moved on. Questions like:

- 'Is he thinking about me?'
- 'Why did he end contact?'
- 'What does his new partner think about me?'
- 'How is his new relationship going?'

While it is within in your jurisdiction to provide answers for these questions, it is also perfectly reasonable to suspect that you are being asked to feed an obsession, and to refuse to play along. Some questions are not respectful to the privacy of others, and some aren't even good for the mental health of the person asking them. Sometimes the questions will be mean-spirited. It is up to you to set your own boundaries and maintain them.

Addiction to Tarot

A good predictive Tarot reading ought to advise the querent for weeks, months or even years. Most people will be satisfied with this and only return to you when they have thought of a new question. Because the cards are randomised, asking a question too often is going to give blurry results. This is because the cards, are probably not truly being manipulated by the universe to line in up in a certain way. Rather, the cards are most likely prompts for your own insightful abilities. Therefore too many readings on one issue are only going to muddle the narrative.

Perhaps because the attention of others feels good, and because the cards can generate 'mystical' feelings, some querents can become obsessed with, or even addicted to Tarot readings.

This behaviour is probably not good for them, and it certainly undermines clear readings. For this reason, you might want to set some rules as to how often you give readings for the same person.

Not liking an answer

Another thing that many Tarot readers have experienced is a successful reading which gave a clear prediction, and which came true in time, but which the querent reacted negatively to because it wasn't what they wanted to hear. If this has happened to you more than once, then you might want to make a decision on whether your job is to make people happy, or rather to make accurate predictions.

If this is happening to you often, then it is also worth considering the way in which you deliver the news. Some querents can deal with a forthright prediction, while others need a degree of diplomacy.

Naysayers

While true scepticism is the suspension of belief until enough evidence is presented to support a conclusion, there are many self-appointed 'sceptics' who missed the memo, and who think the object of the exercise is to first decide something is bogus, and then to build a case for that prejudice. While this is a misapplication of the term, it is prevalent enough that many people use the term 'sceptic' to mean 'naysayer'.

You will probably not end up doing many readings for this type of person. For one thing, they usually proudly announce themselves as soon as something like Tarot is shown to them. They also generally won't invest the time it takes to do a reading, because they already 'know' that Tarot 'isn't real'. They are also unlikely to pay for a professional reading, as that would be feeding a 'charlatan'.

If, however, like me, you have done a lot of free readings for strangers, especially at parties, or at cafes or bars, you might one day read for a naysayer or have to tolerate a 'rational critique' from a naysayer who has been watching you read for someone else. The important thing is not to take offence. Remain friendly. Tarot is not your whole identity.[98] Some people are genuinely curious but they find it hard to shed their 'rational' armour. In almost all cases I've turned the naysaying into a

---

[98] If it is, please let go of this book and go get some help.

great conversation about what it means to be a good sceptic. I've also offered many readings to people to see if they can debunk me, and the result has almost always resulted in them saying things like: 'That Tarot reading was totally different than I expected and now I'm going to have to go away and think about it'.

In many cases they have been totally entranced. In a couple of cases the 'sceptic' ended up becoming a Tarot reader themselves. All in all, only once has a naysayer, a stranger at a bar who had observed me reading successfully for another stranger then requested a reading himself, gone through an entire reading and then called 'bullshit'. As he gave me no other feedback, there wasn't a lot I could do with his critique. He didn't even tell me if had actually gotten the reading wrong. He also didn't tell me that I should refrain from doing Tarot readings. It seems that the entire long winded exercise was so he could display his 'scepticism' to those around him.

I accepted that I had failed to entertain him and moved on.

Outro: Bullshit that works

Many of the biases that may affect a Tarot reading, may also work towards making Tarot both interesting and useful. Because we live inside of our own human psychology, we will almost certainly never reach a complete explanation of how that psychology works, a case of not being able to see the forest for the trees. For this reason, magic and fortune-telling may always occupy the realm of 'the unexplainable' or even 'the paranormal'.[99]

Due to the difficulty of forming appropriate tests, there will probably never be a way to completely pin down the difference between what is 'psychic' phenomena and what is 'psychology'. These 'grey area' pursuits, like Tarot, are therefore potentially useful to us, precisely because they break us out of the false certainty of our general routine habits and into a place where we are open to anything, especially the unusual, occurring.

For this reason, the particular experiences that are explained away by naysayers as biases, may be the very same phenomena that the true believer counts as 'hits'. The underlying purpose of this book has been to present to you the opportunity to think both ways. I do believe that the sceptic has not fully understood what is going on until they have

---

[99] I don't love the term 'paranormal'. It's hard enough to define 'normal'.

(temporarily) played by the rules of the 'true believer' and vice versa. As such, my ultimate goal is that the sceptic becomes more open, and that the true believer becomes more sceptical.

Beliefs ought to be seen as tools rather than edifices. It is quite normal for individuals to hold different, often conflicting sets of beliefs at different times, and attached to the different roles they play. The point of the exercise is then to explore what you can get done. While 'playing' the Tarot reader role, it can help, for the duration of the exercise to 'believe' that you are psychic. This is similar to how an actor delivers a better (and more uncanny) performance if they play at temporarily adopting the belief system and the psychology of the character they are playing.

When one has achieved 'psychic results', the next important thing to ask is *'Could this be bullshit?'* My experience, as a reader, as a querent, and as a sceptical tester of Tarot is that the 'psychic flashes' do happen, regardless of whether they are immaterial thoughts passing from one mind to another, or else simply 'right brain', internally generated, answers that present themselves as coming from outside, but are really just the reader's own mind calculating, and coming up with ideas in a subtle way.

Either way, it has been my experience that these phenomena are accessible to all willing participants, who play the game 'as if' the psychic phenomena can happen. I currently hold the position that the 'psychic' is not an outlying personality, born into a rare talent as a 'chosen one', but rather one who is better at playing this 'game' than other people, and that even sceptics can make good 'psychics', without needing to first swallow an entirely magical belief system.

I feel that the game of Tarot reading and its results are too interesting to be dismissed, or to be left entirely to the 'true believers'. There is something to be gained for almost anyone to try out the Tarot. As such, I urge you to both reach for 'psychic results' and also to remain sceptical. May your journey be fascinating.

—Ari Freeman. February 2024.

If you have enjoyed this book, you might be pleased to know that there is a second volume that will dive deeply into the occult, Kabbalistic, astrological and magical uses for the Tarot as well as my own experiments modifying and 'hacking' Tarot in new ways not seen before. This is entitled *Tarot Magic for the Reality Hacker—Divination for the Modern World* and it will be out in October 2025.

BIBLIOGRAPHY

Carroll, Peter J. (1987). *Liber Null & Psychonaut: An Introduction to Chaos Magic*. Weiser, New York.

Casanova, Giacomo. Machen, Arthur (translator 1894). *The Memoirs of Jacques Casanova de Seingalt, 1725–1798*. Elek Books, London.

Crowley, Aleister. (1944). *The Book of Thoth (Egyptian Tarot)*. Weiser Books, New York.

Donald, Merlin. (2001). *A Mind So Rare: The Evolution of Human Consciousness*. W. W. Norton & Company, New York.

Dukes, Ramsey. (1978). *SSOTBME*. The Mouse That Spins, Cape Town.

Dukes, Ramsey. (2003). *Blast Your Way to Megabucks with My Secret Sex-Power Formula*. The Mouse That Spins, Cape Town.

Forer, Bertram R. (1949). The Fallacy of Personal Validation: A Classroom Demonstration og Gullibility. *J Abnorm Psychol*, 44(1): 118–123. Doi: 10.1037/h0059240.

Freeman, Ari. (2023). *Pragmatic Magical Thinking: Real Magic Explained*. Aeon Books, London.

Leví, Eliphas. Waite, A.E. (Translator) (1896). *Dogme Et Ritual de la Haute Magie*. Rider & Company, London. (Originally published in French in 1856.)

McCarthy, Josephine. (2020). *Tarot Skills for the 21st Century*. TaDehent Books, Exeter.

McGilchrist, Iain. (2012). *The Master and His Emissary: The Divided Brain and the Making of the Western World*. Yale University Press, New Haven, Connecticut.

McGilchrist, Iain. (2021). *The Matter with Things* [Kindle edition]. Perspectiva Press, Location 1271.

Radin, Dean. (2018). *Real Magic: Ancient Wisdom, Modern Science and a Guide to the Secret Power of the Universe*. Harmony, New York.

Schopenhauer, Arthur. (1818). *The World as Will and Representation (Die Welt als Wille und Vorstellung)*. Brodhaus, Leipzig.

Waite A.E. (1910). *Pictorial Key to the Tarot*. Rider, London.

Online articles

Di Monda, Brianna. (2023). Analysis Does Cramp the Painter. https://www.laphamsquarterly.org/roundtable/analysis-does-cramp-painter. Last retrieved 2 December 2023.

McCarthy, Josephine. (2015). Watching the World Through a Window. https://josephinemccarthy.com/2015/07/27/watching-the-world-through-the-window/ Last retrieved 3 April 2024.

McGilchrist, Iain. (2023). RSA Animate – The Divided Brain. https://vimeo.com/31780637 2011. Last accessed 21 November 2023.

Place, Robert M. (2015). A History of Oracle Cards in Relation to The Burning Serpent Oracle and a New Revelation About the Origin of the Lenormand. https://robertmplacetarot.com/2015/10/25/a-history-of-oracle-cards/ Last retrieved 2 December 2023.

Ray, Sharmistha. (2019). Reviving a Forgotten Artist of the Occult. https://hyperallergic.com/490918/pamela-colman-smith-pratt-institute-libraries/ Last retrieved 2 December 2023.

Roberge, Pierre R. Sleeping Brain. https://www.corrosion-doctors.org/Dreaming%20is%20Personal/Brain.htm#:~:text=The%20right%20hemisphere%20of%20the,in%20that%20hemisphere%20during%20REM. Last accessed 3 April 2024.

INDEX

27 club, 124
4Chan, 230
a Christmas Carol (book)
    Ebenezer Scrooge, 262

Abramović, Marina, 246
activist, 31, 241, 247, 256
Adam and Eve, 92, 94, 119, 136–137, 149
Addams Family (television show)
    Wednesday Addams, 228
addiction, 13, 30, 34, 114, 116, 119, 187, 195, 200, 343
advertising, 6, 17
Africa, 75, 99, 127, 154
Agrippa, Heinrich Cornelius, 303, 305
alchemy, 4, 6–8, 11, 77–78, 83–84, 93, 117, 143, 144, 209, 217, 304, 309
Alexander the Great, 95, 97, 297
Ali, Muhammad, 241
Alice in Wonderland (book), 225
Alien (film franchise)
    Ripley, 251
Anansi the Spider, 75

angels
    Gabriel, 139
    Hayyot, 89, 95, 97, 104–105, 143
    Michael, 116
    Raguel, 106
anima, 5, 83, 217, 225, 237, 257
animus, 5, 83, 86, 217, 245, 246, 317
Anubis, 139, 141
Apollonius of Tyana, 301, 309
Ardern, Jacinda, 249
Aristotle, xxiv, 225
associative thinking, 3, 324, 341
astrology
    Aquarius, 10, 89, 104–105, 129, 131, 143, 179–180, 187, 188, 196, 218–219, 221–222, 229, 239, 257–258, 283
    Aries, 10, 86–87, 148, 156–157, 164, 170, 218, 220, 222, 231, 242, 245, 272, 280
    Cancer, 10, 95–96, 151, 158, 165, 171, 218, 220–221, 224, 234–235, 248, 269, 276

350 INDEX

Capricorn, 10, 119, 122–123, 161, 168, 174, 218, 220–221, 229, 239, 252, 273, 283–284,
Gemini, 10, 92, 137, 153, 201, 206, 214–215, 218–220, 222, 231, 248, 259–260, 267
Leo, 10, 89, 98, 105, 143, 148, 176, 184, 192, 218, 220–221, 224, 234–235, 261, 273–274, 276, 280
Libra, 10, 106–107, 153, 160, 166, 173, 218, 220–222, 227, 237, 249–250, 270, 279
Pisces, 10, 132, 134, 151, 200, 205, 212–213, 218–220, 222, 229, 245, 257–258, 280
Sagittarius, 10, 116, 148, 199, 204, 210–211, 218–220, 222, 227, 252, 255–256, 272, 285
Scorpio, 10, 89, 105, 113–114, 143, 151, 177, 185, 194–195, 218–219, 221–222, 227, 237, 255–256, 274
Taurus, 10, 88–89, 90, 105, 143, 181–182, 189, 197, 218–219, 222, 231, 242–243, 259–260, 283–284
Virgo, 10, 101–102, 153, 202, 208, 216, 218, 220–221, 224, 249, 250, 261, 279, 283
atheism, 230, 239, 261
August, Aurora, 120
Augustus, 87
Australian Aborigines, 112
Austria, 291
axis mundi, 137, 142

Baba Yaga, 247
Babalon, 84, 89, 129, 131
Baker, Josephine, 247
Baldur, 112, 137–138
Baphomet, 119
Beach Boys, 138
Beatles, the
    George Harrison, 238
    Lennon, John, 238
        Ono, Yoko, 247
    Paul McCartney, 236
    Starr, Ringo, 243
Beauty and the Beast, 33, 100
belief, ix, xi–xii, xviii–xix, xii, 18, 22, 33, 116, 239, 259–260, 277, 319, 322, 327–328, 337–338, 342–343, 344, 346
Bembo, Bonifacio, 296
Bennett, Allan, 305, 307
Bethlehem, 131
bias
    confirmation bias, xvii, 332, 335–338, 340, 345
    sunken cost fallacy, 339
Bible, 33, 98, 287, 295, 297
    Acts, 192
    Armageddon 141
    Adam and Eve, 92, 94, 119, 136–137, 149
    Book of Revelation, 100, 126, 140, 144, 312
    Cain and Abel, 93
    Daniel, 99–100
    David, 97
    Ezekiel, 89, 95, 105, 143
    Garden of Eden, 92, 136–138, 150, 194,
    Jesus, 82, 88, 103, 109, 111–112, 139
    John the Baptist, 103
    King James Bible, 88, 126
    Kings, 108
    Satan, 98, 119, 121, 122
    Tower of Babel, 126–127
Björk, 249
Blavatsky, Helena, 251, 301, 303–304
Boaz and Jachin, 81, 89, 107
Bonaparte, Napoleon, 97
    Bonaparte, Joséfine, 316
Book of Revelation, 100, 126, 140, 144, 312
Bowie, David, 120
    Thin White Duke, 238
    Ziggy Stardust, 246
Brahma, 142, 314
Brahman, 74, 77
Brando, Marlin, 258

Brer Rabbit, 75
Brera-Brambilla, 296
British Empire, 110, 127, 262
Brown, James, 256
Buddha, 78, 103
Buddhism, xxi, 144, 303, 307
Bugs Bunny, 75
bullshit, xix, 345–346
Bush, Kate, 249
butthurt, 26

Cain and Abel, 93
Caligula, 99
Carnegie, Andrew, 262
Casanova, Giacomo, 298
Catholicism, 81, 99, 120, 139, 141, 150,
    243, 258, 300, 301
Caucacus, 289
chakras, 74, 121, 123, 130, 137, 142
chaos, 33, 77, 104–105, 111, 143
chaos magic, xx
charisma, 224, 234, 255
Charlemagne, 87
China
    Chinese, xvi, xxi, 144, 164,
        286–289, 292
    Dao, xvi, 144
    Taoism, xvi, 144
Christ, 96, 113
    Jesus, 82, 88, 103, 109, 111–112, 139
Christian, Paul, 301, 306
Churton, Tobias, 311
Cicero, Chic and Tabatha, 306
Clinton, Hillary, 251
Cobain, Kurt, 213
coffee ground divination, 315–317
cognitive dissonance, xix, 148, 166, 215
cold reading, xii–xiii
    Forer effect, 322–338
Colman Smith, Pamela, 305, 309–310
Coltrane, John, 241
communism, 131, 241
consciousness, 16, 35, 45, 80–81, 83–84,
        121–123, 135, 143, 150, 207
    altered consciousness, 112
    flow states, 321

sentience, xxii
steam of consciousness, 249
subconscious, 116
conspiracy theories, 207, 230, 241, 304
control freak, 31
corruption, 13, 34, 90, 107, 120–121,
    125, 279
counselling, x, xiii, xxiii, 69, 338
Court de Gébelin, 131, 293, 300
Covid19, 127
Creationism, 230, 239, 241
crossroads, 12, 20, 133–135, 156, 297, 317
Crowley, Aleister, 81, 84, 102, 126,
    140, 143, 236, 263, 294, 300,
    303–305, 307–308, 311–314
    Kelly, Rose Edith, 129
cults, xix, 138, 338
    cult leaders, 14, 32, 121, 255
        Father Yod, 256
        Rajneesh, 256
        J.Z. Knight
    cult personality, 120
Curie, Marie, 251
Curie, Pierre, 251

D'Odoucet, Melchior Montmignon, 299
Darwin, Charles, 260
De Beers (diamond company), 262
de Saint-Just, Louis Antoine, 316
Dee, John, 110, 305
Devil, 13, 15, 34, 64, 90, 98, 119–125,
    130, 133–135, 228, 239, 264,
    273–274, 279, 296
Dietrich, Marlena, 246
Discworld (book series)
    Nanny Ogg, 253
    Rincewind, 75
Don Quixote, 207, 241
double-slit experiment, 17, 73
Doyle, Arthur Conan, 305
Dr Strange (Marvel character), 260
Drag Queens, 245–246
drugs, 45, 111–112, 133–134, 237–238,
    273
    LSD, 106
    MDMA, 121, 137

Dungeons and Dragons, xxiv, 11, 328
  elf, xxiv,
  magic user, 11

earthquakes, 219, 261, 329
ego death, 109, 112, 123
Egypt, 289
Egypt (ancient), 131, 294
Egyptian, 250 ff.
Egyptian (ancient), 74, 76–78, 81–82, 86–87, 107, 130, 136, 140–141, 235, 291–295, 298–303, 311–312, 314
Einstein, Albert, 260
electrician, 30, 110
electromagnetism, 7, 16, 221
Elvis Presley, 8, 258
Empedocles, 4
energy (psychic), xxi, 170, 331
  chi, xxi
  prana, xxi
  virya, xxi
engineer, 6, 30, 110, 242
England, 247, 253, 303, 305, 311
Enlightenment (era), 16, 131, 153
enlightenment (state of consciousness), 94, 103, 121, 137
Etteilla (Tarot writer), 263, 293–294, 299–300, 310–312, 315
Europe, xiv, 4, 77, 154, 287, 289, 291, 294, 298, 300, 316
Evel Knievel, 241

falsifiability, xv
famine, 127
farmer, 30, 97, 242–243, 261
Farr, Florence, 305, 307, 310
fate, xvi, xx, 13, 71, 96, 104–105, 137, 143, 216, 264, 301, 341
  determinism, xxi
  predicting the future, x, xvi, xvii, xx–xxi, xxiv, 37, 39, 43, 241
  karma, xvi, 105, 144
  Norns, 104
  self-fulfilling prophecy, xvi, xvii, xxiii

Urðr, 105
Wyrd, 105
Father Yod (cult leader), 256
fatherhood, 33
Fawlty Towers (television series)
  Sybil Fawlty, 253
Felkin, Robert, 305, 308
fermentation, 76, 113, 115
first nations, 127
Fitzgerald, Ella, 246
flow states, 80, 321–323
Forer effect, xii, 332–334
Forrest Gump (film), 75
Fortune, Dion, 251
France, 131, 289, 291, 298–300, 309, 312, 316
  French, xiv, 19, 247, 293–294, 297–298, 300–301, 304, 309, 315–316
Fred Dagg, 243
Freud, Sigmund, 243, 336
Friends (television show), 198
Fundamentalism, 198, 207
funk (music), 256

gambling, 105, 181, 286, 288–289
Game of Hope, 315–316
Game of Thrones (television show)
  Brienne of Tarth, 243
  Catelyn Stark, 253
  Margery Tyrell, 249
  Ned Stark, 262
  Olenna Tyrell, 253
Ganneau, Simon, 300
gender roles, 30–31, 217
Geopolitics, 125, 144
Germany, 246, 291, 316
Gandhi, 118
Gilgamesh, 100
Gish Gallop, 239
Godfather, the (film), 124, 258
gods
  Amun, 76, 86
  Anansi the Spider, 75
  Anubis, 101, 105, 134, 139, 141
  Aphrodite, 137

INDEX 353

Aphroditus, 116
Apollo, 95, 136–138
Apophis, 89, 104, 111, 126, 143
Artemis, 12, 80–81, 116–117, 132–133
Athena, 86, 106
Atum, 101
Baba Yaga, 247
Babalon, 84, 89, 129, 131
Bacchus, 72, 119
Baphomet, 119–120
Brahma, 142, 314
Ceres, 83
Charon, 88
Chronos, 142
Cronus, 114
Demeter, 12, 83, 165
Devil, 98, 119–125, 133–135
Diana, 80, 116–117, 132
Dike, 106–107
Dionysus, 72, 74, 119
Dis Pater (Pluto), 126
Eros, 92
Eurydice, 92, 94, 135
Eurynome, 142–143
Fenrir, 139
Forseti, 106–107
Fortuna, 104
Freyja, 80, 137
Freyr, 88
Frigg, 83
Gaea, 142
Ganymeda, 129
Ganymede, 129
Geb, 131
Hades, 113–115, 126, 165, 210
Harpocrates, 72, 74, 139–140
Hebe, 129
Hecate, 80, 132
Heka, 76
Hel, 113, 115
Hephaestus, 139
Hera, 83
Hermanubis, 104–105
Hermaphroditus, 116
Hermes, 16, 72, 74, 76–78, 105, 158, 293, 308

Horus, 72, 74, 84, 86, 89, 95, 122–123, 126, 136, 140, 152, 308, 314
Ishtar, 129–130
Isis, 80–81, 83–84, 89, 117, 305, 308, 314
Jesus, 82, 88, 103, 109, 111–112, 139
Juno, 83
Jupiter, 86
Justitia, 106–107
Juventas, 129
Kali, 113–114
Kephra, 132, 134
Khonsu, 132, 140
Krishna, 314
Legba, 88, 132, 134
Loki, 72, 109, 111–112, 119, 138
Lucifer, 129
Luna, 80, 132
Ma'at, 106
Mercury, 76, 122, 199
Minerva, 86
Mithra, 106
Monad, 77
Mother Mary, 78, 82–85
Mother Nature, 12, 33, 83, 85
Mut, 83
Neptune, 109
Norns, 104
Nut, 80–82, 130, 314
Óðinn, 76, 94, 101, 109–112
Ophion, 142–143, 154
Orpheus, 92, 94, 135
Osiris, 88–89, 95, 113, 123, 126, 139, 152, 308, 314
Pan, 72, 74, 119, 122–123, 305
Persephone, 83, 101, 165
Pluto, 114–115
Poseidon, 109
Prometheus, 109, 112, 149
Psyche, 92
Ptah, 142
Ra, 136
Radha, 314
Saturn, 142
Selene, 80, 132
Shai, 104

354   INDEX

Shiva, 125–126
Sopdet, 129
Sothis, 129
Spider Woman, 314
the Fates, 96, 104
Themis, 106–107
Thor, 95, 98
Thoth, 76, 78, 129, 293, 308
Tyche, 104
Typhon, 89, 104–105, 111, 114
Venus, 78, 83–84, 96, 129
Venus von Willendorf, 314
Virgin Mary, 81
Vulcan, 139
White Buffalo Woman, 314
Zeus, 97, 126
Golden Dawn, 2, 81, 99, 102, 115, 120, 123, 143
Goodfellas (film), 124
Gordian knot, 97
gravity, 221
Greece (ancient), 143
Greek, 22, 86, 105, 115, 127, 131, 207, 251 f., 278
Greek (ancient), 9, 26, 73, 76–78, 97, 107, 137–138, 140, 144, 241, 292–293, 295
Greer, Mary (Tarot writer), 316
Grim Reaper, 113–115
guardian, 15, 32, 80, 84, 89, 102
Gunas, 105
Gypsy, 82, 294

Hades, 113–115, 126, 165, 210
Haindl, Hermann, 314–315
Harpo Marx, 74–75
Harris, Frieda, 294, 311–313
Harry Potter, 236
    Hermione, 236
Hawking, Stephen, 260
heavens, 77, 88–89, 114, 126
hedonism, 14, 119, 124, 133, 194–195, 307
Heka, 76
Hendrix, Jimi, 236, 294
Heraclitus, 76

Hermeticism (see also, Golden Dawn), 78, 97, 99, 293, 300
    Hermes Trismegistus, 16, 77–78, 292–293
hieroglyph, 86, 134, 140, 292
Hinduism, xxi, 78, 105, 114, 137, 144, 314
Hippocrates, 9
Hiroshima and Nagasaki, 125, 128
Hobbit, the
    Bilbo Baggins, 75, 232
    Gandalf, 78, 103
    Radagast, 103
Holiday, Billie, 246
Holmes, Sherlock, 260, 305
holocaust, 127
Holy Grail, 95–96, 100, 150
Holy Guardian Angel, 81, 102, 110, 116
Holy Spirit, 81, 89, 130, 140, 150, 170
    Shekhinah, 81, 130, 140
Horus, 72, 74, 84, 86, 89, 95, 122–123, 126, 136, 140, 152, 308, 314
Houdini, Harry, 79
House (television show), 78
Hubbard, L. Ron, 256
Hungary, 316

I-Ching, 315
Icke, David, 241
Indiana Jones (film), 236
initiation, 14, 33, 81, 88, 90, 112, 135
internet troll, 29
intuition, x, xiii, 31, 80, 93, 96, 136, 185, 187, 189, 206, 248, 269, 321, 325, 330
inversion, 33, 111, 188, 282–283
    inversion without liberation, 120
Isis, 80–81, 83–84, 89, 117, 305, 308, 314
Islamic alchemy, 4, 6, 16, 144
Italy, 287, 289, 291, 298, 316
    Italian, xiv, 289–291
Ivan the Fool, 75

Jagger, Mick, 256
James Bond (film character), 236
James, William, xix

Jesus, 82, 88, 103, 109, 111–112, 139
    Christ, 96, 113
Jones, Alex, 241
Judaism, 140
    Jews, 315
Judge Judy (television show), 108
Jung, Carl, xx, 24, 71, 117,
    anima, 5, 83, 217, 225, 237, 257,
    animus, 5, 83–86, 217, 245–246, 318
    Jung, Emma, 253
    Jungian Shadow, 133, 135
    synchronicities, xx, 264

Kafka, Franz, 108
Kahlo, Frida, 246
karma, xvi, 105, 144
Kelley, Edward, 110
Kerouac, Jack, 249
King Arthur, 96, 237
    Guinevere, 225, 237
    Lancelot, 225, 237
    Merlin, 78
    Morgan Le Fay, 225
    Percival, 75
King of the Hill (television show), 243
Kings
    Alexander the Great, 95, 97, 297
    Augustus, 87
    Caligula, 99
    Charlemagne, 87
    Genghis Khan, 97
    King Arthur, 96, 237
    King David, 97
    Midas, 97
    Napoleon, 97, 316
    Solomon, 12, 81, 87, 89, 107–108
    Tzar Alexander, 316
Kingsford, Anna, 251, 303–304
Kuti, Fela, 256

Lady Gaga, 247
landslides, 219
Lenormand cards, 315–317
Lévi, Éliphas, xiv, 79, 119–120, 295,
    300–310
lighthouse, 131

lightning bolts, 126, 199, 219
Little Richard, 246
Logos (philosophy), 76, 80
Loki, 72, 109, 111–112, 119, 138
Lord of the Rings
    Bilbo Baggins, 75, 232
    Galadriel, 82
    Gandalf, 78, 103
Lu Rong, 288
Luther, Martin, 118

MacConneach, Ciaran, vii, 68
Machen, Arthur, 299, 305
Mackenzie, Kenneth R.H., 301, 304
Madmen (television show), 205
    Don Draper, 238
magical thinking, xviii, 341
Manic pixie dream-girl, 226
manifestation, 72, 77, 82, 135, 154,
    170–171, 189, 202, 208–209,
    222, 284, 326, 338
Marat, Jean-Paul, 316
Marilyn Manson, 230
Marquis de Sade, 124
Martin Luther King Junior, 118, 258
martyrdom, 13, 109, 112
    Martyr-complex, 111, 234
Marx, Karl, 262
Marxism, 131
Mary Shelley, 249
Masamune, Gorō Nyūdō
    (swordsmith), 262
Mata Hari, 246
materialism, 16, 67, 231, 242, 252, 261
mathematicians, 6
Mathers, MacGregor, 99, 303–307,
    309–310
    Moina Mathers, 99, 305, 310
McCarthy, Josephine, 84, 101, 130
McKenna, Terrence, 112
mechanics (job), 30, 52, 242
mental health, xix, 15, 33, 334, 343
merchant, 6, 261, 287, 288
Merlin, 78
military, 5, 31, 95, 153, 250, 259, 290, 297
Miranda, Carmen, 246

356   INDEX

Mirandola, Pico della, 295
misses, xv, 330–331
Moby Dick (book), 131
Molko, Brian, 238
Mona Lisa, 232
Monad, 77
   Brahman, 74, 77
morality, 17, 33–34, 88, 90, 98, 106–107,
      120–122, 129, 130–131, 139,
      144, 216, 235, 257, 340
   Immorality, 13, 238, 289, 340
Mother Mary, 78, 82–85
Mother Nature, 12, 33, 83, 85
motherhood, 12, 14, 31, 33, 83–85,
      117, 232
Mr Magoo, 75
Muppet Show
   Miss Piggy, 236
music, xi, 3–5, 17, 60, 222, 249, 310, 321
   funk, 256
   harmony, 163
   musicians, xviii, 8, 30–31, 59–60,
      184, 235, 237, 241, 247, 249,
      253, 298, 305, 321–322, 330
   major scale, 21, 130

Napoleon, 97, 316
   Bonaparte, Joséfine, 316
Nazis, 127
Never Ending Story (book)
   The Child-like Empress, 85
New Age, xvii, xx–xxi, 17, 67, 294, 341
   New Thought, xx, 71
New Zealand, xvi, 243, 249, 305, 308
Newton, Isaac, 260
Nicks, Stevie, 82
nihilism, 129
Nobel Prize, 251
Noblet, Jean, 298
noobs, 12, 15, 223
nudism, 138
Nut (goddess), 80–82, 130, 314

objectivity, xiii, 106, 341
Óðinn, 76, 94, 101, 109–112
   Yggdrasil, 76, 109–110, 112
Orpheus, 92, 94, 135

Orphic Egg, 78, 93, 143, 153
Orsini, Julia, 299
Osho (cult leader), 256
Oswald Wirth, 74, 99, 302–303, 306,
      309, 312

Pannonica de Koenigswarter, 253
Papus (Gérard Encausse), 19–20, 294,
      302, 309–310, 312
Paracelsus, 87, 104, 117, 225
parents, 5, 24–25, 172, 246, 250, 255,
      257, 259–260, 335
Parker, Charlie, 241, 253
Percival, 75
performance, xi–xii, 3–4, 8, 23, 68, 203,
      205, 235, 246–247, 330–331,
      334, 346
Persia, 77, 287, 289, 292
personhood, xxii
Peter Pan (book), 226
Peterson, Jordan, 258
Pharaoh, 78, 86–87
philosophers
   Anaximander, 144
   Aristotle, xxiv, 225
   Empedocles, 4
   Heraclitus, 76
   Hippocrates, 9
   James, William, xix
   Plato, xxii, 241
   Pythagoras, 292, 295
      neo-Pythagorean, 309
philosophy
   post-structuralism, 241
   pragmatism, xix, 90
Pierpont Morgan Bergamo, 296
Pippi Longstocking (book), 226
plagues, 127
Plath, Silvia, 249
Plato, xxii, 241
playing cards, xiv, 4, 286, 288–291, 297,
      299, 316
Poe, Edgar Allan, 238
politician, 31, 118, 160, 240, 250
   Ardern, Jacinda, 249
   Trump, Donald, 241
Pope Joan, 81–82

INDEX   357

Popess, 86, 250
Portugal
   Portuguese, xiv
Post-Traumatic Stress Disorder, 166
Pragmatic Magical Thinking (Book),
   xiii, xviii, 71, 110, 215, 327, 329
pragmatism, xvi, xix, xxii, 20, 23, 90,
   106, 129, 168, 197, 239, 283
prediction, x, xii, xv–xvii, xx, 282, 322,
   328–329
pregnancy, 12, 25, 33, 337
Prima Donna, 14, 30, 234
Prima Materia, 72
Princess Bride (film), 94
Prometheus, 109, 112, 149
psychic, vi, xi–xii, xx–xxi, 227, 243, 303,
   319, 321–322, 324, 326–329
   skepticism of psychics, 322–346
   mediums, 311
   mind reading, xxi, 17, 322–324, 329
psychology, xx, 5, 6, 9, 44–45, 56, 69,
   217, 332, 340, 345
   addiction, 13, 30, 34, 114, 116, 119,
   124, 187, 195, 200
      Tarot addiction, 343–344
   associative thinking, 3, 324, 341
   complexes, 101, 135, 187, 228, 255
      martyr-complex, 111
      victim complex, 234
      Madonna/whore complex,
         237, 336
      knight-beast complex, 336
   narcissism, 234, 239, 337
   parapsychology, 73, 326
   Post-Traumatic Stress Disorder, 166
   trauma, 14, 15, 139, 141, 187, 336
punk rock, 118, 213, 228
Pyramus and Thisbe, 94

Queens (historical)
   Elizabeth I, 247
   Elizabeth II, 253
   Queen Victoria, 249

Radin, Dean, xxi, 326–327
Ragnarök, 141
   Götterdamerung, 141

Rajneesh, Bhagwan Shree (Osho, cult
   leader), 256
Rambo (film), 236
Ramtha (cult), 256
   J.Z. Knight, 256
Rand, Ayn, 256
Randi, James, xii, 243
Rapunzel, 228
Regardie, Israel, 306
reincarnation, 105
religion, xviii, xxi, 33, 71, 88, 89, 90–91,
   122, 125, 130, 188, 230, 304
Ren and Stimpy (television show), 75
Renaissance, 131, 292, 295, 296, 307
Reuchlin, Johann, 295
reversals, 2–3, 18, 263–265, 268, 281
Rhodes, Cecil, 262
Rice, Anne, 249
Rinehart, Gina, 253
river, xvi, 98, 150, 181, 200, 220
Road Runner, 75
Robbins, Tony, 256
Roberge, Pierre R., 325
Robespierre, Maximilien, 266
Rockefeller, John D., 262
Rocky (film), 232
Rolling Stones
   Mick Jagger, 256
Roman, 9, 99, 105, 107, 111, 115, 126, 297
romance, 8, 24, 29, 30, 33, 41, 92, 99,
   150, 158, 191, 221, 227, 228,
   238, 257, 267, 276, 336
Romani, 294
   Gypsy, 293, 294
Romeo and Juliet, 29, 93–94, 225–226,
   228
Rose, Axl, 236
runes, 106, 314

salamanders, 225
Satan, 98, 119, 121–122
   Devil, 13, 15, 34, 64, 90, 98, 119–125,
      130, 133–135, 228, 239, 264,
      273–274, 279, 296
scepticism, vii, ix, xi–xii, xxi–xxiv, 67,
   77–78, 122, 319, 328, 331–341,
   344–346

Schwarzenegger, Arnold, 256
science, xii, xv, xviii, 8, 11, 73, 78, 110, 188, 209, 242, 326
    double-slit experiment, 17, 73
    electromagnetism, 16, 110
    entanglement, 73, 221
    gravity, 221
    physics, xx–xxi, 7–8, 73, 144
    quantum physics, 16–17, 73, 144
    scientists, xiii, xviii, xxi, 6
science fiction, 249, 323
secret chiefs, 304, 307
self-fulfilling prophecy, xvi–xvii, xxiii, 337–338
September 11 attacks, 127
Sesame Street
    Elmo, 225
sex, xviii, 33, 82, 84, 89, 111, 123, 133, 135, 137, 225, 237, 246, 266, 321, 333, 336
    homosexuality, 120, 307
    sexual abuse, 125, 139 141
    sex magic, 121
sex worker
    gigolo, 247
    stripper, 82
Sforza, Francesco, 290, 296
Shekhinah, 81, 130, 140
Sheldrake, Rupert, xxi, 326
Shelley, Mary, 249
Simone, Nina, 236
Simpsons, the (television show)
    Bart Simpson, 226
    Marge Simpson, 253
Sirius, 129, 131
skyhook, 90–91, 130
Snow White, 228
Sola Busca, 166, 290, 297, 310
Solomon (Biblical character), 12, 81, 87, 89, 107–108
    Sopranos (television show), 124
    Carmela Soprano, 253
    Tony Soprano, 256
Source Family (cult), 256
    Spain, 287, 289, 298
    Spanish, xiv, 291

sphinx, 95–97, 104–105, 302
spirit, xxi, 16, 33, 35, 75, 77–78, 81, 84, 88, 89, 104, 110, 112, 123, 133, 148–150, 158, 220
spirits, xxii, 17, 77–78, 80, 83, 89, 102, 227, 303–304, 307, 322, 323
    angels, xxii, 17, 92, 95, 97, 100, 105–106, 110, 116, 129, 140, 154, 260
    demons, xxii
    elementals, xxii, 83, 225
    elves, 83
    fairies, xxii, 131, 137
    ghosts, xxii
    gods (see previous 'gods' entry)
    Holy Guardian Angel, 81, 102, 110, 116
    Holy Spirit, 78, 81, 89, 130, 140, 150, 170
    jinn, xxii
    Kerubim, 88–89, 95, 89
    satyr, 100, 119
    sphinx, 95–97, 104–105, 302
spirituality, xi, 88, 204, 277, 300
Sprengel, Anna, 304–305
stage magician, 79, 243
Star Trek
    Captain Kirk, 256
    Dr Spock, 260
    Leonard H. McCoy, 258
    Scotty, 262
Star Wars
    Darth Vader, 124
    Obi-Wan Kenobi, 91, 103
    Yoda, 93
Steiner, Rudolf, 311
Stella Matutina, 308
storms, 166, 219–221, 260
Stradivari, Antonio (luthier), 262
stripper, 82
Sunset Boulevard (film), 236
Superman, xviii–xix
supermodels, 232
supernatural, xi, 90, 133, 249, 301
suspension of disbelief, xi, 322
Switzerland, 289, 291

Tantra, 142
Taoism, xvi, 144
   Dao, xvi, 144
telepathy, 322–324, 326
temperament (humorism), 9, 10, 11, 218
   choleric temperament, 5, 10, 11
   melancholic temperament, 6, 10, 11
   phlegmatic temperament, 5, 10, 11
   sanguine temperament, 6, 10, 11
Tetragrammaton, 95, 104, 144, 217, 301, 306
Thatcher, Margaret, 253
Tolle, Eckhart, 249
Tower of Babel, 126–127
tradespeople, 6, 261
Trainspotting (film), 124
transcendence, x, 104
Treasure Island, 225
trick-taking (card games), 288, 291
trickery, xi, xiii, xv, xxii–xxiii, 15, 138, 152, 179, 301, 332, 334
   self-deception, xxii, 332–338
   self-fulfilling prophecy, xvi–xvii, xxiii, 332–338
trickster, 73, 77
Tristan and Isolde, 94
Trotskyism, 241
Trump, Donald, 241
Turkey (country), 289
Tzar Alexander I (Emperor of Russia), 316

useful idiot, 29

vampire, 249
virgin, 81, 117, 247
Visconti-Sforza, 290, 296

Waite, Arthur Edward, 1, 130–131, 305, 307–311
Wang, Robert, 306, 308
West, Mae, 246
Westcott, William Wynn, 304–305, 307
Whare Ra, 308
Whewell, William, 188
Wilkinson, William Henry, 248
William Wynn Westcott, 288
Williams, Serena and Venus, 251
Wirth, Oswald, 74, 99, 302–303, 306, 309, 312
witch, 2, 82, 133–134
   Baba Yaga, 247
   Glinda the Good Witch, 247
   Morgan Le Fay, 255
   Witchcraft act of 1735, 311
Wizard of Oz, 108, 132–133, 135, 247
woke subculture, 230
Woodman, William Robert, 304–305
Woolf, Virginia, 249
World War I, 246
World War II, 127, 247
World Wide Web, 144

X-Files (television show)
   Mulder, 236
   Scully, 251

Yeats, William Butler, 305, 307
Yggdrasil, 76, 109–110, 112
yoga, xxi, 84, 121, 142, 144

www.ingramcontent.com/pod-product-compliance
Ingram Content Group UK Ltd.
Pitfield, Milton Keynes, MK11 3LW, UK
UKHW021936290525
459105UK00008B/203